DESIGN BY CHOICE

·Ideas in Architecture·

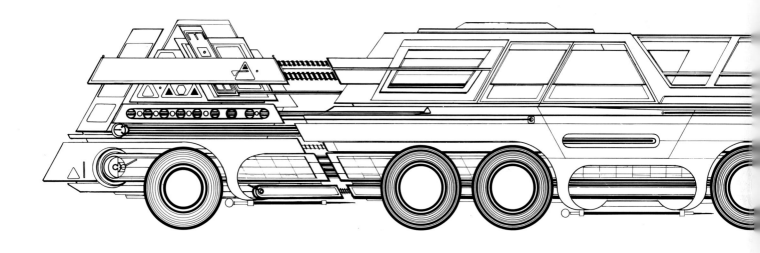

Reyner Banham

DESIGN BY CHOICE

Edited by Penny Sparke

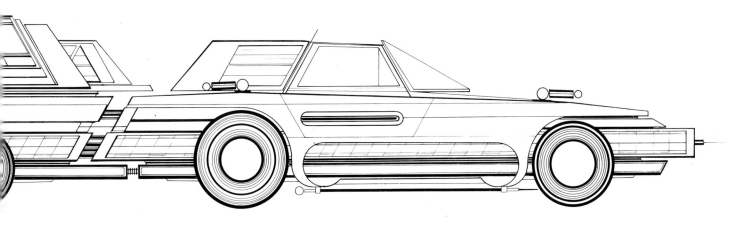

RIZZOLI
NEW YORK

Front cover
JAMES STIRLING and JAMES GOWAN, *Faculty of Engineering Building,*
Leicester University, 1963.

First published in the United States of America in 1981 by
RIZZOLI INTERNATIONAL PUBLICATIONS, INC.
712 Fifth Avenue/ New York 10019

Library of Congress Catalog Card Number: 80-54790
ISBN: 0-8478-0384-8

Series edited by Charles A. Jencks

Printed and bound in Great Britain

CONTENTS

FOREWORD

The splendour (and misery) of writing for dailies, weeklies, or even monthlies, is that one can address current problems currently, and leave posterity to wait for the hardbacks and PhD dissertations to appear later. A periodical article is addressed to the fortunate few (who may number millions) who happen to pick up that particular issue; if it is addressed to anyone else, the readership will immediately know that they are being made use of, and reject it – and thousands of promising careers in writing have died at the first article for exactly that reason.

The misery (and splendour) of such writing, when it is exactly on target, is to be incomprehensible by the time the next issue comes out – the splendour comes, if at all, years and years later, when some flip, throw-away, smarty-pants, look-at-me paragraph will prove to distil the essence of an epoch far better than subsequent scholarly studies ever can.

I am not claiming that any of the pieces anthologized here have that total recall quality, though the reference to Rhomboid Goatcabin in the Mustang essay from *New Society* gives me something of that flash-of-memory sensation and for that reason I am grateful to Penny Sparke for resurrecting it. Indeed, I am grateful for many of her exhumations – some of them I had forgotten completely, or had never considered them my first choices in those particular topics.

For this is *her* anthology, not mine. Its fascination, for me, is that it is one woman's Banham, and I have no doubt that other women, men, persons and creatures, could construct their own, absolutely true and documented, but totally different Banhams. For I have changed my mind – the only way to *prove* you have a mind is to change it, otherwise you might as well be a robot or a magnetic tape – over the quarter-century or so that I have been writing about architecture and design.

And I have also changed my stance or tone-of-voice according to the readership I have been addressing. Obviously, the readers of *Art In America* were very different to those of *New Statesman*, but probably nothing like as different as those of *Architectural Review*, (monthly, cosmopolitan, intellectual, elitist) from the subscribers to *Architects' Journal* (weekly, local, business-like, work-a-day). Of course, many architects read both, and probably *New Society* as well, but they would recognize their own changes of expectation in putting down one paper and picking up another.

But if the tone and style change, it should be clear that one thing does not – my consuming interest, through thick and thin, hardback and limp, in what happens along the shifting frontier between technology and art. I would not claim to have a deeper grounding in technology/science/engineering than have many of my writing contemporaries, but I think I have been effective in deploying that knowledge for explanatory and expository purposes. Again, I have much to be modest about on the art and architecture side in a world that contains the likes of Nikolaus Pevsner, James Ackerman, Anthony Blunt or Vincent Scully, but I think I have been more assiduous than most of them in carrying their discipline down from Olympus into the market-place.

And I have loved every minute of it. Never having believed that journalism is a waste of talents and energy that ought to be reserved for more serious matters, I have treated whatever has come my way, not with levity (as some have claimed) but with the enjoyment of finding things out, and gratitude for having an audience to tell them to. Offence has been taken, I know, by those who insist that profound matters must be discussed only in 'serious' language, but having seen the mess that a Marx, a Mumford, a Levi-Strauss, a Galbraith or a Freud (let alone a Hoggart) can make by trying to handle light matters with heavy equipment, I felt I had license to do the other thing – and a better chance of being understood!

Reyner Banham

INTRODUCTION

There is no easy way of categorizing and describing the work of the architectural writer, Reyner Banham. His writings, which stretch over the last twenty-five years, are characterized by a rich diversity which reflects a flexible and spontaneous relationship with the world. Banham is not a pedantic architectural historian, nor is he interested in self-referential monuments. The context of his architecture and design is strongly humanistic and this perspective constantly determines his choice of subject matter.

Reyner Banham's early career is a mirror image of the diversity that characterizes his writings. Born in 1922, he was brought up and schooled in Norwich and served an engineering apprenticeship in the Bristol aircraft industry during the war. This early entrance into the world of technology was contrasted, after the war, by regular art reviews that he wrote for the *Eastern Evening News* and, later, the *Eastern Daily Press*. From Norfolk Banham came to London to study at the Courtauld Institute of Art in 1952. Michael McNay sums up his early career, 'After apprenticeships in the aircraft industry of Bristol and the art industry of Woburn Square, Dr. Banham was able to identify the thread of a screw as readily as a spandrel, or a triglyph'.

These experiences in two different worlds met in Banham's growing interest in architecture. He found there a focus for all his interests, but few relevant precedents. His reading about architecture began in the 1940s and, inevitably, it was the Modern Movement that he came across first – 'When I began to read up Modern Architecture properly, in 1940 or so, Walter Gropius' Bauhaus and the works of Le Corbusier were already the fixed stars of the greatest magnitude in its firmament. It was a nice, tidy propagandist's firmament, ordered by a cosmology so simple as to be almost simple-minded.'

A resolve to rid Modern architecture of this over-simplification began to dominate Banham's intentions and to these ends he wrote his doctoral thesis (published in 1960 by Architectural Press as *Theory and Design in the First Machine Age*) and contributed articles to *Architectural Review*.

Alongside this move into the respectable world of architectural history, Banham became involved with another, less respectable, series of activities in London in the 1950s. In many ways his time spent with the Independent Group, (a splinter group of the ICA which met initially to discuss the effects of technology and mass culture upon the arts) was more important as a single formative experience than anything else to date. It acted as a catalyst, bringing together many of his boyhood experiences in a provincial town with his later interests. He discovered there kindred spirits – the Pop painter Richard Hamilton, the Pop theorist John McHale, the sculptor Eduardo Paolozzi, the Brutalist architects Alison and Peter Smithson, the photographer Nigel Henderson, and the critic Lawrence Alloway.

The Whitechapel Gallery exhibition of 1956, *This is Tomorrow*, provided Banham with a platform from which to bring all his beliefs out into the open. He described it as, 'an invitation to smash all boundaries between the arts, to treat them all as modes of communicating experience from person to person'. This echoed his own subsequent intentions, affecting the way he began to look at contemporary architecture.

The Independent Group years marked his incursion into Pop culture, into studying the products of mass-production and the mass media. This interest provided an alternative starting point from the conventional one for architectural historians as it allowed for 'expendability', and 'fun' – two major themes in Banham's vision of contemporary society.

He set out, in 1955, in two parallel and interdependent directions; in search for both a contemporary architecture which would meet the needs of the new, democratic, 'admass' society, and a method with which to approach Pop culture. His architectural inquiry took him through a series of discoveries from New Brutalism, to Pop architecture, to technologically-determined structures, to Los Angeles, and finally to Megastructures as he searched for a perfect combination of relevant symbolism and technical competence. He moved from a position of complete faith in the

Opposite
LE CORBUSIER, *Dominican Monastery of La Tourette*, Eveux, near Lyons, 1956–9, detail of the interior near the altar of the Holy Sacrament.

Page 10
NORMAN FOSTER, *Willis Faber Office*, Ipswich 1975.

Page 11
DENYS LASDUN, *National Theatre on the South Bank*, London, 1976, detail.

Page 12
RON HERRON, *The Walking City*, designed for the Archigram Exhibition at the Institute of Contemporary Arts, London, January 1973 (*above*).

PETER COOK, *Plug-in City*, 1964, maximum pressure area, section (below).

Page 13
Moulton Standard Bicycle designer Alexander Moulton, 1964 (above).

Volkswagen Beetle Export, 1953 (below).

Page 14
Olivetti ELEA Computer, 1958–9.

Olivetti Lettera 32, 1963 (*inset*).

Page 15
Bertoia Chairs, designer Harry Bertoia, c. 1956.

The
Paylis
Terrace

The
← Olivier
Theatre

The
Cottesloe ↘
Theatre

The
Lyttelton
Theatre

Box
Office ↘

CITIES: MOVING

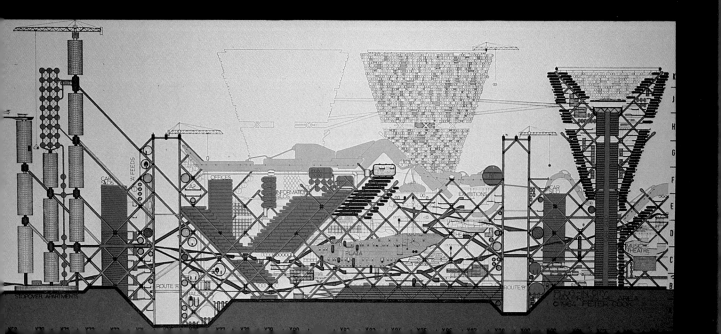

architect to a distrust of his omnipotence and back again, with many shades of grey between these black and white extremes. Simultaneously his interest in the mass environment urged him to come to terms with the aesthetics of expendability and to an analysis of object symbolism in terms of consumer expectations and aspirations.

The mid-sixties foray into Pop architecture seemed to bring the two inquiries together and it looked as if Banham had found an ultimate cause with which to ally himself. However, it proved to be a stylistic cul-de-sac, and Banham moved on, taking, once more, two parallel routes; the first looking for a democratic architecture that was possible rather than utopian, and the second consolidating his interests in objects in which expendability was a reality rather than a clever metaphor.

Banham's interest in industrial design was encouraged by a visit to Germany in 1959, to the Hochschule für Gestaltung at Ulm where the study of design was allied, under the leadership of Tomas Maldonado, to related disciplines including sociology, anthropology and semiology. This broadening of the design context undoubtedly appealed to Banham who had evolved, in embryonic form, a similar approach to design during his years with the Independent Group.

On the other side of the Atlantic the annual Aspen conferences provided a picturesque setting for many of Banham's serious thoughts about design. In 1974 he edited a book of papers from Aspen conferences of the previous two decades in which he commented, 'IDCA appeared to be addressing itself to problems that needed attention – Aspen's first attempt to tackle the problems of the environment for instance, was as early as 1962, long before the topic had become "hot and sexy"'.

America had more than Aspen to offer Banham. His visit there on his Graham Foundation scholarship from 1964 to 1966 was almost a 'return of the native' experience as his early absorption of American films and pulp novels had already prepared him for a culture that was democratic and visually exciting. In the US Banham rediscovered the American Moderns, experienced the unselfconsciousness of much American architecture and design, and, above all, discovered Los Angeles. This prompted his first thorough study of a total environment. His 'historical monograph' of LA, published in 1971, combined descriptions of avant-garde architecture and Pop phenomena like hamburger stalls and painted surfboards, creating a microcosm of the world which Banham inhabits – a world in which not only architects but the public put their creative stamp on the environment. He concludes the book with this statement: 'The common reflexes of hostility are not a defence of architectural values, but a negation of them, at least insofar as architecture has any part in the thoughts and aspirations of the human race beyond the private world of the professional.'

The rhetoric of the American environment – and growing dissatisfaction with the British – finally persuaded Banham to set up home there and after a period of about 15 years teaching architectural history at University College in London, he took up the offer of a professorial post at the State University of New York at Buffalo. During the blizzards of his first winter there he became aware once more of America's dependence on technology – this time it was 'snow-mobiles and commercial radio that made Buffalo bearable'.

Opposite
Eames Chair and Ottoman, designer Charles Eames, 1956.

At Buffalo Banham has continued to write about architecture and design and to review new books on the subjects. Banham has written for many periodicals over the last twenty-five years, contributing regularly to the *Architectural Review* and *Architects' Journal* in the 1950s, *New Statesman* in the late 50s and *New Society* in the mid-1960s. His style of writing has developed and changed alongside his intellectual evolution. McNay writes that, 'Banham thinks of his books as his serious statements and his journalism as the formulation of ideas that may be quite transient.' This is not a denigration of the shorter pieces but rather a description of their different function. Many of his articles are 'essays' for his books – particularly his architectural pieces – but the others, on a cross-section of mass culture, serve to translate the ephemeral values within this area of culture into an equivalent language which adequately describes them.

Banham's literary devices cannot be separated from his general ideological stance as they serve to communicate his special vision of the world. His democratic definition of culture is paralleled by his spontaneous and creative use of language which echoes the spirit of his subject matter. He describes a Hells Angel's motorbike, 'As like or not, they now have ape-hanger handle-bars, a single-tube frame, sissy-bars at the back, and a livery of Big, Bad Orange paint'; and the accumulative effect of his alliterated, hyphenated and often invented compound adjectives creates a strong visual image which evokes the power of the bike. Banham has learnt from the ad-man the technique of selling through evocation and suggestion, – devices highly appropriate to the subject matter he selects. (There is a strong parallel with Tom Wolfe's 'New Journalism' and other exponents of the same style on both sides of the Atlantic, which manifest a similarly playful, racy style to simulate the message of Pop culture and make the break with the 'old culture' complete.)

Banham's writing is characterized by its attention to detail – both of the language he employs and of the object he describes. However journalistic and ephemeral much of his writing may be, it serves, collectively, to mirror a universe which is unified by Banham's perception of it. In the end it is his vision that counts. His often utopian, always humanistic commitment to a world of equal opportunities, where the imagination defeats dry rationalism, points the way to a freer society and a new liberated role for the arts within it.

*   *   *

This selection of essays is divided into two parts. The first section consists of a number of Banham's articles about architecture and the second section contains a representative selection of his writings about Pop culture.

The articles in the first section have been chosen to show the main themes that run through Banham's career as architectural historian, theorist and critic. Two major themes recur – 'architecture as expression' and 'architecture as technology', reflecting the twin interests of his early career. Both these approaches towards the built structure depend ultimately upon the notion of a participant or 'consumer' who experiences the architectural solution whether in an active or a passive capacity.

In his reassessment of the Modern Movement Banham's humanism emerges in his desire to emphasize the expressive nature of much that was built or envisaged. This point is reiterated in his articles about misjudged heroes and unrecognized pioneers.

Banham shows his dissatisfaction not only with the aesthetic of Functionalism, but also with its dishonest relationship with the machine. For a while he is swayed by the 'architecture as services' argument and writes, 'one could create a neutral technological frame which was simply a support of structure and service within which people could express themselves freely', but soon returns to his earlier interest in the aesthetic problem of architecture when he realizes in 1966 that 'It does still matter to people what buildings look like'.

Banham's re-examination of the Modern Movement led him to an approach to architecture which he subsequently applied to the post-war world. His search for a combination of technical competence and honesty and a sensitive manipulation of form which takes account of contemporary symbolism introduced him to a vast cross-section of architecture from the most commercial to the 'fine art' end of the spectrum, permitting him to write equally persuasively about it all.

In the second section of essays, Banham's involvement with Pop culture is represented. These articles show his interest both in a definition of and an approach towards it, and in its manifestations as symbol-laden social phenomena. Banham's introduction into this area of culture as a subject for serious study occurred during his Independent Group days and remained a constant feature of his writings for magazines like *Architects' Journal, New Statesman* and *New Society*. His main interest lies in the styling and symbolism of consumer objects and the products of the mass media and in the way that they stand for 'Dreams that money can just buy'.

The subject matter that he returns to throughout his career falls into a number of distinct categories which have been dealt with separately in this selection. Of these by far the most popular are objects of transport, especially cars, closely followed by mass-produced consumer goods with a mechanical bias, ads, science fiction films, and a number of other mass media products that appeal to the public imagination.

Banham has said that Pop 'depends on a massive initial impact, but small sustaining power'. His writings about Pop conform to the first prerequisite by hitting the reader firmly below the belt, but I think that, unlike the phenomena they describe, it is quite clear that their ability to pass the test of time has been proven beyond any doubt.

Penny Sparke

Opposite
NORMAN FOSTER, *Willis Faber Head Office*, Ipswich, 1975, main escalator hall.

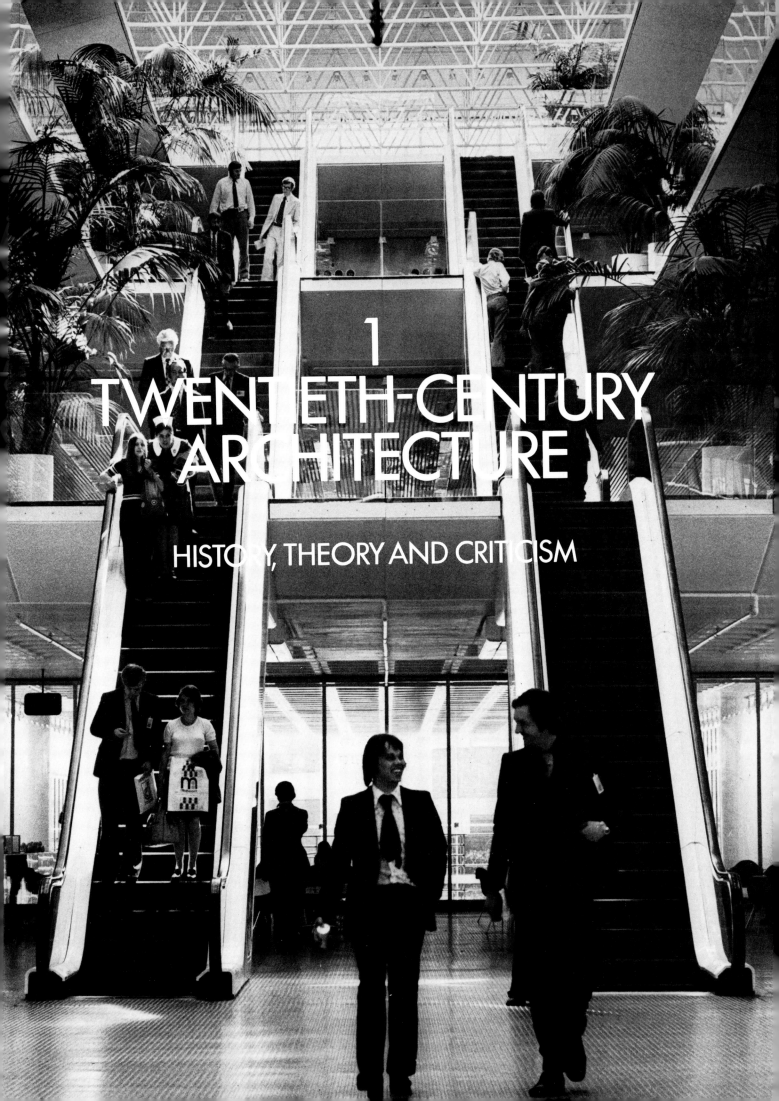

1
TWENTIETH-CENTURY ARCHITECTURE

HISTORY, THEORY AND CRITICISM

1.1 HISTORY AND PSYCHIATRY

In this article, originally published in Architectural Review, *May 1960, Banham discusses the need to redress the balance in the picture of the Modern Movement as portrayed by the architectural historians, Pevsner and Giedion, and begins to examine the 'Zone of Silence – 1910–1926' that they both omitted. Banham declares that he wants to reassert the importance of the Expressionist phase of Modern architecture that has been largely ignored and to define a new role for the architectural historian. This article provides the ideological framework for most of Banham's historical pieces written in the 1950s.*

The written history of the Modern Movement in architecture is a product of that movement's second, or Academic phase, much as Vasari's *Lives* of the great Renaissance artists was a product of the second, or Mannerist phase of humanistic art. So closely is historical writing associated with that second phase of Modern architecture, that its limits in time may be set, conveniently, by two works of the Movement's most favoured historian: Sigfried Giedion's *Bauen in Frankreich* ushered in the period in 1928–9; his *Space, Time and Architecture* began to undermine its intellectual basis in 1940–1.

The period, dominated by CIAM and the fight to establish Modern architecture outside the countries (Holland, Germany, France) that had brought it to birth, was one of consolidation, not of innovation, and contributed surprisingly little that was new to the Movement's stock of ideas. In many senses this is true of the historical writing of the period as well. Not that an historian is often able to make any startling new contributions at the best of times – sensational new documents rarely make more than marginal rectifications to the main body of evidence available, and radically new interpretations of the evidence are nearly always forced by the weight of the evidence itself.

But when an historian's primary sources are all embedded in the live traditions of an existing body of live men who are all of his own generation or the generation immediately preceding, two further effects also seem to come into play. Firstly, the 'evidence' seems to consist only of the most current of current opinion, and the facts that support it; secondly, the facts about the previous fifteen to twenty years are such common knowledge that no one really considers them worth recording. These factors, rather than any deliberate *Suppressio Veritatis*, seem primarily responsible for that peculiarity of all Modern Movement historiography of the academic phase, summed up in a statement by Bruno Taut: 'With the outbreak of the War (1914) the history of modern architecture may be considered closed.'

In Pevsner's *Pioneers of the Modern Movement*, which concludes, effectively, with the Deutscher Werkbund exhibition of 1914, a similar historical concept appears to be at work – but only *appears*, since the explicit programme of the book is to cover the Pioneers, the confusion deriving from the fact that some of the Pioneers lived to become masters of the next phase. In *Bauen in Frankreich*, the history appears to stop even further back, in the nineteenth century; works of the late twenties are made to appear directly derivative from buildings completed before 1900, and in his introduction Giedion speaks of going back to ultimate beginnings and ignoring all the 'débris' that had accumulated on top of them.

The upshot was the creation of a Zone of Silence, extending from about 1910 to 1926, the period when most

of the Masters of Modern architecture were perfecting their personal styles, as individuals, and the International Style, as a group. The débris that accumulated in this period was – near enough – the historical evidence for how these styles were developed. Much of this was probably beyond discussion at the period, either because it was too obvious to all those present, or because the historians were naturally reluctant to air, in public, the dirty linen of their friends (this is still a problem for a person writing about the period today).

In the process of creating this Zone of Silence, two alternative misconceptions were propagated – one, always in favour with some group or another, that there were scandals to be hidden; the other, the official line until fairly recently, that the Modern Movement is a direct continuation of the Rationalism and Functionalism of the nineteenth century. As a polemical device this latter proposition was immensely useful, since it meant that Modern architecture could be defended against the Philistines and sold to the undecided on grounds that they could accept and respect – honesty about function, materials, structure, respect for hygiene, economy and rationalization of construction.

So rare was direct discussion of the aesthetic or symbolic content of Modern architecture in this period, that the exceptions strike the eye, and have acquired a status out of all proportion to their intrinsic content. In this group one might name the first English-language edition of Moholy-Nagy's *New Vision* (*von Material zu Architektur*) and the sheaf of constructivist-slanted essays published in England in hard covers as *Circle*. However, the third work that is often found shelved alongside these two in libraries is of far greater consequence. The Museum of Modern Art's great catalogue of the exhibition *Cubism and Abstract Art*, edited by Alfred Barr, is the monument of the one grouping that really kept stylistic, aesthetic (and thus culturally interesting) discussion of Modern architecture alive. We owe to the Barr-Johnson-Hitchcock circle the phrase 'The International Style' and we owe to them also, as the organizers and inspirers of the exhibition, the other great catalogue, still a standard work, *Bauhaus 1919–1928*. These last two volumes together, like the two halves of the charge in an atom bomb, contained enough critical mass to detonate and demolish the whole myth of the Modern Movement as a persistence of the nineteenth century into our own times. Yet for a long time nothing happened, in spite of the trickle of revisionary information initiated by *Space, Time and Architecture*.

What was needed, probably, was some telling incident to form a positive trigger – in my own case this was a statement in an early talk on the BBC Third programme, to the effect that the Dutch de Stijl movement had considerable influence on the Bauhaus. Reference to the pages of *Bauhaus 1919–1928* produced ample visual justification for this proposition, but it also produced a positive statement that *de Stijl* was of little consequence in Bauhaus history. Such patent contradictions between fact and propaganda certainly stimulated my own earliest researches into the history of the Modern Movement; they may well have been the stimulus for others, notably Bruno Zevi's book on *de Stijl* under the title *Poetica dell'Architettura Neoplastica*. By the beginning of the fifties, the existence of the Zone of Silence was widely noticed, its contents the subject of interest and speculation.

However, serious research and reappraisal had not gone far before they were overwhelmed by that anomalous and largely irrelevant wave of neo-Palladianism to which reference was made in *Architectural Review*, 1960/1/ii. Yet when that wave receded it left the intellectual climate of the younger Modern architects permanently changed. Firstly, it seems to have broken their unthinking and purely conventional acceptance of the traditional posture of Modern Movement architects, ever poised for a bold step forward into some diagrammatic utopia. The loss of this compulsive progressivist reflex seems to have hurt politics more than it has hurt architecture. It may well be that this mass defection from Left solidarity was only a part of a more general disintegration of progressive opinion, but it had special consequences for younger architects – they emerged from their Palladian deviations with the habit of listening to the opinions of historians, and some expertise in deciphering their utterances. For this they had been prepared, of course, by fairly long acquaintance with the works of Pevsner and Giedion, but in the post-Palladian phase historians have come to the front as men with a specific and unique contribution to make, and history, as a subject of academic discourse, has acquired a new standing in the world of architectural education.

But the history of Modern architecture has also been presented with a new task – that of the revision of the great myths on which the Movement's esprit de corps is nourished. Although this extends far enough back to include a re-appraisal of the work of the Grands Constructeurs of the nineteenth century, the main task is seen as the elucidation and explanation of the events covered by the Zone of Silence. A generation has grown up that believes – rightly and wrongly – that Modern architecture underwent a major crisis somewhere in that period, and that the details have been kept from them. Though they are almost completely wrong in supposing that there has been any deliberate suppression of fact, they are clearly right about the crisis when the missing facts are examined.

Furthermore, the filling-in of the blanks gives meaning and value to contemporary reactions to the crisis. To take an outstandingly difficult case; the work of Gropius in the early twenties – a degree of embarrassment clearly surrounds his Sommerfeld House, an Expressionist log cabin of 1921 that makes patent nonsense of any suppositions of continuity between the Pioneer and Master phases of his work. The general response of the younger generation on first discovering this house has been to suppose it to be the product of (*a*) a moment of almost psychotic aberration, or (*b*) craven submission to the importunities of his client.

The filling-in of the surrounding facts, however, demolishes both propositions. The client, though strong-willed, was no fool and retains to this day a lively and sympathetic interest in Modern architecture. Nor can an aberration be convincingly propounded – the surrounding facts include, for instance, the exactly contemporary Otte house which makes a smooth transition between the log-cabin aesthetic and Modern architecture as commonly understood, since, in it, Gropius uses the same over-all form, even to the dormers, in combination with very pure, white-rendered surfaces.

But the surrounding facts also include Expressionist/Dadaist Berlin in political turmoil. Against this George Grosz background, one also perceives Bruno Taut making town-planning projects à la Finsterlin, and Hans Scharoun designing blancmange-shaped office blocks with Gothic portals, and Mendelsohn's Einstein tower just completed. And against this background Gropius emerges as what he has always been, a master of rationalism and restraint. One sees why the younger generation demands to be told '*all* the facts

on modern architecture'.

Now, if Expressionist Berlin does so much to give sense and context to the Sommerfeld house, it does quite a lot, still, in the same way for the Bauhaus buildings in Dessau, designed only four years later by a man who was still Walter Gropius, and – with suitable dilutions – this applies also to buildings he designed later still, such as the Siemensstadt flats, and to experiences he had undergone earlier, such as working with Peter Behrens. Our view of Gropius is impoverished out of all proportion to the number of facts involved if any part of his career is omitted from the account.

The same is true of the career of any other master, and since those careers add up – or rather, multiply together – to form the Modern Movement, our view of the Movement is disproportionately impoverished by those parts of their careers that have been swallowed by the Zone of Silence. In fact, the situation is worse than that, the silence covers *whole* careers – Mart Stam's for instance – writings, such as Paul Scheerbart's – and movements, such as Elementarism. But since this period, these movements and ideas were those in which Modern architecture as we know it was created, those members of that movement who could not be present at the time, because they were not yet born or were in Finland or Brazil, are in ignorance of their own origins. The urgency of the demands to know 'What really happened in Modern architecture', to be apprised of every discoverable fact, to have every accepted valuation checked and every movement, however obscure, shaken out for any original ideas it contains – the urgency of all this, which is the consumer-pressure on the producers of historical writing, is the urgency to know 'How did I get this way?' History, considered under this light is not, in Alan Colquhoun's telling phrase about Giedion, 'The quest for respectable grandfathers,' but a psychiatric enquiry into the springs of action, the grounds of inhibition.

If the older historical dispensation approaches the evidence much as a herald might approach a family tree, to see what glorious bearings may be quartered into the blazons of Modern architecture, the new historiography puts the movement on the couch and asks embarrassing questions. A father-figure like Auguste Perret who appears as a scion of a noble line of classicists on one count, may appear as a structural pervert on the other; an influence like Mondriaan, whom the 'official' view may see as an exemplar of simplicity and purity, may be seen from the other side as a man in the grip of an almost catatonic fixation, unable to do anything but repeat the same image over and over again. However, the psychiatric simile cannot be pursued too far in detail – though it remains overwhelmingly true in general. The confirmation comes most aptly in a phrase used to describe the passionate interest in the content of the Zone of Silence, viz 'Using facts to pervert the history of the Modern Movement'.

Against accusations like the last – which are perfectly true if one inserts such a word as 'accepted' in front of 'history' – the new-style historian needs a double armour. Firstly, because his main sources will be the public or private utterances of men still alive, he needs a diplomatic talent that will enable him to break confidences without giving offence. The historian who persistently accedes to demands for decent silence will sooner or later lose the respect of his readers. But, even more important than the ability to spill secrets inoffensively, is the ground on which he decides to spill them. His integrity as an historian must be beyond question, and this, under present circumstances, means that the amateur historian, the historian with architectural connections, is out. It is very noticeable that the prestige of

Sir John Summerson's utterances about Modern English architecture has gone up since he ceased to be an apologist for the English Modern Movement and that the big question-mark about Sigfried Giedion is still his involvement with his subject matter as secretary of CIAM.

The one secure ground on which an architectural historian can stand is outside architecture. Since he cannot be an architect, his professional qualifications must be as an historian, since he cannot get by without some professional qualification that an architect can trust. He is now regarded more and more as a sort of specialist consultant, like an acousticist or a traffic engineer, and is expected to tell the truth even if it hurts. But he cannot get away with this unless he stands firmly on a professional qualification that proves his grounding in an orderly method, that proves an objective attitude towards the evidence.

Obviously, this does not rule out the amateur contribution, particularly in field-work – the enthusiast who is prepared to work through *Bottin* in search of early houses by Lurçat, or swings his camera on to a factory in Krefeld on the off-chance that it may be Mies van der Rohe; the self-appointed commandos who storm doors in Hollywood in the hope of seeing interiors from Frank Lloyd Wright's concrete block period, or stir the dust in Italian museums in pursuit of ground-plans by Sant'Elia. These men – who are also a phenomena of the new history – are the prospectors and surveyors who fill in the blanks on the map, but the final drawing of the map, and the indication of the areas that still need further field-work, these need the authority of a trained professional mind that the field-workers can trust; therefore, preferably, a professional with some field-work behind him, like Theodore M. Brown, the author of the recent book on that highly symptomatic figure from the Zone of Silence, G. T. Rietveld.

The position remains, in any case, that the appointment of historians to a cure of souls, to the guardianship of the conscience, even the sanity, of the profession, places upon their shoulders a responsibility that they have not been asked to carry before. Nor is this likely to be a passing phase – the detachment of architecture from its grand traditions, extending from the Pyramids to the Crystal Palace, has clearly been broke for good, it cannot hope to regain its Vitruvian innocence. Without the ballast of an equivalent millenial tradition, architecture will have to be consciously trimmed and steered as it proceeds, and someone will have to plot its course continually. That someone is the historian: it is not for him to give orders or indicate destinations, but his plot of the track to date must be accurate. The most difficult and embarrassing part of this new task will be to pass judgment on the tendency that so much disturbs the older historians of Modern architecture – the tendency to Modern Movement revivalism (discussed in *Architectural Review*, 1960/1/iv–vi). Although this tendency affects mostly the younger historians' own contemporaries it also touches some of the Masters, and requires him to say how far the curved forms of, say, Ronchamp are to be regarded as conscious revivals of Gaudi or early Mendelsohn (hardly at all in the present writer's opinion) just as much as he is required to pass judgment on the revivals of the Dutch 1920s to be seen in some aspects of Neoliberty, and in different aspects of Team X projects (in both cases fairly conscious and deliberate).

But to revert to the psychiatric simile, his diagnosis must be as nearly infallible as is humanly possible, and to achieve this he must be as nearly objective as is humanly possible, and as reliably skilled in interpretation as is humanly possible. The responsibility that awaits him is not a light one.

1.2 SANT'ELIA

Banham's interest in Sant'Elia stems from the lack of attention that had previously been given to him and the important role that he feels that Futurism in general plays in the Modern Movement's adoption of the machine as an expressive symbol. In this article, originally published in Architectural Review, May 1955, *he discusses the source material of this exciting architect and shows how central an understanding of his expressive work is to the history of the Modern Movement.*

The Modern Movement can have left behind few monuments as baffling as the memorial to the war dead of the town of Como. Seen from a steamer coming down the lake its white form – a truncated dipylon gripped between powerful canted buttresses – suggests the remains of some grandiose engineering project, such as a suspension bridge, abandoned before completion. Seen from the land, its stance astride the axis of the inevitable Via Vittorio Veneto, and its flanking hemicycles of cypresses, make its monumental intentions unmistakable. Yet it is quite free of the usual flabby symbols of Fascist military rhetoric; all is fine-drawn, stark and abstract. It is, as the red CTI guide-book of 1936 truly says, 'una severa costruzione architettonica'.[1]

The red guide offers one other piece of information on the monument: that it was built by the 'ing. e arch. Terragni, su disegni del caduto arch. Sant'Elia'. The architectural information in CTI guide-books is usually perceptive and well informed, but most students of Modern architecture would find the monument so unlike what they know of the manner and intentions of the fallen architect Antonio Sant'Elia, that they would suspect that what they see is much less his work than that of the engineer and architect Giuseppe Terragni, fallen, in his turn, in another world war, some six years after the guide book was written.

But how much do we really know of Antonio Sant'Elia, Futurist and architect? A very well-read student of the Modern Movement, who used the resources of the RIBA and Victoria and Albert Libraries to the full, going on even when the catalogue had lost interest in the subject, would be acquainted with: a longish footnote in Dr. Pevsner's *Pioneers;* four paragraphs in *Space, Time and Architecture;* a collection of essays entitled *Dopo Sant'Elia,* which includes the text of the *Manifesto of Futurist Architecture;* two pages in P. M. Bardi's *Belvedere;* a dim little book by Alberto Sartoris, whose accidental importance, as we shall see, outweighs its patent demerits; two articles in *Casabella* in the early thirties, and one in *Architettura;* and six pages of involved and high-flown exegesis of the Manifesto, in Zevi's *Storia.* This may seem quite a respectable literary memorial for a man who never built a building, but the entire body is bedevilled by an inescapable defect – it is based upon a very limited knowledge of the existing evidence about the architect. Most of the Italian material is also spoiled by jingo rhetoric before the last war, and political embarrassments after it. The student who has consulted all these books and periodicals will have seen no pictures of the Monument, and only ten of his drawings. Four of these, all skyscraper projects, are from the *Città Futurista* exhibition of 1914; one is a sheet of drawings dated 1913, which can be cut up to look much more numerous, and the rest, which appear only in the obscure second edition of Sartoris's book, come from another source altogether – and suggest, faintly but tantalizingly, unknown aspects of Sant'Elia's personality.[2]

The student who commanded this material would know Sant'Elia's views on architecture, as they appear in the Manifesto, would have only the vaguest idea what those ideas were to look like in the round; he would know that his memory was honoured by Sartoris, Terragni and the Italian rationalist architects, but also by the apologists of Fascism; that he was born in 1888, and was thus younger than the great masters of the twenties, finally qualified in 1912, *summa cum laude,* joined the Futurists in the same year, and set up his own office in Milan, but had to waste his talents detailing other people's competition projects; and that he died, under conditions of almost too-conspicuous gallantry, in the fighting round Monfalcone, October 10, 1916. His last words, according to a well-nourished legend, were: 'To-night we sleep in Trieste, or in Paradise with the heroes.'

Essentially, this information is all that is needed to form a true estimate of Sant'Elia's historical position, and his contribution to the Modern Movement, but most of us would be hard put to interpret the evidence, or to know which saying illuminates which drawing, and vice versa. The basic obstacle is the fixed image we have in our minds of Futurism as a closed aesthetic system with a single aim, the praise and illustration of movement. But though studies of motion represent the great contribution of the Futurists to twentieth-century art, it should not be thought that the delight in speed, noise and machinery which gives rhetorical vigour to the Manifestos of 1909 and 1910 remained the sole object of the Manifestos even of 1912, still less of 1914. The situation was quite otherwise, and after the Milan group had fused with Soffici and the Florentine Cubists in 1912, the leading Futurists began to retrace their steps. Lesser figures like Balla and Russolo might continue to pursue and refine the theme of motion, but the founder of the movement, F. T. Marinetti, and its greatest exponent, Umberto Boccioni, were both on the way back to a static and classicizing ideal, achieved by the latter, who died two months before Sant'Elia, in the form of an open and understanding imitation of Cézanne in the last two or three paintings he produced.

In the case of Marinetti the change is harder to see. One who is essentially a public figure and popular performer must inevitably repeat his accustomed verbal formulae, and his earliest phraseology carries through by its own momentum into 1914. But the title of his most carefully worked out policy-manifesto, which appeared in March of that year – *Geometrical and Mechanical Splendour, and the New Sensibility of Number*[3] – though it promises a greater change than the text exhibits, clearly reveals the new tendency. Sant'Elia, who was not a foundation member of the group, but rather the 'Beniamino della squadra', took his style from the leaders, and everything which remains of his thought and work is marked by this transitional frame of mind, between motion and stasis, between empiricism and classicism, with the world of machinery and an aggravated sense of patriotism as the only stable elements to which a man might look for support.

The *Manifesto of Futurist Architecture* is almost exactly contemporary with that on *Geometrical and Mechanical Splendour,* and was certainly written very much under Marinetti's influence. It has never been translated into English – very little Futurist literature has – and though this is not the place to examine it in detail, its main drift must be known before Sant'Elia's drawings and projects can be understood.[4] It is arranged in the common Futurist form of a general prologue, analysing the present condition of the aspect of life due for Futurist attack, followed by sets of tabulated propositions about what should be done. In this case the prologue opens with the statement that there has been no architecture since 1800, but only a hotch-potch of decorative styles.

So-called renovators of the art have simply added new variations to an old game, undisturbed by the complete revolution and mechanization of modern life, and our cities remain sunk in the squalor of the centuries, instead of answering the needs of to-day. Thus a great art is debased to an empty game of revivals, as if we, with our turbulent mechanized life, could live in buildings designed for the needs of five centuries since, and students are forced to copy the past, instead of studying the true needs of the contemporary city.

The problem of Futurist architecture is not one of finding another style of detailing, but of starting afresh on sound foundations, using every resource of science, abandoning all that is heavy and antique. Architecture has been worn out by traditions, and must be remade by force. Precise structural calculation, the use of concrete and steel, exclude architecture in the classic sense. We no longer believe in the monumental, the heavy and static, and have enriched our sensibilities with a taste for lightness, transience and practicality. We must invent and remake the Futurist city like an immense assembly yard, dynamic in every part; the Futurist house like a giant machine, without painting or sculpture, enriched only by the innate beauty of its lines, extraordinarily brutal in its mechanical simplicity; and streets must be buried storeys deep below the buildings, served by escalators and high-speed conveyors.

We must abolish decoration, and solve the problems of Futurist architecture by strokes of genius and the use of scientific techniques. Everything must be revolutionized: roofs cleared, cellars opened up, façades devalued, and attention transferred to the grouping of masses and disposition of planes on the broadest scale.

An end to monumental commemorative architecture!

The reader who has been hanging on to his hat in the gale of prophecy that blows through this remarkable document – he will have noted the anti-monumentalism twenty years before Mumford, the house/machine equation eight years before Le Corbusier, mechanistic Brutalism nearly forty years before Hunstanton – has further buffets to follow in the tabulated propositions which make up the rest of the Manifesto.

Sant'Elia proclaims:

(1) that Futurist architecture consists of precise calculation, boldness and simplicity, concrete, steel, glass and lightweight materials

(2) that it is not, for all that, merely an arid combination of practicality and utility, but remains an art ...

(3) that diagonal and elliptical lines are dynamic by their very nature and a thousand times more emotive than horizontals and verticals

(4) that decoration as something stuck on to architecture is an absurdity

(5) that just as the ancients drew the inspiration for their arts from the world of nature ... so we should draw ours from the mechanized environment we have created

(6) that architecture must be understood as the art of disposing the forms of a building according to finite and stable laws

1 SANT'ELIA, *Città Futurista*, c. 1913–5.

2 SANT'ELIA, *Città Futurista*, c. 1913–5, sketch for a street.

3 SANT'ELIA, *Study for Milan Central Station*, 1913.

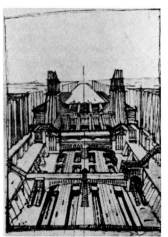

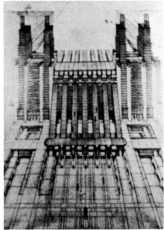

4 and 5 SANT'ELIA, *Studies for Milan Central Station*, 1913.

(7) that architecture must also be understood as the power to harmonize man and his environment

(8) that an architecture such as this breeds no permanence, no structural habits. We shall live longer than our houses, and every generation will have to make its own city.

If these eight propositions reveal his sources – Adolf Loos, Boccioni, Marinetti and so forth – they also carry deeper the tone of prophecy. Not merely the short-term prophecies of the superficial aesthetic of the Expressionists, as in (3), but also in the subtler and more durable prophecy of the essential philosophy of the International Style, for (5) and (6) bring together, probably for the first time, the idea of mechanism and the idea of absolute aesthetic laws, the Machine Aesthetic. But we can go further than this: (2) rejects, as every great architect of the twenties was to reject, the essentially Victorian concept of Functionalism, while (7) and (8) adumbrate a philosophy astonishingly close to that of Buckminster Fuller.

Yet to have prophesied the common intellectual currency of the twenties is not enough to make him a Pioneer of the Modern Movement, any more than statements about beauty following function, uttered in the 1850s, can make Horatio Greenough a founding father of contemporary American architecture. To have bracketed together machinery and aesthetic law, or steel, concrete, daring and calculation, would only guarantee Sant'Elia an honoured place on the side-lines, like C. R. Mackintosh, who anticipated many of the forms of Modern architecture, without arriving at its essential intellectual basis. What gives an architect his place in the family tree of the Modern Movement is the manner in which he gives plastic form to certain basic assumptions about architecture and mechanism – and in the absence of completed buildings, this brings us back to the question of Sant'Elia's drawings.

As has been mentioned above, the apparently extensive literary record of his life and work contains very few drawings, and the literature normally available to an English speaking student, only one, from the *Città Futurista* set, 1. Other drawings from this set have appeared in Italian publications, there is the single sheet which appeared in *Dopo Sant'Elia* and in *Belvedere*, and there are the other five which appeared in the second edition of Sartoris. This is precious little to have survived from an artist who according to Reggiori,[5] made hundreds, and died less than forty years ago.

However, when Sartoris issued the first edition of his book in 1930, it contained no drawings at all, and a rather huffy introduction by Carlo Ciucci explains that this is solely due to one who, though bound by the strongest moral ties to assist those who wished to honour the dead architect, had repeatedly put obstacles in the way of the publication of his sketches. The implication of this is clearly that the main corpus was already within one person's control, and there is internal evidence in the book to suggest who this might be, for in the very full bibliography there is listed a de luxe edition of Marinetti's book on Sant'Elia 'di 13 copie con allegata una opera originale di Sant'Elia' – though no example of this edition with original drawings bound into it seems to survive. Circumstantial confirmation of Marinetti's responsibility is offered by a corpus of ninety-four drawings, all but four of them unpublished (except those mentioned below) which were given to the Museo Civico in Como in 1945, by the architect's family it is said, yet within three or four months of the death of Marinetti at Bellagio, just up the lake.

These drawings may have been out of Marinetti's control even before his death since some of them appear in Sartoris's second edition, dated somewhat uncertainly 1944, but even so it seems fairly certain that the paucity of published drawings must be attributed to Marinetti's unwillingness to trust others to honour a memory to which he was deeply attached. As has been suggested, the five drawings from the Como corpus which appear in Sartoris's second edition do give intimations of a more complex artistic personality, and the totality of this corpus,[6] of which the *Città Futurista* set form less than one-eighth part, give so immensely broader and deeper a view of Sant'Elia that revisions of the common estimate of his stature are clearly required.

About a dozen of the drawings belong to the *Città Futurista*, or are connected with it in some way, such as 2, with its Wellsian valley-section streets, graded for different classes of traffic, or 3 and 4, studies for the reconstruction of Milan Central Station which lead on to 5, the station for the *Città*. The exterior view, 3, looks as if it must have some part in the prehistory of Erich Mendelsohn, but 4, looking out over the tracks, certainly prefigures one of the characteristic dream-images of the urbanism of the twenties – the airstrip between skyscrapers of Le Corbusier's Plan Voisin de Paris.

The other eighty-odd sketches represent terra incognita. They do not exhibit much of the Viennese influence which has been suggested by some non-Italian writers, and this is hardly surprising in view of the Futurist loathing of Austria-

6 and 7 SANT'ELIA, *Sketches for a Villa and for a Theatre*, c. 1913–5.

Hungary. Yet, in spite of the outburst in the Manifesto against 'pseudo-avant-garde architecture from Austria, Hungary, Germany and America', there are unmistakable traces of International Art Nouveau in drawings such as the villa, 6, or the frequently redrawn project, 7, for a theatre. Yet here, framing the apparently cast-iron Gothic detailing of the central bay, one sees great stone buttresses of simple geometrical form which do show some affinity with the Monument. But, in fact, there are nearly a score of drawings which show closer affinities that this, and reveal a designer whose intentions in the modelling and disposition of forms were of a simplicity and boldness far ahead of those of his older contemporaries Gropius, Lurçat, Mies and Le Corbusier at that time, though his functional and planning intentions remain inscrutable in the complete absence of any plans among these drawings.

These purely formal exercises are called mostly 'dinamismo architettonico' or 'torre faro'; 8 and 9 are typical of the former, purely abstract group, 10 and 11 of the lighthouse projects. They all exhibit large plain areas of flat unadorned surface; bold arrises; thin refined re-entrants, as on the Monument, wherever a rounded form shoulders back on a rectangular one; the use of canted cut-backs in vertical surfaces, or of upright buttresses rising out of sloping planes; all imbued with a highly sculptural sense of form, of moulding and cutting large masses of apparently homogeneous material. But beside a sculptor's sense of form, one can also sense that of a civil engineer, of the nineteenth-century bridge and dam-builders, or of one who, as Sant'Elia had done, had occupied a responsible position in the works department of the city of Milan, and of the Villoresi Canal, even before his qualifying exams. Not unnaturally, it is when this particular and forceful formal sensibility is employed on substantial functional problems, especially industrial ones, that his talents begin to resemble those of a major designer.

The factory project, 12, is perhaps not the most exciting of these, though its combination of high, sculptural accents with the low shed between does pre-echo Mendelsohn again, in this case the factory at Luckenwald. But in projects like the two-level bridge, 14, or the even more proto-Mendelsohnian airship-hangar, 13, one can see a truly imaginative, but well-informed, appreciation of the possibilities of reinforced concrete, and can educe some idea of how Futurist architecture was to be not merely 'an arid combination of practicality and utility, but an art . . .' by virtue of the dynamic potentialities of diagonals and ellipses. However, it is in three power-station projects that we see the culmination of this engineer-sculptor sense of formal manipulation.

The theme of the generation of electricity was clearly much in the minds of the Milan group in 1913 and 1914, and it contributed a characteristically rhetorical image to Marinetti's *Manifesto of Geometrical and Mechanical Splendour*:

> There is nothing in the world so beautiful as a great generating station, humming with power, holding back the hydraulic pressures of a mountain chain, storing the power for a wide landscape, integrated by control panels gleaming with switches and commutators. These powerful images are our only models . . .

This passage, another example of Marinetti pioneering an aspect of machinery as an emotionally-loaded symbol that was to have a respectable career in the avant-garde thought of the twenties, also shows the change which had come over Futurism by 1914. For however mechanistic and emotive this image may be, it does not deal with noise, speed and physical impact, but is static, clean, subdued and essentially abstract. Sant'Elia parallels this with the superbly

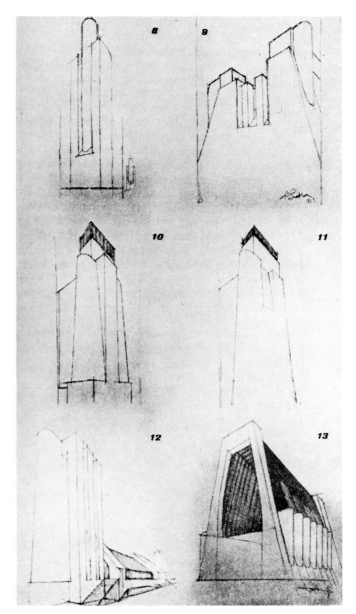

8, 9, 10, 11, 12 and 13 SANT'ELIA, *Sketches from the Unpublished Drawings at Como*. 8 and 9 are typical of 'dinamismo architettonico', 10 and 11 of the lighthouse projects; 12 is a sketch for a factory and 13 for an airship-hangar.

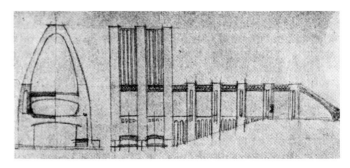

14 SANT'ELIA, *Two-Level Bridge*.

rhetorical composition of 16, with its sense of soaring *excelsior* and the shouldering up of the massive buttresses at its base; with the elegant understatement and simplicity of 15, which surely cannot have long to wait for realization by some Scandinavian architect; and in 17 with a design as prophetic as any of the propositions of the Manifesto. The block of the generator shed, with its ranked cylinders of the chimneys, its tall canted window and high transformer-tower (or condenser-stack) anticipates in general form and in

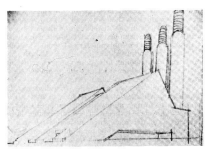

15 and 16 SANT'ELIA, *Sketches for Power-Stations*, c. 1914.

17 SANT'ELIA, *Sketch for a Power-Station*.

some details, the aspect of power-plants designed by intelligent engineers in the last twenty years. It is far in advance of the worn-out classicism of Tony Garnier's almost contemporary power-house in Lyons, and few architects since have conceived of forms which so truly summoned up the mechanical and geometrical splendour of the theme as this sketch of Sant'Elia, done in 1913.

* * *

Where does this leave us with the various problems raised by the person and work of Antonio Sant'Elia. As to the Monument, we now see that, allowing for the fact that he despised monuments, this is the kind of monument he might have built. For obvious reasons he could not have designed a war memorial for 1915–18, but its flavour of frustrated engineering, its plain and simple modelling, its canted buttresses, and its general form combine to give it a place as an appendix to his works – and if a certain stiffness,

and the rather unpleasantly Novocentista flavour of its base must be credited to Terragni, one should also recall that it is unlikely that the original architect would have been able in his own lifetime to erect a structure so blankly devoid of cornice or detailing.

The other two problems, that is: sources and stature, can only be dealt with under the important proviso that our conclusions are subject to there being no other drawings still in existence. The certainty with which Sartoris and Ciucci assumed that Sant'Elia could not be properly illustrated without the Marinetti drawings suggests that these were already, in 1930, either the largest, or the most important surviving collection, but this does not rule out the possibility that stray sheets, like that in *Dopo Sant'Elia*, may still turn up, and the decencies of art-historical method therefore require a certain caution.

Still, given this proviso, we can say that the problem of Austrian influence needs to be reconsidered, at least. One has the impression that it depends, to some extent, on a misapprehension of the scale of the *Città Futurista*, for if one examines the drawing by Otto Wagner which Professor Giedion compares with the most famous of the *Città* drawings,[7] one sees that its scale and intentions are roughly comparable with the bridges over the Seine in Paris, and is perhaps 50 feet high from its Beaux-Arts basement to its Art Nouveau cresting. Sant'Elia's project, on the other hand, 1, must be practically 270 feet high from the lowest visible circulation level to the top of its ranked radio-masts, and there are at least six visible circulation levels, anyhow, as against Wagner's two. On this kind of scale, what are compared to decorative details on Wagner's project are, in fact, quite large structural units. There certainly are Viennese influences to be detected, but they are more convincingly found in, say, the actual draghtmanship of 14.

But these details are merely the surface flourishes upon a highly individual manner of conceiving architectural form, and the sources of that manner, with its simplicity and broad glyptic planes, are very difficult to identify in the Europe of 1910–14. Thus, though it is only too easy to see in Wagner where the architecture leaves off and the engineering structure begins, Sant'Elia's *Città* exhibits a completely integrated structural conception, and blends different materials as equably as, say, the Library Wing of Glasgow Art School. That Sant'Elia could have seen pictures of this celebrated elevation is unlikely, and we are driven back to an enquiry as to the men he met in the course of his practice and training – who taught structures at Milan Polytechnic, or Bologna,[8] whom did he work under on the Villoresi Canal, what engineering plants did he know, could he see in magazines, or were pointed out to him by Marinetti and Boccioni? Or was there still a constructive tradition descending from Antonelli's work in Turin and Novara, passed on to d'Aronco and the Stilo Liberty?

The fact that names and places do not immediately spring to mind is a warning that we have come to accept a rather narrow view of the sources of the Modern Movement, and inspires one to hope that some Italian student is currently gathering the personal memoirs of the survivors of what must have been an exciting period before it is too late.

As to Sant'Elia's stature in the Modern Movement, it seems unlikely that further drawings will seriously upset the estimate which one may now form, given the extended and deepened appreciation of his intentions which the unpublished drawings provide. Though he had no direct followers, he clearly ranks with Adolf Loos as an early abolisher of decoration, but whereas Loos seems often, as a consequence, to find himself stuck with a collection of rather dull boxes, Santa'Elia is rarely stuck, but goes on to create forms which are exciting in virtue of their mechanistic inspiration. In fact, putting the total corpus of drawings against the text of his Manifesto, we see that he was among the very first to combine a complete acceptance of the machine-world with an ability to realize and symbolize that acceptance in terms of powerful and simple geometrical form. The acceptance is more complete than Le Corbusier's, the forms more powerful than those of Gropius.

To say, as Professor Giedion has done,[9] that he intended 'to introduce the futurist love of movement into his city as an artistic element', seems now an underestimate of his mental calibre, and a misunderstanding of his place and time in the development of Futurism. The drawings entitled 'Dinamismo Architettonico' make it clear that 'movement' as a quality of individual buildings has a very special meaning in his hands, while an examination of the *Città Futurista* drawings suggests that far from trying to 'introduce' move-

ment, Sant'Elia is basing his whole design on a recognition of the fact that in the mechanized city one must circulate or perish. He seems to have foreseen the technological cities of the fifties, each of which, in Gerhard Kallmann's neo-Futurist phrases,[10] 'is a dramatic demonstration of motion-existence articulating space. At the centre of congress motion surges upwards ... in towers that pin-point the sky ... horizontally it articulates highway ribbons charged with a continuity of energy missiles; omnidirectionally it radiates outwards by aeroplanes arriving and departing,' and having seen all this he tried, and may yet prove to have succeeded, to give this concept of the city a comprehensible architectural form which should enhance its character and facilitate its essential functions. Even though he left behind no completed buildings, he was a Pioneer of the International Style, and the first to conceive the planning of cities as fully three-dimensional structures, and his position in the family-tree of the Modern Movement is thus assured.

1.3 THE GLASS PARADISE

Like Sant'Elia, Bruno Taut's Glass Pavilion, with its debt to the German poet Paul Scheebart, plays an important part in the development of Expressionism within Modern architecture. Banham describes the symbolic and expressive power of this building and stresses the fact that Modern Movement writers have ignored this vital aspect of its evolution. This article originally appeared in Architectural Review, *February 1959.*

The public were less surprised by Lever House than was the architectural profession – and this was logical, for had not a massive body of opinion-making machinery been telling them, since the mid-twenties, that Modern architecture was just a lot of glass boxes? Architects, on the other hand, knew that between the glass legend and the concrete fact there was a great gulf fixed – a gulf forty years wide and as deep as the building industry.

In spite of near-misses like Gropius's Faguswerke, and any number of exhibition buildings, in spite of Mies van der Rohe, Lever House was still the first of the glass towers to realize a seminal concept that has lurked in the mind of the Modern Movement since before the First World War. The reasons for this extraordinary lack of phasing may be traced back to the Movement's own view of itself, and particularly to its tendency to try and tidy up its own history as it goes along.

The respectable genealogy of the glass legend is primarily the work of two men: one was Hermann Muthesius, father of the *Deutscher Werkbund*, who wrote in his *Stilarchitektur und Baukunst* of 1902, of the beauties of the Crystal Palace and the Galérie des Machines, station halls, covered markets, and most of the totemic objects of the glass dream – a pioneer re-assessment of the nineteenth century. The other is Sigfried Giedion, whose *Bauen in Frankreich* of 1928, related the architecture of his contemporaries back to Muthesius's canon of nineteenth-century masterpieces, and interpolated, with great historical subtlety and erudition, a philosophy common to both. His contemporaries were, of course, delighted to find that they were following such distinguished precedents, most of which were unknown to them until they opened the book.

But if these precedents were, in practice, unknown to them, what precedents did they follow, what motives drove them? What, in fact, had been said and done to further the glass dream between 1902, when Muthesius pointed the way, and 1929, when Giedion's book was shortly followed by others by, e.g., Arthur Korn or Konrad Werner Schulz, which dealt specifically and exclusively with glass in building.

One can point first to two respectable contributions, Meyer's *Eisenbauten*, before the First World War, and the *Ingenieurbauten* of Lindner and Steinmetz after it, which both drew attention to buildings of the type originally praised by Muthesius, but were not particularly slanted toward glass. One sees also that Bauhaus teaching, and the example of the Bauhaus buildings in Dèssau must have turned men's minds in the direction of transparent membranes, even though Le Corbusier's first *pans de verre* were still, so to speak, around the corner of a white rendered wall. But in all these there is no sign of the singing tones of prophecy, the incantatory repetitions that give a material those symbolic powers, over and above the recommendations of reason, that make it a live component in architecture.

It is to Germany, in the months immediately preceding and immediately following the First World War, that we have to turn to find that prophetic tone, to the period bracketed by the completion of the glass wall of the Faguswerke, late in 1913, and the second, 1920, glass-tower project of Mies van der Rohe. Both of these are accounted works of the party of reason, yet both, on examination, are found to have some curious cousins. Mies's glass towers have been justly called Expressionist, while their contemporaries, from Gropius's side, include the first Bauhaus proclamation with its gushing rhetoric about buildings 'like crystal symbols', and a three-spired Gothic cathedral on its cover.

All this is commonly written off as an aberration due to 'post-war Berlin'. But if it was, then it was an aberration that gripped a generation, and must have more in it than meets the eye. In fact, there is a great deal in it, a great deal of the Modern Movement's disreputable ancestry, but as far as the glass legend is concerned, there are two dominant strains, both traceable back to the Werkbund's exhibition in Cologne in 1914. The importance of that exhibition for the glass dream is known, and acknowledged in every history by an illustration of one of the staircases of Gropius' office block in its glass hemicylinder. But that is only half the story.

There was also at Cologne for that exhibition a pavilion devoted to the glory of glass exclusively, a pavilion that demonstrably had a far greater immediate effect on the imagination of German architects than Gropius's did, for sundry descendants of it can be identified in designs done after the war, including Mies's first, faceted design for the Friedrichstrasse skyscraper. This pavilion cannot be comfortably fitted into the history of the Modern Movement – particularly if that history, like Giedion's, is slanted for continuity – because it is so wrong for its time: a primitive geodesic dome of steel and glass, raised on a drum of glass bricks containing staircases with glass treads and glass risers, a design imbued with the homogeneity and visual certainty that Gropius's office block so conspicuously lacks, even allowing for differences in function and form.

The Glass Pavilion was the work of Bruno Taut, and so far exceeds every other design from his drawing board that one may properly enquire what lies behind it. The clue is given by Konrad Werner Schulz: it was 'Paul Scheerbart gewidmet', and this Paul Scheerbart was 'der literarischer Vorlaufer und Anreger moderner Glasarchitektur'. Now, the statement that the literary forerunner and instigator of Modern glass architecture was Paul Scheerbart will probably come as a

1 OSCAR KOKOSCHKA, *Paul Scheerbart (1863–1915).*

complete surprise to English-speaking readers and to many German-speakers as well. In German architectural literature his name is unknown outside the works of Schulz, Platz (two brief references in his *Baukunst der neuesten Zeit*) and some forgotten books by Bruno Taut. In English, there is a glancing reference in Giedion's *Walter Gropius: Work and Teamwork*, but not a word in *Space, Time and Architecture*.

The oblivion into which Scheerbart's name has fallen suggests – and how rightly – that he is not to be numbered among Modern architecture's respectable ancestors. Handbooks of German literature, unanimously unaware of his architectural interests, record an almost spherical Bohemian layabout – and Kokoschka's portrait confirms this – a fringe-member of the Futurist-Expressionist Sturm group, born in 1863 and dead in 1915, the author of fantasticated novels, mostly short and decorated by his own hand in Yellow Book style. Many of these novels can best be described as contra-science fiction, astral pantomimes, moon romances, astral novelettes and what-have-you. Beyond this, his output included appendices to the Munchausen legend, Harem romances, an *Eisenbahnroman* that appears to be the pioneer of that genre of literature whose chief ornament is the *Madonna of the Sleeping Cars*, a 'Hippopotamus' novel (of which more in due course), and a telegraphic romance called *The Mid-Ocean Hay-fever Sanatorium*, in whose very title one perceives something of the vein of practical logic that runs through his one work specifically devoted to the arts of buildings, *Glasarchitektur*, published in 1914.

Dedicated, as one might have guessed, to Bruno Taut, it is a slim, soberly-presented volume, quite unlike his novels in typography and format, and runs about a chapter to a page – some of the chapters no more than single thoughts noted in a couple of sentences – for 125 pages. These chapters are only loosely connected, though not much more loosely than those of Le Corbusier's *Vers Une Architecture*, and like that work they expound an unpredictable mixture of uninhibited vision and sharp practicality. Both the vision and the practicality draw their strength from the things that Scheerbart knew at first hand or had seen with his own eyes – glazed verandas, palm-houses, public halls, searchlights, zeppelins, sanatoria, mirror-panelled café interiors, theosophist publications, the Cologne pavilions of Taut (oxplicitly) and Gropius (by inference), and much more besides. the vision he offers is a compound of all these, torn from their contexts, and re-assembled by a mind unrestrained by conventional ideas and received opinions, but buttressed by a shrewd idea of what will, and what won't work, 'The vision of a glass world ... as entirely delectable as the gardens of the Arabian Nights ... a paradise on earth ... we shall show no longing for the paradise of heaven', begins with something that was common knowledge to Scheerbart and most of his readers, the glazed conservatory. This he envisaged becoming ever larger and more important until it had to be emancipated from the house, and set up independently in the garden. The glass-world citizen then abandons his old house and moves into the conservatory, which is aesthetically linked to the garden (floodlit at night) by glass walls and screens that extend its structure into its surroundings. As a habitable environment, the conservatory-house, which Scheerbart seems to envisage as something like Taut's Glass Pavilion, has double walls of coloured glass carried in a reinforced concrete frame clad in mother-of-pearl or mosaic. Its floors were to be of coloured ceramic tiling, its furniture of glass with brightly enamelled steel legs and upholstery of glistening glass-fibre cloth. Artificial light was to enter the rooms from sources between the double-glazing, and from hanging lamps of oriental style, the heating under the floor.

The landscape in which the jewel-like house and its floodlit garden are situated is to be a diffuse metropolis, with air-navigation beacons winking from the tops of its taller buildings. Illuminated trains, cars and motor-boats, like blazing jewels traverse the night scene, while overhead, zeppelins, brightly-lit themselves, and shedding light over the land, cruise toward an air-terminal in a park of experimental glass buildings, one of which is a hangar whose roof-space is occupied by an exhibition of models of historic airships, all with their own miniature lights ablaze. The shore line of the Swiss lakes, the outlines of the smaller Alps are picked out in brilliantly lit glass hotels, the summits of the higher peaks are floodlit in colour. Venice – or a new movable Venice – is a cluster of huge pyramidal buildings, glazed and illuminated and doubled by their reflections in the calm sea. Tourists, no longer hurrying from distraction to distraction, move calmly from the contemplation of one glass wonder to another.

About this vision certain things need to be said. Its inspiration was certainly personal – Scheerbart, it appears, was often poor, cold and miserable in squalid surroundings, and had an acquired hatred of the ill-lit and oppressive atmosphere of congested masonry cities. Hence the diffuse planning of the glass dream-world, the gardens and the greenery. Hence, too, the dedicatory motto he pronounced at Taut's Cologne Pavilion:

> Das Glas bringt uns die neue Zeit
> Backsteinkultur tut uns nur Leid
> (Glass brings us the new age
> Brick culture does us only harm)

and his insistence that the 'metropolis in our sense' must be dissolved. But Scheerbart, unlike some of the glass-enthusiasts of later generations, was under no illusion that glass was in itself a universal panacea. He had too much practical sense for that, and knew the weaknesses and side effects of its use. He knew that it was all too pervious to heat, and insists frequently on the need for double-glazing. He knew also of the greenhouse effects it can produce, and insisted that glass architecture was for the temperate zones, and not the tropics nor the polar regions. He knew that his call for 'Mehr Farbenlicht!' (More coloured light!) that runs through the whole book, could only reasonably be answered when electricity was cheaper and more plentiful than at the time he wrote. When hydroelectric power came in, he prophesied, then even private persons will have floodlighting in their gardens. He knew from Taut that the making of convincing models of glass buildings awaited more tractable materials than the picture-glass and brass strip then in use, and looked forward to developments in transparent plastics (he names a forgotten proprietary product *Tektorium*). Beyond that again, he looked forward to even better materials than glass for full-size buildings, and identified laminated glass (zwischen zwei Glasplatten eine Zelluloïd-platte) which had only just come in, as an example of what should be looked for from a lively and developing technology, for:

> We stand at the beginning, not the end, of a culture-period.
> We await entirely new miracles of technology and chemistry.
> Let us never forget it.

This optimistic view of technology puts him at one with the Futurists, whose works he certainly knew, and in this, as in his long-range prophecies, he is clearly of the party of progress, a member of the mainstream of Modern architectural thought. Where he is conspicuously outside that mainstream is in the detail aesthetics of his vision. Whether or not he knew any Tiffany interiors, he certainly knew and

Opposite
2–4 BRUNO TAUT, *Glass Pavilion*, Werkbund Exhibition, Cologne, Germany, 1914, plan and elevation drawings, and contemporary photograph.

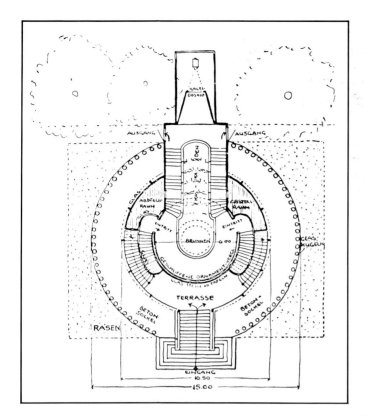

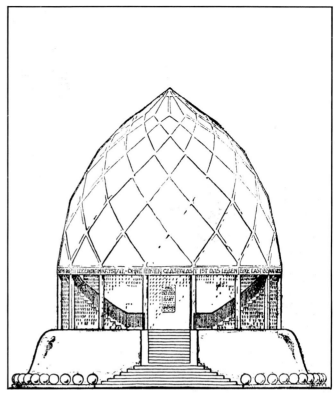

admired individual pieces of Tiffany glass, and its aesthetics, notably the nuanced colours that he calls 'die Tiffany-Effekte', inform many of his visualizations. To this must be added an insistence on ornament based on mineral forms and vegetation – perhaps like Louis Sullivan's – and a strong strain of conscious orientalism that directs his thoughts on light fittings, cloths and fabrics, floor coverings, tile-work and so forth.

Here, in fact, we see him headed against the supposed tide of Modern Movement ideas. As Charles Mitchell pointed out some time ago, the idea of good modern design for which we have settled is a profoundly classical idea, in opposition to the anti-classicism of much nineteenth-century thought. Scheerbart was no classicist, and for an entirely logical reason: 'Hellas ohne Glas' (Greece without Glass). Equally logically he admired those cultures that delighted in coloured glass, in the Orient and in Gothic Europe. Equally logically again, he combated the classicist polemics of Adolf Loos (by implication if not by name) against ornament.

But – and still perfectly consistently – he also saw Gothic architecture as the true forerunner of the great glass and iron structures of the nineteenth century that he admired quite as much as Muthesius ever did, and in this linking back of the Grands Constructeurs to the Gothic spirit, he is at one with the French Rationalist tradition from Viollet-le-Duc to Auguste Choisy, the tradition that produced most of the buildings that were featured in *Bauen in Frankreich*. Again, his orientalisms, Gothicisms, his interest in theosophy and light-mysticism, which all seem a mile away from mainstream Modern Movement ideas, are no distance at all away from the frame of mind in which Johannes Itten created one of the greatest glories of the Modern Movement, the Bauhaus preliminary course. The Bauhaus connection cuts even closer than this – much of the text of the first proclamation, where it deals with eliminating the barriers between brain-worker and artisan, directly echoes the apocalypse of Scheerbart's *Immer Mutig* (the Hippopotamus novel referred to above) where 'Kings walk with beggarmen, artisans with men of learning' and the three-spired cathedral in Lyonel Feininger's woodcut on the cover is now seen to be topped, not – as has been supposed – by three stars of Bethlehem, but by three navigation lights for Zeppelins.

One could pursue the matter further, into the ever-ramifying but ever more attenuated influence of Scheerbart as it runs on into the twenties including perhaps the glass towers of Le Corbusier's Plan Voisin de Paris, for they are close cousins to Mies's Friedrichstrasse project, and their form with emphatic vertical accents was later written off by Le Corbusier as a mistake peculiar to German architecture. But the mere pursuit is not the point – it is the necessity and attractions of the pursuit that are the point. Why, in a word,

Opposite
5–9 BRUNO TAUT, *Glass Pavilion*, Werkbund Exhibition, Cologne, Germany, 1914, interior views.

do we have to re-write the history of the Modern Movement?

Not because that history is wrong; simply because it is less than lifesize. The official history of the Modern Movement, as laid out in the late twenties and codified in the thirties, is a view through the marrow-hole of a dry bone – the view is only possible because the living matter of architecture, the myths and symbols, the personalities and pressure-groups have been left out. The choice of a skeletal history of the Movement with all the Futurists, Romantics, Expressionists, Elementarists and pure aesthetes omitted, though it is most fully expressed in Giedion's *Bauen in Frankreich*, is not to be laid to Giedion's charge, for it was the choice of the Movement as a whole. Quite suddenly Modern architects decided to cut off half their grandparents without a farthing.

In doing so, Modern architecture became respectable and gutless; it entered on what Peter Smithson has justifiably called its Academic phase, when it became a style with books of rules, and could be exported to all parts of the Western world. but having set itself up as something more than a style, as a discipline of pure reason, it had to double-talk fast and frequently to explain its obsession with certain materials, particularly glass and that smooth white reinforced concrete that never existed outside architects' dreams and had to be faked in reality with white rendering. Clearly, these materials were symbolic, they were totemic signs of power in the tribe of architects. But while concrete has never lacked respectable medicine-men, from Auguste Perret to Pierluigi Nervi, to maintain its mana, the image of Gropius as the official witch-doctor of glass has never looked very convincing. On the other hand the fanaticism of a Bruno Taut possessed by the spirit of Paul Scheerbart, as by a voodoo deity, has much more the air.

This is not to say that we now throw away the history of glass in Modern architecture as it has been established so far – the position of Muthesius and Gropius among its prophets is not demolished, only diminished. We have to find some space for Scheerbart, as Giedion now clearly recognizes. The problem, which is not to be settled by a single article, is – how much space? As to his right to that space there can be no further doubt, for if one applies to him the normal test for missing Pioneers, that of prophecy uttered in the right ears at the right time, he scores more heavily than many other writers of his day. Not only were his architectural writings known and in varying degrees influential among the generation of Gropius and Mies van der Rohe, but at a time when many spoke of steel and glass, he also spoke of water as the natural complement of glass, of the need to temper the white glare of light through glass by the use of coloured tinting, he spoke of America as the country where the destinies of glass architecture would be fulfilled, and he spoke of the propriety of the 'Patina of bronze' as a surface. In other words, he stood closer to the Seagram Building than Mies did in 1914. To put him back into the history of Modern architecture is to shed upon it precisely what he would have us shed upon it – 'Mehr Farbenlicht!'

1.4 MENDELSOHN

Expressionism, along with Futurism, form, according to Banham, important areas for study for the historian of Modern architecture and Mendelsohn's work, from his war sketches to the Einstein Tower to the later geometrical buildings, provide a good example of form combined with expression. Banham compares him with the Dutch Expressionists and shows their influence, and that of America, upon him. This article originally appeared in Architectural Review, *August 1954.*

The large reproductions of a sketch for the Einstein Tower, and the short and baffled accompanying paragraphs, which have been all that most of the major international architectural periodicals have been able to produce as memorial notices to the talent of Erich Mendelsohn (1887–1953), are a tribute to the myth which has been built around his name, rather than the buildings which he designed. His has been an extremely difficult achievement to assess, but the blanket description of Expressionist which is normally applied to his work has only made assessment more difficult. Like Futurist, the term Expressionist has become a dirty word in architectural criticism, and it serves nowadays as a mask for our unwillingness to pay attention to a whole group of architects who lie outside the respectable genealogy of the descent of the Spirit of the Modern Movement.

The term may with some certainty be applied to his work of about 1919, and the Einstein Tower is, indeed, a monument to that phase of Expressionism which reached its apotheosis in Dr. Caligari, but the differences between the first great doctor of the German Cinema, and Dr. Mabuse, the last, are not as great as those between the Mendelsohn of 1919 and the Mendelsohn of 1932. Like Dr. Mabuse, the last works of his German period seem, by implication, to reject Expressionism as the employment of the insane, and to substitute for it a more sensible and humane view of the world, and the aim of this article is to sketch in the stages by which this transformation was effected, and to suggest some of the causes which have obliterated this change of mind from the popular mythology of Modern architecture.

The point of departure of any study of Mendelsohn must always be the well-known sketches of the War years, and the related series of sketches which followed the interruption of 1917–19. These have made a major contribution to the myth, and seem to be regarded as a kind of master-key to the labyrinth of his imagination. But when one re-examines them one finds only that the labyrinth is more involved, and the imagination more diverse than one had supposed. They are not stylistically homogeneous, either among themselves or with his work of the early twenties, and it is in their stylistic aberrations that they are most revealing. The corpus of pre-1917 drawings contains, for instance, a whole series of rather pretty and feeble variations on themes which seem related to Hoffman's Palais Stoclet, and another group which shows no signs of this classicized Art Nouveau manner, but, drawn in heavy black brush-strokes, seems to depend on Max Berg and Fritz Höger.

However, elements from both these series – an Art Nouveau sense of linear decoration, a whiff of the Beaux-Arts, a debt to the 'plastic' Expressionists of the previous generation – these elements do appear, dramatically metamorphosed, in the justly celebrated series of factory and warehouse projects which, to most of us, are typically Mendelsohn. But in this series there also appears a new element – an unmistakable tone of high Futurist excitement about the world of the machine. These projects are surely attempts to realize the Marinettian vision of 'immensi cantieri tumultuanti', and of the Futurist building which was to rise like 'una macchina gigantesca' above the roaring abyss of the streets. And in Sant'Elia's manifesto of 1914 one finds, most suggestively, a categorical demand for an architecture of ellipses and diagonals, since these forms are 'dynamic by their very nature, and are a thousand times more emotive than perpendiculars and horizontals'.

To these literary imperatives one may certainly add a shrewd appreciation of the expressive possibilities of Behrens's Turbinenfabrik and the Galerie des Machines, both of which Mendelsohn was later to praise in public utterances. But closer examination of the actual drawings will bring further interesting light to bear on his creative mind at this period. The powerful plastic sensibility, which shapes the aggressive forms of these projects, often models them in a manner which seems quite alien to the nature and performance of the material which is supposed to compose them. The forms which he employs express a romantic feeling about the materials, rather than a technical understanding of them, just as the over-all shape of the building is

1 ERIC MENDELSOHN, *Early ink sketch showing traces of pre-1914 Expressionism.*

2 ERIC MENDELSOHN, *Project for a Factory,* 1917, sketch and axial plan.

intended to express something about the process conducted within, but seems not to be governed by an interest in the space or flow requirements of that process. This idea, of shapes being able to express certain emotions or attitudes, is the great legacy of nineteenth-century academic thought to the aesthetics of Expressionism, and this academic affiliation is unexpectedly confirmed by the symmetrical Beaux-Arts plans which are appended to some of these projects. In this, however, Mendelsohn is no more than the child of his time, as one may see by comparing these projects with the immediately pre-war work of Gropius. When designing a building to house a real industrial process – the Fagus Factory – Gropius and Mayer make no pretensions to over-all symmetry of plan, but when he was called upon to design a building to express a state of mind about machinery – the so-called factory at the Werkbund exhibition at Cologne – Gropius not only relapses into the Great-West-Road pretentiousness of hiding his machine hall behind an arty office block, but makes that office block symmetrical and aligns his machine hall on the axis of it. And one does not have to look very hard at the Werkbund complex to see that it contains more than one anticipation of Mendelsohn's work of the twenties.

But, as far as the War years are concerned, the development of his style followed the lines laid down in the first series of factory projects – the shapes become more bulgy and pressurized, but the basic principles of conception and composition remain the same, and the fruition and termination of this development was the Einstein Tower. Contrary to commonly accepted belief it must be emphasized that the tower closes a chapter in his career, and has no progeny in his own work; it is the end of Mendelsohn the Expressionist.

The commission came to him as a result of some observatory projects of 1917 which he had showed to Professor Findlay-Freundlich, one of Einstein's collaborators, and made him a natural choice when the German Government decided to show its change of heart towards the deviser of the Special and General Theories of Relativity by building him an observatory for the spectrographic study of galactic recession. The subject matter was a perfect one for a crypto-Futurist to build expressively, and its realization gave tangible form to all the tendencies latent in the wartime sketches. Its plan is as snugly axial as that of a beetle, its outward forms have an almost manually-moulded appearance, as if the 'eyebrows' over the windows had been pushed up by a giant thumb, and these shapes are quite arbitrarily false to the material of which they are composed; for, under the rendering, the building is almost entirely of brick. Nevertheless, these moulded shapes have a certain sculptural sense about them, and are consistent within their own disciplines, and the plan is perfectly adequate to the fairly simple functional programme. On the other hand the manifest dynamism, the aggressive directional tendency, of the exterior treatment is curiously inapt to a structure whose purpose is to stand still and look upwards and all round – and Mendelsohn, regarding the rising structure in the light of his experiences in 1919 and 1920, seems to have had his own doubts about the value of dynamism of this sort.

The experiences which may have produced such doubts were themselves precipitated by the Tower itself – for the sketches and plans for it were shown in an exhibition of his drawings at Paul Cassirer's gallery in Berlin – under a title, *Architecture in Steel and Concrete*, which seems to be the basis for the legend that the tower is a reinforced concrete structure. His outré designs clearly hit an appropriate note in Dadaist Berlin, and the exhibition was well received and widely noticed. Among those who noticed it was H. T. Wijdeveld, who invited Mendelsohn to supply material for a special issue of the magazine *Wendingen* which he edited from Amsterdam, but before this issue appeared in print (October 1920) the architect himself was in Holland to lecture to the *Wendingen* group, and study contemporary Dutch architecture at first hand.

Those who knew him at the time confirm that he was very impressed by his Dutch experiences, and the evidence of his writing and designs makes it clear how profound the consequences were. *Wendingen* was the mouthpiece of that group of second-generation Dutch Modernists who married Art Nouveau and Arts and Crafts ideas in the style now usually called Amsterdam Eclectic; a group which included the feverishly inventive talents of de Klerk, and the hardly less brilliant designers Kramer, Kropholler and the Eibink-Snellebrand partnership. No group then practising in Europe could be more likely to appreciate the Expressionist art of Mendelsohn: they knew their Poelzig as well as he did; like him they commonly designed with maquettes of soft plastic materials; the stylistic development of the Eibink and Snellebrand office closely parallels his, and their villa plans are in every way the peers of his for organic qualities and freedom from straight walls; and in de Klerk's post-office of 1917 Mendelsohn could see an architecture which was dynamic in the literal Futurist sense of being elliptical and in parts diagonal.

But if the dynamic members of *Wendingen* stood very close to him in some ways, they were separated from him by their understanding, common among Dutch progressive designers, of Frank Lloyd Wright. The influence of the great Chicagoan on the Dutch Rationalists – Oud, van t'Hoff and others – is in the textbooks, but it was *Wendingen*, not *de Stijl*, which published a special issue on him, and any visitor to the suburbs of Amsterdam can see how much the Eclectics borrowed from him – displayed wooden structure, handicraft surfaces and, most particularly, free picturesque planning whose asymmetry was very different from the prim axiality of Mendelsohn's work. One should remember that *de Stijl's* reaction against *Wendingen* was hardly under way at this juncture, and was barely visible to the eye in built architecture – Oud was still using handicraft surfaces, Rietveld's manifesto-house outside Utrecht was not completed until the time of Mendelsohn's second visit in 1923, and any distinction between the two schools was about to be smeared over by Dudok and the early work of van Boeken. Any manifestations of *de Stijl* then visible would have appeared to the visitor, as they appear today, no more than an excited rectangular pimple on the face of a consistently developing national style.[1]

Mendelsohn saw, both in Amsterdam and Rotterdam, no more than variants of a common style drawing on Art Nouveau, Wright and handicrafts, practised in a manner which was extravagant in the north, and restrained in the south. The real division of Dutch architecture in 1919 was between *Wendingen's* tendency to put expressive aesthetics first, and the tendency of the Oud-Rotterdam circle to put social and functional considerations first. All this he saw and understood, for he wrote to his wife: 'Oud is functional, corresponding to Gropius, Amsterdam is dynamic. Analytical Rotterdam refuses vision; visionary Amsterdam has no use for cold objectivity. Rotterdam will pursue the narrow path of construction until it dies of cold; Amsterdam will perish by the fire of its dynamism.' This letter is one of the vital documents on Mendelsohn's development, but it has hitherto been subjected to the wrong kind of interpretative treatment.

3 ERIC MENDELSOHN, *Pleasure Pavilions*, 1920, 2 sketches and an exterior view.

4 ERIC MENDELSOHN, *Double-Villa*, Charlottenburg, Berlin, 1922.

5 ERIC MENDELSOHN, *Hermann Hat Factory*, Luckenwald, Germany, 1923 (destroyed). Detail of the power-house (*above*), and general view of the factory with the dye-vat on the left (*below*).

Energy has been lavished (by Whittick among others) on exegesis of the word *dynamic* – a matter which could have been cleared up by a quotation from the *Manifesto of Futurist Architecture*, and some illustrations of the work of de Klerk and Kramer – energy which would have been far better expended in relating this document to Mendelsohn's own position in 1919. For the letter continues: 'I stand by my intermediate position ... dynamism *plus function* is the challenge'. The middle-of-the-road attitude to Dutch architecture which he here proposes clearly implies a qualified acceptance of the *Wendingen* position, and thus, by extension, a qualified acceptance of his own Einstein Tower frame of mind. But when one examines the sketches and designs of the years following 1919 one sees at once that 'qualified acceptance' is a bleak understatement – the sight of the dynamic fantasies of Amsterdam produced a violent self-examination, a state of mind in which alarm was mingled with 'There, but for the grace of God, go I'.

In the sketches, the stylistic homogeneity which had been evoked by 1917 is split: on the one hand the curvilinear Expressionist manner is screwed up to a pitch of contorted frenzy which utterly outbids his previous conceptions, but had no effect on his built work; on the other hand there appears a new style altogether, chunkily rectangular, asymmetrical, and commonly executed in slashing horizontal shading. In built work this new manner appears pure, and purely Dutch, in the 'tile-hung' double villa at Charlottenburg, completed in 1922; a building whose sources are unmistak-

ably Rotterdam, but whose rectangularity is clearly not from *de Stijl*, in spite of the fact that he had, by now, made the acquaintance of van Doesburg. Equally Dutch are the Meyer-Kauffmann factory, the Sternefeld house and the Haifa competition projects of 1923 – these last being so characteristically Dutch that one sees the justice of von Soergel's attempt to link Wright, Dudok and Mendelsohn in a kind of international remote-control master-pupil relationship. But the accent of the Haifa projects, and of the Weichmann silk stores, is more violent than that of Dudok, or that of Richard Neutra, with whom Mendelsohn was collaborating at the time, but who seems unlikely to have had much influence on the new manner, since the other product of their partnership was the remodelling of the Tageblatt corner in Berlin, and that is the one really Expressionist work of the early twenties.

But the outstanding work of this stage in his career is undoubtedly the Steinberg-Herrmann factory at Luckenwald, completed in 1923. It is also the most instructive, for now, after nearly ten years of the celebrated factory projects, one can see the architect at grips with an industrial problem in reality. The product, alas, had not the brio quality of the Futurist dream – there is nothing very dynamic about a hat, however elliptical its plan-form – and yet the overall layout of the factory does take up the axial symmetry of the pre-1917 sketches. This is all that is taken up, however, and the meaning of the symmetrical plan is severely compromised by the fact that the main runs of the work-halls are at

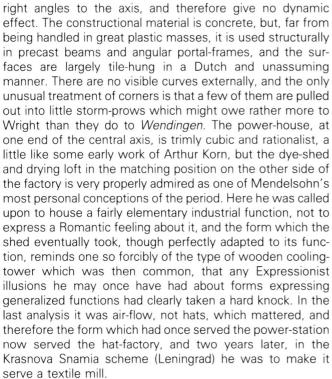

6 ERIC MENDELSOHN, *Bejach House*, c.1927, east, north, south and west elevations, and a photograph of the east façade.

7 ERIC MENDELSOHN, *WOGA Flats*, Berlin, 1928.

right angles to the axis, and therefore give no dynamic effect. The constructional material is concrete, but, far from being handled in great plastic masses, it is used structurally in precast beams and angular portal-frames, and the surfaces are largely tile-hung in a Dutch and unassuming manner. There are no visible curves externally, and the only unusual treatment of corners is that a few of them are pulled out into little storm-prows which might owe rather more to Wright than they do to *Wendingen*. The power-house, at one end of the central axis, is trimly cubic and rationalist, a little like some early work of Arthur Korn, but the dye-shed and drying loft in the matching position on the other side of the factory is very properly admired as one of Mendelsohn's most personal conceptions of the period. Here he was called upon to house a fairly elementary industrial function, not to express a Romantic feeling about it, and the form which the shed eventually took, though perfectly adapted to its function, reminds one so forcibly of the type of wooden cooling-tower which was then common, that any Expressionist illusions he may once have had about forms expressing generalized functions had clearly taken a hard knock. In the last analysis it was air-flow, not hats, which mattered, and therefore the form which had once served the power-station now served the hat-factory, and two years later, in the Krasnova Snamia scheme (Leningrad) he was to make it serve a textile mill.

Thus one sees that the contact with Holland had been instrumental in producing a fundamental change in his mode of conceiving architecture. He no longer thought in terms of roundly-modelled forms, broad-based like a blancmange, but now in terms of structural assemblies of geometrically simple units which presented themselves to the eye as tidily profiled edges, or areas of flat or vertical filling. He still seems to think in terms of perspectives and exteriors, but these seem now to be conceived as sharply angular solutions to corner sites, rather than as buildings in the

axially-planned round. Pure plain Dutch influence continues to appear in his works, whether small – like the Bejach house and the Boat-club project – or large – like the very Amsterdam-looking flats on the WOGA-Universum development. But riding through this continuing influence is the development of a new style of publicity-architecture which was to be of critical importance in the shaping of the visual world of Western Man, and made, quantitatively, a greater contribution to product design than the more elevated conceptions of the Bauhaus and *l'Esprit Nouveau*.

This new style is not so much a continuance of the Einstein manner, as it is often supposed to be, as a crossing back of his Dutch experience on the original Futurist inspiration. Its development is consistently from mechanistic self-assertiveness towards a bland and sweeping precision, and though Borax and Streamstyling are its undoubted progeny, they were incidental to a development whose main trend was in a different direction – a direction which had barely been revealed when the Nazis brought his German career to an end.

The Futurist dream had never been dead, though it had been jolted, and stripped of its vocabulary of form by his Dutch experiences, and it is from Holland, paradoxically, that the best evidence of Futurist continuance has come. It appears in another *Wendingen* publication, the text of his lecture of 1923 'The International Coherence of Modern Architectural Thought', delivered during his second visit to Holland. The theme was once more the opposition of Dynamics and Function, and in words at least he temporizes between approving and disapproving the machine – passages of almost Futurist rhetoric being counterpoised against cautious passages in which architecture and mechanism are carefully held apart. But the marginal illustrations to the text are even more instructive than the lecture, since they include, among much else, skyscraper projects by Gropius, Mies, and Hans Scharoun, pages from *l'Esprit Nouveau*, buildings by Berlage, Frank Lloyd Wright and Max Berg – an international gallery of advanced architectural thought. But this series of thumbnail illustrations opens with a sequence of images as impeccably Futurist as those in *Vers une Architecture* – lathe, foundry, power-house, locomotive, aircraft, cunarder, and then his own Tageblatt corner and Tatlin's Constructivist memorial tower.

This places his earliest reklame architecture firmly between mechanism and Constructivism, and this Futurist position was to be powerfully reinforced by his visit to America in 1924. There, it is true, he stayed a few nights with Frank Lloyd Wright, and was lectured on Louis Sullivan by no less a person than Fiske Kimball, but there he also saw for the first time the fully and unrestrainedly mechanized environment of the Futurist dream, the tower-cities for which the infant Moholy-Nagy had wept. His *Architect's Picture Book of America* is a photographic vision of high-speed multi-level circulation at the feet of towering buildings, the window lines soaring up into a sky that is still light while the headlamps of the traffic slash horizontally across the bottom of the photo-image. Man populates that roaring abyss, the street, from which the Futurist's buildings were to rise like gigantic machines. This is his view of America, and, curiously enough, it contains none of the great factories at Detroit, no early work of Albert Kahn – though it does include two Detroit street-cars whose importance will appear later.

Characteristically, it is a view which, when it observes a grain silo, seems uninterested in the classical regularity of the great simple cylinders, but insists instead on the tangle of pipes, staircases and services on the side about which Le Corbusier was always so careful to remain silent. And it is a view which verbalizes itself in pure Futurist rhetoric in the letters which he wrote during his stay in America:

> Boilers, turbines and conveyors built in sizes which have completely exploded the original scale of the Power-station, all subject to the law that the expressive power of any material is limited, and must in time give way to newer and more fully mechanized materials; the fantastic drama of great Piranesian tubes from which are born purely technical achievements that point the way to the future and leave functionalism behind as a merely transitional condition. The Power-energy of the future advances inexorably upon us because it is driven forward by these new emergents.[2]

If the handicraft excesses of *Wendingen* had driven him out of his old admiration for dynamism, his Futurist response to America and its mechanical enormities had driven him into a new one. It is precisely because this post-American dynamism is new that the Tageblatt corner cannot be made to fit with the rest of the reklame designs. It belongs to the older concept of dynamism; its great nodding 'tara' is merely Poelzig vulgarized; it is the last outpost of his Expressionist past. The new accent begins to appear, rather tentatively, in the Herpich store of 1924 with its hard smooth surfaces and radiused bays, but the vital step forward is taken with the projects for the Mosse exhibition stand and the Autophil petrol pumps from later in the same year. Here his Dutch experiences, and some possible contact with Russian Constructivists then in Berlin, were confronted with a theme which, in the petrol pumps, was undeniably Futurist – and he responds with a formal resolution of the problem which anticipates in an astonishing way the pressed-steel Borax which his influence was to father in America some fifteen years later.

In the next year the classic Mendelsohn cliché, the cylindrical glass staircase-drum appeared. But it was not a

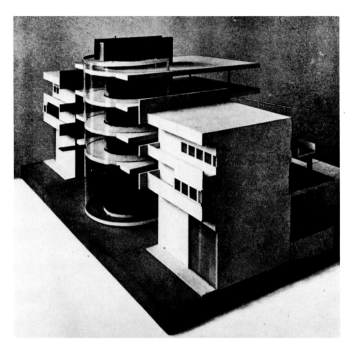

8 ARTHUR KORN, *Competition Project for a Shopping Centre*, Haifa, Israel, 1923, model showing the glazed stair-drum.

9 ERIC MENDELSOHN, *Schocken Department Store*, Stuttgart, 1926–8, axonometric drawing.

Mendelsohnian invention, and it was not he that made a cliché of it. It had first appeared in Gropius' Werkbund building, and had been revived in a Haifa competition project of Arthur Korn's in 1923 – and he and Korn seem to have been in quite close touch in the early twenties. What Mendelsohn did was to give this architectural device a formal certainty which it had lacked in the Gropius version by building out its rotundity with projecting horizontal fins, and tying it back to the rest of the building by running these fins as cornices across the flat of the façade. He first used the device on the Krasnoya Snamia engine house, and then on the Cohen and Epstein store of 1925, where it is in effect a scale model for the Schocken store at Stuttgart, whose design must have been put in hand early in 1926. Here a full-sized department store staircase rises in a projecting glazed drum at one end of the main front of the building. The wrap-round cornices are used to tie it back to the side façade, and the main street front has a contrasting system of fenestration with long brick panels separating horizontal bands of glazing. A similar use of horizontal bands of windows, with more than an air of homage to Louis Sullivan in their framing, appears in the Petersdorf building in Breslau, and there a vertical drum is used to sweep off the end of the façade in a manner which, having only one cornice per floor, suggests rather forcefully the part which the street-cars of Detroit might have played in the development of this shiny and mechanistic style – one might be looking at the prow of a multi-decker tram.

And these three shops are his total employment of a device which is normally regarded as a cliché in his work. Already in the Mosse Pavilion for the Cologne exhibition, with its very wide-swept run of fenestration round the end, and even in the stupefying juke-box façade of the Wertheim project (also 1929) there are signs that he was about to go off on another tack, signs which are justified by the WOGA-Universum development, the Schocken store in Chemnitz, and Columbushaus in Berlin. In these there emerges a new way of managing large urban sites, with broad bland façades sweeping round to follow the run of an existing street or shape the traffic-flow in a new one. This last German manner of his, with its horizontally banded frontages free from either horizontal or vertical projections, smooth, professional and urbane, looks as if it may have been the road to a rapprochement with the International Style; the Galeries Lafayette project had already shown a large pure prism, trimly rectangular in form, and topped with publicity and lettering in a manner which suggests more than a smattered acquaintance with Constructivist thought. But whether this rapprochement was to take place is now but an historical speculation; the coming of the Nazis cut short a development which might have brought commerce and the International Style together in a manner which might have eliminated the excessive caution of the former, and the distrust of the latter – how much Peter Jones's in Sloane Square owes to this last German phase of Mendelsohn!

*   *   *

Looking back then over the period between Dr. Caligari and Dr. Mabuse we see Erich Mendelsohn practising three different styles subsequent to Expressionism, with which he had completely finished by 1922 – the Dutch manner from 1922 to 1929, and the first reklame style in parallel with it, followed by the second reklame style from 1929 until he left the country. There is nothing here so consistently Expressionist as to justify the Mendelsohn myth, as it seems to be understood by such writers as M. F. Roggero whose recent book on Mendelsohn virtually ignores the successive impacts of his Dutch and American visits, or Bruno Zevi, whose *History of Modern Architecture* contains what is probably the most compact recension of the myth. This admits that the Stuttgart store is different from the Einstein Tower (and discusses none of his other buildings) but insists on the continuance of an Expressionist aesthetic[3] – a position which is quite untenable if one compares the Stuttgart store with the orthodox Expressionist detailing and massing of Rudolf Steiner's exactly contemporary Goetheaneum.

But the reason for Zevi's position is easy to see. For him any stick will do to beat the dog of Rationalism, and to him, as to the Rationalists themselves, it is Mendelsohn's departures from the International Style which are conspicuous, not his approximations to it. The conventional myth of Mendelsohn is much more use as a polemical weapon than is the true image of an original and changeable designer, so Zevi has a vested interest in its continuance. And since the historical victory has gone to the International Style, rather than one of the variant possibilities of the twenties, we are all now the children of Rationalism, and, noticing Mendelsohn's aberrations from our canon of form rather than his conformities to it, we tend to accept the Zevian estimate of him.

But there is another and more specific incentive to concentrate our view of Mendelsohn into a single image of Expressionist disorder, and that is Borax.[4] His ultimate

10 ERIC MENDELSOHN, *Exhibition Hall*, Cologne, 1928.

responsibility for the formal language of American product-design cannot be denied, but to hold him responsible for the enormities of its misuse is as stupid as it would be to blame Voysey for the swarming horrors which are the undoubted offspring of The Orchard, Chorley Wood. Borax has its triumphs, as well as its disasters, but our attitude towards it tends to be comparable to that of our forbears toward the Baroque. The empurpled rage of the Burlingtonians before the work of Borromini is chicken-feed to the almost pathological fury of Max Bill confronted with the products of General Motors: 'Thanks to the speed with which efficient salesmanship is spreading this catchpenny trash all over the world, it looks as if the ultimate collapse of our civilization could not be averted much longer.' This is an extreme case, no doubt, but a similar seizure of the critical faculties seems to affect most of our pundits when faced with the confident convexities of a Buick, and in such a state of seizure they see, through Borax-coloured spectacles, the Einstein Tower and the Stuttgart staircase as Mendelsohn's characteristic works. This composite image of the two towers always proves to be the substance of the Expressionist myth, and will presumably remain so until some doctorate-seeking drudge raises Borax to the status of a major style, and subjects it to the familiar disinfecting routines of art-history. Or until we drown our ignorance of his work in a flood of knowledge of what his achievement really amounted to, and recognize that he was less a vulgarian than an original and a non-conformist.

1.5 THE LAST FORMGIVER

In Le Corbusier *Banham discovers the supreme manipulator of expressive, symbolic form and in this obituary on Corb's death, stresses the vital role that this genius played in twentieth-century architecture. He describes Corb's grasp of the contemporary aesthetic and the way that he has evolved a language of architecture that has influenced many followers. This article originally appeared in* Architectural Review, *August 1966.*

All genius is embarrassing, and never more so than in the immediate aftermath of death. Supporters of the deceased giant busy themselves with the public record to ensure that the good (in defiance of the normal entropy of reputation) shall live after him. Detractors, convinced that their hour has finally struck, emerge from the woodwork – only to find that everyone is applying the law of *de mortuis* to the last letter of *nil nisi bonum*. When the dead genius has attained a measure of acceptance as widespread, total and unquestioning as that enjoyed by Le Corbusier, when his supporters are in such total command of the media of communications as were Corb's, the chances are that the festering resentments of the detractors, when they finally burst through the crust of conventionalized approval, will provoke a reaction so destructive of his reputation that it may take a generation or more to set the record straight.

Apart from the deliciously truthful memoir of his domineering and satyrish attitude to women which appeared, amid gasps of scandalized horror, in *The Guardian*[1], the writers of Le Corbusier's necrologies have seemed determined, by their vacuity, sentimentality, name-dropping and ignorance, to make the reaction – when it comes – so explosive and disastrous that the reputation will be destroyed finally and forever. The gullibility, for instance, of those who praised his ability to 'extract lyricism from technology' (etc., ad nauseam) would be comparable to that of the courtiers who failed to observe the non-existence of the Emperor's new clothes, but for the fact that the non-observation of the demonstrably non-existent had gone on so long that the clothes had become old, the topic so boring that – apart from a few brave voices like that of Denys Hinton in his letter to *Architects' Journal*[2] – small boys had given up trying to point out the obvious to their CIAM-besotted elders.

The observable facts of his built designs are that most of his most celebrated 'machine age' effects were achieved with very primitive building technologies, descending, in later designs, to plain fakery (those spray-on walls at Ronchamp, those sky-hooked vaults of the Law Courts at Chandigarh). The writings of his declining years revealed an ever-deeper ignorance of the intellectual disciplines that kept the technologies of his life-time moving, and he delighted himself (with the childishness of an old man) in such 'technological' discoveries as the interference patterns produced by superimposing two transparent grids.[3] This discovery (*sic*) has little that is interesting, or even significant, to do with the progress of technology, but the fact that

1 Le Corbusier.

2 LE CORBUSIER, *Chapel of Notre Dame du Haut*, Ronchamp, 1953.

these patterns caught his eye five years or more before Op Art hit the galleries, points to something that is significant about Le Corbusier and interesting about the times in which he lived: he was the fashion-master of his age. He was ever first in the hearts of his fellow professionals because he was always first on the beach-heads of aesthetic (never technological) adventure. Just as the US marines never stormed an atoll or captured an island without finding 'Kilroy was here' chalked on some handy surface, so no sudden rush of aesthetic adventure in architecture between 1925 and 1965 ever reached its objective without finding slogans in the old master's familiar hand already scrawled across the scene. As Alison Smithson once said, with the kind of resigned exasperation usually reserved for discussing elderly relatives, 'When you open a new volume of the *Oeuvre Complete* you find that he has had all your best ideas already, has done what you were about to do next'.

This is by no means a gift to be despised. To enjoy this kind of command over the quasi-conscious and semi-rational preferences and prejudices of men, has been the source of vast political power to some, immense wealth to others, has founded religions that brought empires to their knees. History has not been shaped solely by deep social groundswells, inexorable economic forces, new sources of power or improved means of communication. It has also been decisively shaped by unforeseeable individuals (Lenin, Gandhi, Martin Luther King – but also Christian Dior, Elvis Presley, Jackson Pollock) whose power to utter the right word, turn the necessary gesture, has made great trends conscious and comprehensible, defined the forms in which history, and their contemporaries, could recognize the drift of events.

The *quality* of the utterance or gesture made by these historical formgivers has no bearing, it seems, on its charismatic effect. Gandhi could speak foolishly, King irresponsibly, Lenin stupidly, without their ceasing to be great and compelling leaders. Corb could be as flashy as Presley, as ridiculous as Dior or as mulish as Pollock on a bad Monday, and yet his slightest doodle would be as persua-

sive as his longest-pondered design to architects of most generations in most parts of the world. The bitterness of British architects seasoned in the service of the Raj, who complained that Le Corbusier was offering to solve the architectural problems of India on the basis of a merely tourist acquaintance with the sub-continent, was made the more sour by their helpless recognition that these solutions would impose themselves on practically everybody – including themselves, as like as not. Within the confines of architecture as currently practised, and the compass of architectural history as currently studied, his achievement is overwhelmingly clear – he was the outstanding formgiver of what may prove to be the last form-dominated epoch of architecture. He was, perhaps, less fundamental a formgiver than Auguste Perret, whose trabeated conception of concrete structure underlies even Le Corbusier. He was less radically inventive than Frank Lloyd Wright, but far more imitable. The evidence of the eyes is that for thirty years he discovered, codified, exploited, demonstrated – even invented – and gave authority to more forms than any other architect around. To walk across the grass at Alton West is to inhabit a total environment created largely and consciously in his image, but to drive down Sunset Boulevard is to be constantly reminded that men who never heard his name have been able to go to work on clichés borrowed at second- or third-hand from his notebooks. From him the Modern Movement in architecture learned most of its international language of architectural expression, and the fact that this language expresses practically nothing of interest for the second half of the twentieth century is the Movement's fault, not his, and detracts nothing from his personal achievement in imposing it.

Below
3 LE CORBUSIER, *Apartment Block (Unité d'Habitation)*, Marseilles, 1952.

Opposite
4 and 5 LE CORBUSIER, *The Secretariat*, Chandigarh, India, 1958 (*above*), and *Centre Le Corbusier*, Zurich, 1967 (*below*).

1.6 THE MACHINE AESTHETIC

In this article, originally published in Architectural Review, *April 1955, Banham sees Le Corbusier as a crucial figure in the Modern Movement, not this time as a formgiver but as a characteristic self-deceiver in his relationship with the machine. Banham realizes that the Moderns used the machine in a symbolic rather than a technological way and that Functionalism is a myth that should be exposed. He contrasts it with the American design style 'Borax' which is honest about the appeal of 'styling' and, therefore, a more relevant aesthetic for the present day.*

Architects are frightened of machinery, and have been so ever since engineering broke loose from the back pages of Vitruvius and set up on its own. Even where they have paid lip service to 'the Machine' they have paid it to a simulacrum of their own invention; they have been prepared to do business with it only on their own terms, and only with those aspects of it which lie closest to architectural practice. When Adolph Loos hailed engineers, in 1898, as 'our Hellenes' he may have been speaking far less metaphorically than we have so far suspected, since his fellow-Viennese Otto Wagner had already looked to engineers to restore 'powerful horizontal lines, such as were prevalent in Antiquity'. Similarly, to admire the ranked cylinders of a grain silo was not so great a feat of visual athletics to those who had been trained to accept the lumpish columniation of the temples at Paestum.

The 'Machine Aesthetic' of the Pioneer Masters of the Modern Movement was thus selective and classicizing, one limb of their reaction against the excesses of Art Nouveau, and it came nowhere near an acceptance of machines on their own terms or for their own sakes. That kind of acceptance had to wait upon the poets, and particularly Marinetti, whose *Futurist Manifesto* of 1909 not only opens with the first car-crash in European literature, but contains the pioneering value judgment '... a roaring racing car, rattling like a machine gun, is more beautiful than the Winged Victory of Samothrace.' Such an opinion could only be expressed in the rare atmosphere of pure poetry, and the grey eminences of architecture continued to square up to the problem slowly, picking their ground with care. They had committed themselves to a Machine Aesthetic of some sort, and the words of Marinetti must have stuck like barbs in the flesh, but to accept his viewpoint would have been to let go of architecture as they understood it. The selective and classicizing approach had therefore to continue – as one sees in the pre-1914 factories of Peter Behrens, which are a long step toward a mechanistic architecture, but remain, for all that, neo-classic temples in form and silhouette.

Both at the Bauhaus, and in the circle of *L'Esprit Nouveau*, this approach continued, in however disguised and complicated a form, making it possible to bracket together architecture and machinery with the least mental strain for the architectural side. Bauhaus masters may expostulate that they set up the design of machines as an exemplar of method, and did not posit any formal resemblance between machinery and the bare, spare rectangular architecture they produced, yet Malevich, in *Bauhausbuch* No. 11, hopefully says of his own filleted and rectilinear aesthetic 'thus one may also call Suprematism an aeronautical art.'

But Bauhaus theory, as we receive it now, is very fragmentary, and one should be chary of invading this difficult field until the group psychologists have been into it, for it is the Bauhaus *atmosphere* which needs to be studied.

L'Esprit Nouveau is a more immediately rewarding field, with its neat corpus of signed articles and all pseudonyms known, and its effect upon the growing concept of the Machine Aesthetic is clearer and easier to follow. In this body of articles one will find, in extenso, the manipulation of the superficial aspects of engineering in the interests of a particular conception of architecture, and in those articles which were later published as *Towards A New Architecture* one can see Le Corbusier advancing a view of machinery which progresses shortly from special pleading to false witness.

One should perhaps be careful of imputing any sinister intent in all this, and exercise towards the author that charity which is due to one who, in the world of engineering, was not even a provincial, but a complete backwoodsman. His background in his native Chaux-de-Fonds was watchmaking, still in an eighteenth-century condition compared with the production-line industries; his architectural apprenticeship was with Behrens and Auguste Perret, both old-time classicists and the latter a self-confessed reactionary whose model in concrete was wooden framing; and his 'industrial experiences,' if indeed they were with the Voisin company, were in an aircraft industry which was barely out of the box-kite phase. These facts remembered, his naive belief that machines are by their very nature highly finished can be understood – a watchmaker could hardly think otherwise – and so can the extraordinary penetration with which he views the pre-history of flight: 'To wish to fly like a bird is to state the problem badly ... to seek a means of support and a means of propulsion is to pose it properly.'

But can such naivety explain the crooked argument of the chapter in *Towards A New Architecture* entitled 'Automobiles'? Its crookedness is disguised by the fact that the argument is partly verbal and partly visual. The hinge of the verbal argument is the virtue of standardization; the hinge of the visual is the confrontation, sustained over several pages, between automobiles and the Parthenon, and the totality has been read by two generations of architects and theorists as meaning that a standardized product like a motor-car can be as beautiful as a Greek temple. In its context that is how it must be read, but the *tertium comparationis* of the argument is a disingenuous pretence – none of the motor-cars illustrated is a standardized mass-produced model; all are expensive, specialized, handicraft one-offs which can justly be compared to the Parthenon because, like it, they are unique works of handmade art. Mass-produced vehicles like the Model T Ford are not allowed to sully these classicist pages.

Naivety? Sharp practice? Or wishful thinking? A certain aesthetic *parti-pris* is undoubtedly there; a desire that certain wishes should come true; that architects should in reality be able to assume the moral stature of engineers on whom, in the opening chapter, Le Corbusier had wished the virtues of the Gothic Craftsman and the Noble Savage: 'Engineers are healthy, virile, active and useful, moral and happy.' It would be difficult to write this kind of nineteenth-century fustian with one's tongue in one's cheek, and an intention to deceive would be very difficult to maintain against him, since he does not even seem to see how the parenthetic caption to one of his motor-car illustrations, *Carrosserie Ozenfant*, undermines his argument by conjuring up the presence, not of a moral and virile mass-production engineer, but either a luxury carriage-builder, or his artist-son who was Le Corbusier's pictorial collaborator.

This same Amedée Ozenfant was later to depth-charge the whole argument by pointing out that 'M. Ettore Bugatti as well as MM. Voisin, Farman and the Brothers Michelin had all been art-students' so that even Voisin, the patron of *L'Esprit Nouveau*, was not an untainted engineer happy in his morality and usefulness.[1]

Wishful thinking cannot be ruled out; nor a desire to find support for one's aesthetic prejudices in some human activity which can be admired without qualification, and this clearly opens the way for extensive self-deception. The particular wish-confusion which lies at the bottom of this complex structure of deception and distortion is easiest to identify in *La Peinture Moderne*, an otherwise excellent book which Le Corbusier and Ozenfant made out of another series of *Esprit Nouveau* articles which had appeared in parallel with those on architecture. Here they say of Purism, their own style of painting: 'Le Purisme a mis en evidence la Loi de la Sélection Mécanique,' and this law, which they clearly intend to share the status of Darwin's Law of Natural Selection, they explain as follows: 'It establishes that objects tend toward a type which is determined by the evolution of forms between the ideal of maximum utility; and the demands of economical production, which conforms inexorably to the laws of nature. This double play of forces has resulted in the creation of a certain number of objects which one may call standardized' – and, the argument runs, are therefore good, and have been selected as the Purist's subject matter. The relation between the law and the paintings only concerns us in one respect here: the authors have set up an abstract model of the design process in mass-production, and the paintings will show us what class of objects we have to interpolate as the last term of the proposition in order to test its truth.

These Purist objects prove to be bottles and jugs, pots and pans, glasses and pipes, of forms which approximate to the cylinder, sphere and cone which had been canonized in Post-Impressionist painting, regular geometrical forms with simple silhouettes. If we make these the last term in the Ozenfant-Corbusier model of the design process, we get a proposition of this order: objects of maximum utility and lowest price have simple geometrical shapes. To most architects this proposition would appear watertight, but to most production engineers it would appear too abstract to be useful, and demonstrably false in its outcome.

To them, Utility, in the Rationalist sense which the authors clearly intended, is a marginal factor – only one among a number of other factors bearing upon sales. When the American Ford Company issued a questionnaire to discover what qualities buyers sought in cars, most answerers headed their lists with such utilitarian considerations as road-holding and fuel consumption – a result which sales-analysis did not support – but when asked what *other people* looked for most headed their lists with chromium plate, colour-schemes and so forth. To manufacturers, utility is a complex affair which, in certain products for certain markets, may require the addition of ornament for ostentation or social prestige. Similarly, the demands of economic production do not, as the authors of the model supposed, follow the laws of Nature, but those of economics, and in fields where the prime factor in costing is the length of the production-run a simplicity, such as would render a handicraft product cheaper, might render a mass-produced one more expensive if it were less saleable than a more complex form. High finish, too, is another Purist mirage, for the quality which interests engineers is not finish but tolerance – the factor by which a dimension may vary from the designed figure without injurious effects. This renders high finish a

1 Le Corbusier in his studio.

purely negative characteristic, and where it is extensively applied to any object it is nearly always the product of handicraft labour, and has some bearing on sales – for reasons of consumer preference, as in luxury cars and watches, or performance, as in air-liners and surgical equipment.

All these qualities then – summed up as simplicity of form and smoothness of finish – are conditional attributes of engineering, and to postulate them as necessary consequences of machine production was to give a false picture of the engineer's methods and intentions. But such a picture was clearly of the greatest polemical utility to the Purists in their search for a justification of their aesthetic preferences. It is also clear that they were not alone in this, for the Machine Aesthetic was a world-wide phenomenon, nor was its mythology noxious at the time, for it answered a clear cultural need in offering a common visual law which united the form of the automobile and the building which sheltered it, the form of the house, the forms of its equipment and of the art-works which adorned it. Nor – and this is the heart of the matter – was its falsity visible at the time, for automotive, aeronautical and naval design were currently going through a phase when their products did literally resemble those of Functionalist architecture. The Intelligent Observer, turning from one set of smooth simple shapes to the other, would see apparent and visible proof of the architect's claim to share the virtues of the engineer.

But these days were numbered. Already, in 1921, aeronautical design was launched upon a train of development in which a third quality, not mentioned in Le Corbusier's original Support-Propulsion formula, was to domi-

2 *Pennsylvania Railroad Engine*, designed by Raymond Loewy, 1937.

nate the field. That quality, now common to all forms of motion research, was Penetration, and in pursuit of ever better factors of penetration typical aircraft forms were to ingorge their structure, and turn from complex arrays of smooth simple shapes, like those of Functionalist architecture, to simple arrays of mathematically complex forms. At the period when the crisis of this development was reached in the early thirties, with the general change-over to monoplane configurations and retractable landing-gear, the process was doubled in the field of automotive design, where the liberation of bodywork from horse and buggy concepts is aptly symbolized by the way in which the Burney Streamliners rendered Walter Gropius's architecturally-conceived Adler cars obsolete in a bare eighteen months. Within another eighteen months the slump had done some rough surgery on the motor industry, lopping off its weaker members and leaving a few giants battling for mass markets and low production overheads. The consequent philosophy of long manufacturing runs and rapid repeat orders led inevitably to vehicles which were very different from the handmade art-works which had graced the pages of *Toward A New Architecture*. It was not merely that pressed steel technology works most efficiently with broad smooth envelope shapes, but also that the need to chase the market led to the rapid evolution of an anti-Purist but eye-catching vocabulary of design – which we now call Borax.

The tone of architectural response to these developments was to complain that machine-designers were failing in their task – a tone which had been set by a caption-writer in *Cahiers d'Art* as early as 1926, who had accused the engineers responsible for an artless coaling-gantry of the normal splay-legged type of being 'soaked in Romantic Expressionism' – an inexplicable performance unless one believes the Law of Mechanical Selection, and shares its preference for elementary solid geometry. Under the turbulent conditions of the thirties most intelligent men had bigger and more urgent things to occupy them than the complaints of architectural Purists – the world was too conspicuously going to the dogs in other fields. But after the Second World War, in which a whole generation had been forced to familiarize themselves with machinery on its own terms, the disparity between the observable facts and the

architects' Machine Aesthetic had become too obtrusive to be ignored. In the Jet Age these ideas of the twenties began to wear a very quaint and half-timbered look.

This, of course, made it easier for some feeble intellects to 'adopt a modern style,' and we are all familiar with the dandified figures in their draughty and obsolescent sportscars who practise Modern architecture as if it were a finished period style, with all the answers in the books. Such men are academics, since their authority is the past, and their skin-deep Modernism is soon seen through. But there is another class of Modern Movement academics whose position is tougher – those, like the Swiss critic Max Bill, who seem genuinely to desire a universal product aesthetic, and are sincerely alarmed by the defections of whole categories of manufactured objects from what they conceive to be the true principles of design. Unaware that these principles stem from false or irrelevant premises, but committed to a mechanistic concept of architecture, they are left to rail against the growing vulgarity of the world, to become 'laudatores temporis acti', living justifications of Ozenfant's post-Corbusian jibe that '...lovers of machinery by preference collect implements long out of date. Imagining that they worship mechanism, in reality they offer sacrifice to a taste for antiques.'

In these men the architect's fear of machinery re-emerges, and they set up the outworn categories of the Machine Aesthetic as a defence against situations which cannot be managed by purely architectural standards. But to do this seems not only cowardly, but also presumptuous; why should other aspects of design be subservient to architectural preferences? To blame the automobile, for instance, for not answering to a code of visual practice adapted to buildings is as inconsequential as it would be to censure the apple for not having a rough bark, or the peach-tree for not having a downy skin. It is not merely that the car and the building are made of different materials, that one is mobile and the other static, but that the manner of consuming the two products is so different. Like the tree, the building is a long-standing investment. Compared with it the motor-car is, like the fruit, a deciduous affair. Its season is the four or five year retooling cycle of the big manufacturers, and like the fruit it must have an appetizing exterior.

In this situation Borax is entirely proper, though there are plenty of other design situations, notably architecture, in which it is grossly inappropriate. Basically its propriety to automotive design lies in its symbolic content, which is concerned, more than anything else, with penetration. When this symbol-language was young it had an architectural connection, for the only available language of penetration was the misplaced dynamism of Erich Mendelsohn and his imitators, but as the public grew more familiar with the appearance of racing cars, jet planes, spaceship projects and the like, a whole new iconography of penetration-symbols became available to the automobile stylist. Its aptness to the automobile cannot be denied. It is forward-looking – and its very iconography refutes Max Bill's attempt to equate it with half-timbering. Its theme is germane to the business of transportation, and its symbols are as firmly built into the technical history of the product as were the useless flutings, guttae, triglyphs and so forth of Greek Doric temples. Amateurs of the Parthenon have thus no logical defence against Borax, nor, indeed, have believers in the Law of Mechanical Selection, for the contemporary motor-car is precisely the result of the interplay of utility and economical production – if those terms are realistically defined as factors of the mass-market for which cars are produced.

This is not an attempt to set up Borax as next week's fashionable gimmick, or to require a suspension of value judgments in front of it. There is plenty of bad Borax about, some of it is as mean and skimpy as a great deal of contemporary architecture, and more of it is inflated and overblown than is any recent building. It is a design language which can be used badly or well, but the good and the bad are not identified by applying to it tests which are not germane to it, and to set up an exclusionist standard, which is what any universal criterion of taste like the Machine Aesthetic must eventually become, is simply to deny ourselves the enriched experience which a variety of product aesthetics can offer us. No-one can less afford such an impoverishment of the mind than the architect, but his study of machinery must have a firmer basis. The Machine Aesthetic is dead, and we salute its grave because of the magnificent architecture it produced, but we cannot afford to be sentimental over its passing. It is an outworn piece of mental equipment and, as Le Corbusier also said in the days of *L'Esprit Nouveau*: 'We have no right to waste our strength on worn-out tackle, we must scrap, and re-equip.'

3 *Adler Limousine*, designed by Walter Gropius, c. 1931.

1.7 STOCKTAKING

Banham maintains in this article, originally published in Architectural Review, *February 1960, that two forces affect contemporary architecture. The first is the conservative pressure of tradition and the second is technology which encourages a more progressive, open-ended approach to the architectural problem. This latter 'back to basics' argument provides the foundation of a radical architecture which will question basic assumptions like permanence in architecture.*[1]

Reyner Banham, in taking stock of the impact of tradition *and* technology *on architecture today, finds it necessary to re-define these terms. For his purposes both words are used in a specialized sense.* Tradition *means, not monumental Queen Anne, but the stock of general knowledge (including general scientific knowledge) which specialists assume as the ground of present practice and future progress.* Technology *represents its converse, the method of exploring, by means of the instrument of science, a* potential *which may at any moment make nonsense of all existing general knowledge, and so of the ideas founded on it, even 'basic' ideas like* house, city, building. *Philosophically it could be argued that all ideas, traditional or otherwise, are contemporaneous, since they have to be invented anew for each individual, but the practical issue is not thereby invalidated. For the first time in history, the world* of what is *is suddenly torn by the discovery that* what could be, *is no longer dependent on* what was.

Tradition

Architecture, as the professional activity of a body of men, can only be defined in terms of its professional history – architects are recognized as architects by their performance of specific roles that have been assigned to the profession in previous generations. Any significant attempt to extend or alter those roles will be dismissed, by most of the profession and even more of the public, as something other than the business of architects as architects. As James Cubitt wrote recently 'Designing roundabouts or doorknobs is not architecture. The idea that it is arises from a misconception of the purposes of the Bauhaus, primarily a school of industrial design. Architecture is, and always will be concerned, roughly speaking, with "carefully balancing horizontal things on top of vertical things".'

In spite of the much debated 'revolution' in architecture in our time, the roles of architects have not been significantly extended, and certain extensions of role – into product-design, for instance – seem to have been tacitly abandoned since the nineteen thirties. There are probably a number of reasons for this, but most of them, including the legally enforced codes of conduct that architects have created for themselves, are traceable to a feeling that modification of the accepted roles beyond a certain point threatens the integrity, or even the identity, of the profession.

Quite apart from certain obvious worries about such marginally extra-professional activities as contracting, this self-stabilizing tendency operates also in a more generalized and diffuse manner to preserve the status quo. We have seen a notable example of this in the past decade, one that has done much to precipitate the present confused state of world architecture. Using student opinion – articulate but disengaged from the daily routine of business – as a barometer of opinion, one could distinguish, shortly after 1950, a strong feeling that architectural theory was leaning so far towards sociology and technology as determinants of architectural form that – in practice – architectural form was not being determined at all, or – alternatively – such form as was being determined was not architectural. There were demands to *get back to architecture* – a classic response, closely resembling that which Charles Eames described in his 1959 Discourse at the RIBA as a reliance on 'the lore of the operation'. Whether or not this situation brings with it the dangers to which he also referred – 'The danger of this procedure is that operational lore, being an integration of experience rather than apparent intelligence (i.e. available information), sacrifices sensitivity in order to gain stability' – whether or not this is true, it has happened, and constitutes one of the two major pressures to which architecture has been subjected in the last decade.

The first phase of this return to operational lore was Anglo-Italian, an appeal to the classical tradition; not to the nearer end of that tradition as summed up in, say, the work of Auguste Perret, but to the beginnings of Modern classicism in the Italian Renaissance. Its symbol was the Vitruvian Man, its slogan 'Divina Proporzione', its hero Palladio, its prophet – quite coincidentally – Rudolf Wittkower. The appeal was not to the forms and details of Renaissance architecture, but to the underlying proportional mathematics, as set out in Professor Wittkower's *Architectural Principles of the Age of Humanism*, and echoed after a fashion – equally coincidentally – in Le Corbusier's *Modulor*.

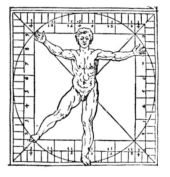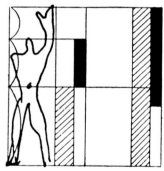

1 Man (Vitruvian and Modulor) as geometry.

The upshot was not neo-Georgian, but an aggressive axiality of plan, and a reliance on modular devices as planning tools. This particular moment has passed, and not left much behind – some projects for 'Palladian power-stations', some hotly-discussed fifth-year student thesis projects, now forgotten, and a slowly waning admiration for things Italian – of which the slowest-waning, perhaps, is the reputation of Luigi Moretti, whose *Casa del Girasole*, discovered by Anglo-Saxons in 1952, was for some years a test of taste.

But, in a more generalized sense this moment in the history of Modern architecture has left much behind. It marks the beginning of the persistent belief in modular number patterns as disciplines inherently beneficial to architecture – a belief now institutionalized in the Modular Society, where, however, attempts are being made to give it a footing in something more solid than vague sentiments inspired by reliance on operational lore. Somewhere in this moment too lie the origins of the present addiction to formality of the middle and elder generation among US architects – the use of classical pavilion forms by Ed Stone and Walter Gropius in their recent embassies in New Delhi and Athens, or by Mies van der Rohe in his Baccardi building, or the use of multi-axial symmetries and vaulted coverings by Philip Johnson, in such examples as his Shrine at New Harmony. In the case of Johnson – early a devout Wittkowerian – the apparent historicism is backed by the resounding proclamation of faith: 'Hurrah for History. Thank God for Hadrian, for Bernini, for Le Corbusier and Vince Scully.'

Scully, through his celebrated lectures at Yale, has – like Wittkower, Colin Rowe, Bruno Zevi, and others – done much to give history teaching a new dynamic, and thus to add a richness to the traditions of operational lore that has not been there since the death of Soane and Schinkel. What is new in this situation is the way that the revived interest in history has not come about in countries whose great architecture is all in the past, and the future has nothing to offer, but in countries – like the US – who appear to have a wave of great architecture ahead of them in the immediate future, and one of the effects of this new sense of history has been to produce a reassessment of the work of the masters who will set the style for that future. Thus, just before the 'rediscovery' of history, there was a current of opinion that tended to evaluate Mies van der Rohe's architecture in 'technological' terms as a theoretically endless accretion of 'additive' units. After the rediscovery of history, this view, propagated by Richard Llewelyn-Davies and Gerhard Kallmann, was replaced by an emphasis on Mies as a classicist, on the axial symmetry, regularity and modular organization of his planning, and his debts to German neo-classicism.

Aside from these returns to the classical lore of the architectural operation, another, older stream of latent historicism has burst forth on the surface again, after a period when it was buried by classicist enthusiasms. This is the strain of historicist defeatism – entirely lacking in the intellectual exaltation of the classical revival – that was first manifest in a muted, self-effacing way as the new Empiricism of the Scandinavian North in the late forties, and now reappears in a more aggressive and wilful form as 'Neoliberty' in Italy. Both movements exhibit the same tendency to rely on purely *local* operational lore, one might almost say the lore of the local building industry, rather than the lore of architecture at large. Both also rely on the lore of materials, declining to use new ones because they are visually 'unreliable' under weathering and use. Both have been interpreted as relying also on the lore of public taste, not wishing to put up buildings that the average citizen cannot understand (i.e., not putting up buildings that he hasn't seen before). It is worth noting that most of these observations are also true of the architecture of the English New Towns, where the same frame of mind appears to have governed the town planning as well.

Neoliberty also introduces another problem of acute interest in the present state of architecture, but this must be left over, for the moment, in order to consider the general import of these historicist trends. The blanket term most commonly in use to cover all the tendencies in Modern architecture that deviate from the Functionalist norms of geometrical purity and plan-wise asymmetry, is Formalist. The term is fair enough, provided limitations are placed around its usage. There is little sign at the moment of out-and-out Formalism, of shape-making for the sake of shape-making. Even the paper-projects of an architect like Marcello d'Olivo keep within certain bounds, and those bounds are within the limits of the lore of the operation – nothing like Action painting has happened to architecture yet. For this reason, the deviation from the canons of Functionalist form does not constitute 'Une Architecture Autre', as Odo Kulterman appears to believe (to judge from his article in

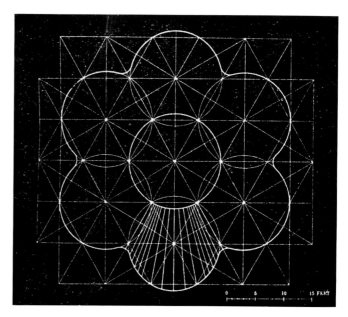

2 Philip Johnson, *Geometry of Shrine*, at New Harmony, Indiana, 1960.

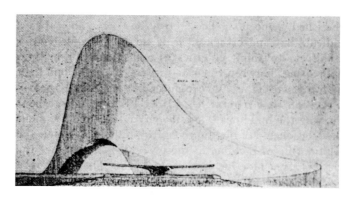

3 Great Wall of d'Olivo's Rayad University.

Baukunst und Werkform, 8, 1958). If the concept of an Other Architecture has any place in this survey, it is in the article on Technology that follows this one. New shapes notwithstanding, it is still the same old architecture, in the sense that the architects involved have relied on their inherited sense of primacy in the building team, and have insisted that they alone shall determine the forms to be employed. Formalism it may be, but it remains Formalism within the limits of a professional tradition, albeit that traditon is now wide enough to span from the neo-libertarians to d'Olivo, from Mies van der Roche to Bruce Goff.

But to return to the specific significance of Neoliberty. It is a revival, but not of an historical style in the sense that Doric or Gothic are historical styles. Art-historical niceties about the precise degree of modernity that Liberty (Art Nouveau) can claim, do not affect that it is not a style enjoying long-ingrained cultural approbation, like the great styles of the remoter past, but a style of our own time, propagated through international magazines and exhibitions by men conscious of living in a machine age.

Its revival implies a recognition that the allegedly anti-traditional Modern Movement has a tradition of its own. Reliance on the traditional lore of the operation no longer necessarily means relying on a tradition older then oneself – the men who made the tradition are, mostly, still alive. However, a further new factor, over and above the recognition of a new tradition, is the existence of two different ways of looking at that tradition. On the one hand, it may be accepted as a tradition of the sort we have known before, passed from master to pupil, teacher to student, almost subliminally as a succession of ever-mutating attitudes and preconceptions, constantly in process of change as the needs and aspirations of successive generations came to bear upon it. This, if it existed, would be the mainstream of Modern architecture today. But the stream has practically vanished, and consists of isolated individuals, like pools in a drying torrent-bed – and the pools are drying out, too. Two years ago, one could have pointed to Wells Coates and André Sive as mainstream Modernists, in the sense of men inhabiting a live Modern tradition, but not any more. For the most part, this kind of smoothly-developing Modernism exists nowadays in the work of large offices such as Skidmore, Owings and Merrill, or Yorke, Rosenberg and Mardall, or in solitary originals like Bakema, Goldfinger or Denys Lasdun. It also exists, with pronounced local characteristics, in Brazil and other Latin American countries.

But what, then, of the men who ought to be the great mainstreamers, the four architects whom Henry-Russell Hitchcock identified as the masters of the twenties and thirties? J. J. P. Oud long ago made his private retreat into local professional lore. Mies van der Rohe has isolated himself in a bronze tower more pure than ivory, driven there by a logic that would have worked equally well in a vacuum where Modern architecture did not exist. Gropius has become the Dean of the Formalists, Doric in Athens, Islamic in Baghdad. And Le Corbusier?

While it is generally conceded that the apparent formalisms of a Frank Lloyd Wright were a law unto themselves, justified by the dimensions of an almost Michelangelesque personality, there is clearly a widespread feeling that the apparent formalisms of Le Corbusier answer to some law obscurely, but vitally, inherent in the business of architecture. No sooner were the implications of Ronchamp apparent than a dozen pens were at work explaining that its forms were not a wilful contradiction of everything that Le Corbusier had done before, but the fulfilment of certain aspects of himself, or Modern architecture in general, that had lain dormant. It is clear that Ronchamp is not Formalism in the commonly accepted sense, because it does not gain the one secure advantage of formalizing within the tradition – that of communicability. No one doubts that Ed Stone's Delhi Embassy, or Saarinen's in London, look like representational government buildings, but the argument over what Ronchamp looks like is still proceeding, the only basis of agreement being that it does *not* look like a church.

The attempts to explain why Ronchamp is as it is, and how it is connected with the true nature of Modern architecture, bring out the other way of regarding the Modern tradition itself – not as a man-to-man communication of attitudes and concepts, but as an immutable and scientifically ascertainable succession of historical facts. Such an approach is in direct conflict with the 'traditional' view of the Modern tradition, and has been described as 'using facts to pervert the history of Modern architecture' by supporters of that view. It has also led to persistent allegations of modern eclecticism being levelled against younger architects who hold to the 'scientific' view of recent history. Very often this is true, particularly at student level where the formal vacuum of half-trained minds can as easily be filled with pickings from the twentieth century as from other centuries. But much of this alleged eclecticism has been the stimulus, mask, or vehicle of radical attempts to establish 'what really happened in Modern architecture'.

The most important aspect of this view of the tradition is its all-inclusiveness. The other type of tradition proceeds by what might be called 'selective amnesia,' each generation

4 LE CORBUSIER, *Chapel of Notre Dame du Haut*, Ronchamp, 1955. Exterior of the chapel from the south-east.

5 ALISON and PETER SMITHSON, *Secondary Modern School*, Hunstanton, Norfolk, 1954. The link between the single storey block and the main block, with the water-tower behind.

6 ALISON and PETER SMITHSON, *Secondary Modern School*, Hunstanton, Norfolk, 1954, main block.

forgetting anything that had ceased to be of interest in order to find room for new matters of interest that had come up in its own time. The new view, on the other hand, demands total recall – everything that wasn't positively old-fashioned at the time it was done is to be regarded as of equal value. The Futurists must be discussed in the same breath as the Deutscher Werkbund, de Klerk must be put alongside Rietveld, Maybeck alongside Wright. The guardians of the Modern tradition, such as Sigfried Giedion, have been called in question for forgetting too much, and – it is claimed – distorting the truth by over-selectivity. In revenge, every discarded formal and functional device that was dropped or ignored by the developing mainstream must now be re-examined and, wherever applicable, re-used.

Much of what results – projects and a few finished buildings – is, indeed Modern Movement revivalism, the resurrection of usages (though rarely of total building forms) of the architecture of the twenties, or even the forties – David Gray's house at Lowestoft can serve as an example of the former, the Smithsons' school at Hunstanton of the latter. But Hunstanton – the building by which the much-battered term 'New Brutalism' is commonly defined – immediately raises another problem altogether. Wherever the scientific and all-inclusive attitude to recent history is found, it is nearly always accompanied by a similar attitude to the use of materials. The mystique of materials 'as found' involves (a) a resolute honesty in their use (paralleling the refusal to allow a selective attitude to historical fact) and (b) an insistence that all the qualities of a material are equally relevant.

Thus, in the Hunstanton School, steel is given a far higher valuation than the rather abstract one implicit in Mies's work. Its visual quality as a rolled product with makers' trade marks embossed on it is given value, the nature of its ultimate performance under stress is acknowledged in the use of plastic theory by the engineer responsible for the structural calculations. Or, to take another work that has been abused for modern eclecticism, the development at Ham Common by Stirling and Gowan differs from its acknowledged sources (such as Le Corbusier's Jaoul houses) by using brickwork calculated to the limits of the load-bearing capacity – a decision that is more responsible than any twenties revivalism for the use of the dropped windows, with their inverted L-shape.

This, finally, brings us to the most significant aspect of the rigorous scrutiny of the history of the Modern Movement: the rediscovery of science as a dynamic force, rather than the humble servant of architecture. The original idea of the early years of the century, of science as an unavoidable directive to progress and development, has been reversed by those who cheer for history, and has been watered down to a limited partnership by the mainstream. Those who have re-explored the twenties and read the Futurists for themselves feel, once more, the compulsions of science, the need to take a firm grip on it, and to stay with it whatever the consequences.

The consequence, in some cases, appears to be to whisk them straight out of Formalism and Modern historicism altogether, to make them abandon the lore of the operation, and make use of 'apparent intelligence' instead. But this may be only an appearance – certainly John Johansen's Airform house has the appearance of a radical reversal of attitude for a one-time neo-Palladian of the strictest sort, but equally certainly, many of the most apparently liberated spirits of our time, the intellectual freebooters of the borderland between tradition and technology will not, in the last resort, renounce the lore of the operation. Thus Charles Eames, who has introduced the concept of operational lore into architectural thought, and made with it a plea for the acceptance of scientific attitudes of mind, could still say, toward the end of his Discourse

> Yet, in this circumstance I have described, and in these tools that I have described, I see and feel something which is a real continuity in the architectural tradition.... The real planning, the real architecture, the building of the future, is going to be built with something similar to these tools, and part of these circumstances. My plea is that it fall under the head of that great name, architecture, which embraces it.

Technology

Architecture, as a service to human societies, can only be defined as the provision of fit environments for human activities. The word 'fit' may be defined in the most generous terms imaginable, but it still does not necessarily imply the erection of buildings. Environments may be made fit for human beings by any number of means. A disease-ridden swamp may be rendered fit by inoculating all those who visit it against infection, a bathing beach may be rendered fit by removing land-mines left over from the last War, a natural amphitheatre may be rendered fit for drama by installing lights and a public address system, a snowy landscape may be rendered fit by means of a ski-suit, gloves, boots and a balaclava. Architecture, indeed, began with the first furs worn by our earliest ancestors, or with the discovery of fire – it shows a narrowly professional frame of mind to refer its beginnings solely to the cave or primitive hut.

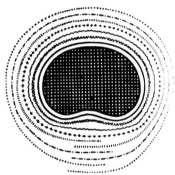

7 Personal architecture – vest to overcoat.

The service that architects propose to perform for society can often be accomplished without calling in an architect in the sense discussed in the article that runs parallel to this, and the increasing range of technological alternatives to bricks and mortar may yet set a term to the custom-sanctioned monopoly of architects as environment-purveyors to the human race. These alternatives, whose justification is measurable performance rather than some cultural sanction, extend, however, beyond the provision of technological services, and include analytical techniques as well, so that it becomes possible to define 'home' without reference to hearth or roof, but simply as the integration of a complex of intrapersonal relationships and main-services. To do so would, in fact, be to depart so far from the operational lore of the society which we inhabit as to provoke alarm and discomfort even among the scientists and technicians who, within their specialities, regularly employ these techniques. Nevertheless, a moment's reflections on such phrases as 'TV Theatre' or 'Radio Concert-hall' will show how far technological advance has made nonsense of concepts that were hitherto building-bound, and yet has gained popular social and cultural acceptance.

Under the impact of these intellectual and technical upheavals the solid reliance of architects, as a profession, on the traditions of that profession must eventually give way. Yet the Functionalist slogan 'a house is a machine for living in' gives nothing away because it begins by presupposing a house. Far more seditious to the established attitude of architects is the proposition that, far from caravans being substandard housing, housing is, for many functions, sub-standard caravans. Outside the context of architectural discussion this would be a pretty radical criticism of current architectural concepts, but within the profession it stands simply as a marginal criticism of some aspects of housing that need improvement in detail.

8 R. Buckminster Fuller, inventor of the Geodesic Dome, in his office at Carbondale, Illinois, surrounded by models of geodesic structures.

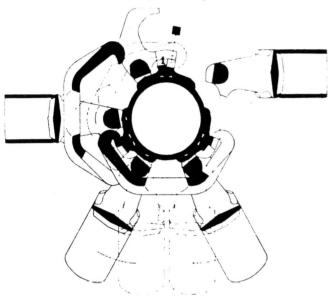

9 Machinery of Wachsmann frame-joint.

10 FREI OTTO and ROLF GUTBROD, *West German Pavilion Expo '67,* Montreal, 1967.

This may be taken as typical of the profession's professional attitude to the impact of technological and scientific alternatives for the art of building. The profession tolerates a few peripheral radicals, whose ideas call the whole professional apparatus in question. Such a man is Buckminster Fuller, recently made a member of AIA, and thus accepted as relevant to architecture in the professional sense. But it is clear that Fuller is admired for his structures and accepted as a formgiver, while his elaborate body of theory and fundamental research into the shelter-needs of mankind is mostly dismissed unread. An extreme technologist more to the profession's taste is Konrad Wachsmann, whose work does not question the need for buildings but concentrates a fanatical watchmaker ingenuity on the solution of certain problems within the given context of built structure – and here it may be noted that while his celebrated joint for the space-frame roof of the B36 hangar was associated with a fairly radical structure, his equivalent work on the General Panel House was associated with a dwelling concept of the utmost banality. Again, the research and teaching being undertaken by the Hochschule für Gestaltung at Ulm, while it asks some searching questions and produces some truly radical answers, does so within a mental concept that substantially accepts the limits that the architectural profession has set itself. In many ways, Le Corbusier's Murondin project for installing sophisticated mechanical services in mud-huts showed a greater radicalism of approach than either of these last two examples.

In any stocktaking of the present condition of architecture, then, it must be accepted that the human environments under consideration are constructed environments, static, more or less permanent and designed to operate without the consumption of too much mechanical energy. These last two provisos are both rather relative since no discussion of the present state of architecture could decently ignore the tented structures of Frei Otto and other semi-permanent exhibition environments, nor could it ignore the fact that some of the most permanent and static structures being built today – such as atom-proof command posts or office blocks in extreme climates – can only be kept fit for human activities at the cost of pouring vast quantities of mechanical energy into them in the form of air-conditioning and artificial light. Within these provisos, the mechanization of the total environment in which architects are called upon to work still acts as a powerful stimulus to their professional activities. Automobiles, the ever-present symbolic objects that typify the present epoch of technological culture, are the irritant that causes constant revision of a number of cherished concepts. These revisions are not always radical, but, nevertheless, it is no longer possible for architects to think of cities as collections of buildings with spaces between them, but as collections of buildings with streams of metallic objects flowing round them – a revision that requires them to think differently about the way the buildings touch the ground, differently about the relationship of building to street, differently about the relationship of building to those who look at it, since the viewers may now be passing it at sixty-plus mph on a gently rising curve or in an underpass whose sides may effectively blank off the whole of the lower storey when the viewer is on the axis of the main façade.

Conversely automobiles as the manifestation of a complex and agitated culture-within-a-culture producing discrete objects which are themselves environments for human activities, provide a standard of comparison for the activities of the architectural profession. They may ruefully compare the scale of the constructional work produced by the automobile culture with that entrusted to architects; they may enviously admire the apparently close communion that exists between users and producers, the direct way in which designers and stylists seem to be able to apprehend the needs of motorists and satisfy them, and they may also draw from the work of stylists some sobering conclusions about the possibility of tailoring aesthetics to fit the aspirations or social status of the clients. The concept of 'the style for the job', which was most recently enunciated in *Architectural Review* by James Gowan in December 1959, has frequently been explained or criticized in terms of the gradations of automobile style for different parts of the market, always with the assumption (sometimes justified) that these gradations are the result of scientifically accurate market research.

However, there is no ambition to imitate automobile form – the only exception to this rule appears to be the 'styling' of the Smithson's House of the Future on the assumption that mass-produced houses would need as high a rate of obsolescence as any other class of mass-produced goods. Such a sentiment is rare, however, because the operational lore of architecture seems not to include the idea of expendability. On the other hand, the forms of the more permanent products of technology are liable to imitation – to cite a notorious example, the development of cooling towers for power-stations has been paralleled by a series of pseudo-cooling towers from Eric Mendelsohn's Hat Factory of 1921, to Le Corbusier's Parliament House for Chandigarh.

This sincere flattery of technology is one facet of the almost fetishistic regard afforded to certain classes of engineers, an admiration that has undergone an important change in the last decade. The respects paid by the early masters of Modern architecture to the engineers they admired was not paralleled by any attempt to mimic the forms of their work – where will you find Freyssinet echoed in early Corbusian design, or Maillart in Max Bill despite the latter being the great bridge-builder's devoted biographer? Yet nowadays the desire to incorporate engineering forms into architectural designs is so overwhelming that engineers like Nervi, Candela, Torroja and others enjoy a status both as collaborators with architects, and as the creators of imitable forms, that engineers have never had before.

Just how far this is merely the employment of engineers as alibis for fancy formalisms is difficult to assess, though Robin Boyd made some pertinent suggestions on this subject in 'The Engineering of Excitement' (*Architectural Review*, November 1958). Over and above this is the possibility that the freeing of floor-space from intermediate supports which new vaulting techniques and space-frame trusses make possible, is being used in one way and explained in another. Great clear spans make possible a free and untrammelled functional disposition of interior spaces – this is one of the promises of Fuller's domes, for instance. But they also clear the floor for free and untrammelled exercises in architectural sensibility – which seems to be what happened, in fact, inside the geodesic dome furnished by Roberto Mango at the 1954 Triennale di Milano.

Such situations are not as rare as might be supposed – Mies van der Rohe's project for a theatre in a giant aircraft-hangar is another debatable case in point – and they represent the continuance of a trend that has been with us since the beginning of the century; the marriage of the logical objectivity of abstract aesthetics to the experimental objectivity of advanced science. It goes back to Perret, it also has roots in *de Stijl* and Constructivism. In the guise of the 'logical Formalism' of Mies van der Rohe it has served the important function of easing the acceptance of curtain

11 Custom designed owners of Oldsmobile.

12 ALISON and PETER SMITHSON, *House of the Future*, Ideal Home Exhibition, Olympia, London, 1956, view of living area.

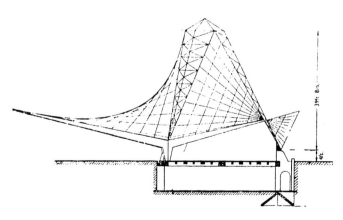

13 Roof of Candela's Coyoacan Chapel.

14 R. BUCKMINSTER FULLER, *His Own House*, Carbondale, Illinois, 1960.

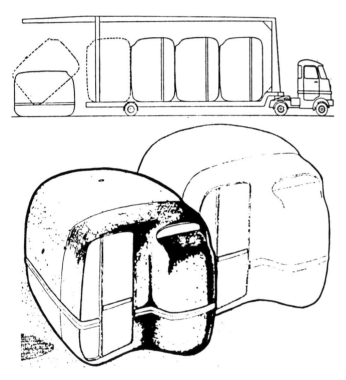

15 Complete Coulon/Schein plastic dwelling units.

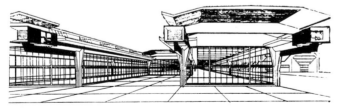

16 Zanuso integration of structure and services.

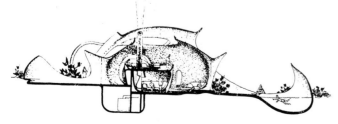

17 Airform liberation from professional lore.

walling and other additive pre-fabricating systems as 'architecture' in a sense that can be assimilated to the lore of the operation.

However, it should be noted that when prefabrication gets out of the direct control of architects, into the hands of engineers, it almost invariably ceases to be rectangular in its format. Fuller's work is again a case in point, so is that of Jean Prouvé, which has persistently relied on tapered portals, sloping walls and curved members. However, there is a division of mind here between architects and engineers that goes much deeper. The operational lore of the architectural profession has assimilated prefabrication as a technique applied to fairly small repetitive components to be assembled on site. Such an arrangement leaves the determination of functional volumes still securely in the hands of architects, and the physical creation of those volumes securely in the hand of traditional-type site labour.

But prefabrication, for most of the creative minds in the plastics business, means something quite different. It means – as Michael Brawne has suggested ('Polyester Fibreglass', *Architectural Review*, December 1959) – the fabrication of components large enough to be effective determinants of functional volumes. Thus, the Monsanto House has only four large components to form the whole of one of its cantilevered rooms (bar the lateral windows) while some of the products envisaged by the French group around Coulon and Schein call for the off-site fabrication of complete functional volumes such as bathrooms and kitchens, a procedure which both has structural advantages and makes it possible to complete most of the fabricating work under controlled, laboratory conditions. The result seems likely to be a house put together from large non-repeating units – except for the joiners which, like railway corridors, must be universal fits. In larger structures room-units might be carried in an independent frame, but in either case the result should be that service-rooms, which need to be connected to the public mains, might be treated as expendable clip-on components, thus obviating some of the difficulties of the Appliance House project, which runs the risk of degenerating into a series of display-niches for an ever-changing array of domestic machinery.

However, such ideas have hardly touched the general body of architecture at all as yet. Much of the most painstaking and valuable research that can be shown, has been undertaken in conditions that presuppose the existence of rectangular buildings. Much of this work has been structural, concerned chiefly with prefabrication techniques, a field in which, for instance, the Ministry of Education and independent commercial experimenters can be found advancing, from the other end, into territory already being prospected by the Modular mathematicians. Elsewhere, as with the Nuffield Trust, a great deal of solid, plodding work, that most architects would rather not undertake, has been accomplished in the fields of space requirements and the physiological effects of daylighting and colour. The fruits of such work, because of the 'logical Formalist' connection discussed above, often wear a characteristic air of grid-like simplicity which, it should be noted, derives more from the mental disposition of the men involved than from the findings of the research programmes.

Where research has been surprisingly thin has been in office-design, in spite of the large sums involved (although there has been some clever ad hoc rationalizing in this field) and in domestic work, in spite of the vast amount of housing still necessarily being built. Even clever ad hoc rationalization could show results in housing, but, as was said at the beginning of this article, the operational lore of our whole culture renders domestic architecture practically proof against scientific attitudes. On the other hand, it should be noted that via market and motivation research, and the long accumulation of sociological data, extensive scientific inroads into the 'sanctity of the home' have already been made, and when domestic designers can master their fairly long-standing distrust of sociologists, and their new-found distrust of 'Hidden Persuaders' they may well find that a great deal of very suggestive research is already at their disposal.

In the meantime, science and technology touch architecture chiefly at the level of structural justification and organizational confusion. One specialist consultant makes the building stand up, six others render it largely useless by means of the services that are intended to make it usable. By and large, architects have established a peaceable and fruitful technique of working with their structural engineers. In England, engineers like Samuely, Arup and Jenkins, in France men like the late Bernard Laffaille and René Sarger, in the USA men like Fred Severud, Mario Salvadori and Paul Weidlinger or offices like Smith, Hynchman and Grylls, could claim to have played a dominant and valuable role in the architectural developments of the last ten years, but no other body of consultants could claim anything of the sort – though some architects might, nowadays, find a good word for the more enterprising type of quantity surveyor.

The fact remains that heating. lighting, ventilating, air-conditioning, acoustics, office machinery and other more specialist services seem for the moment incapable of assimilation to the harmony established over the years between structural engineers and architects. The few breaks in this unpromising situation appear to derive from lighting engineers and acousticists with architectural training, and from a few liberated spirits, notably Louis Kahn with his 'topological' science blocks for the University of Pennsylvania, or Marco Zanuso with his integrated structure-and-air-conditioning schemes.

This may be a bulldozer solution for a problem that Mies van der Rohe, for instance, believes should be solved in secret. But it is a solution that brings us to the point of fusion of the technological and traditional aspects in architecture today. Kahn is sympathetic to, and has been classed with, the Brutalists. On both sides, enterprising and intensive scrutiny of tradition and science appears to suggest a way out of a dilemma, if not a solution to a problem. But it is a balancing feat that may prove to need acrobatic skill and expertise in brinkmanship as architects edge temerously along the margin of the scientific disciplines and never quite put a foot over into the other camp. From the scientific side there is neither such caution nor such finesse. It appears always possible that at any unpredictable moment the unorganized hordes of unco-ordinated specialists could flood over into the architects' preserves and, ignorant of the lore of the operation, create an Other Architecture by chance, as it were, out of apparent intelligence and the task of creating fit environments for human activities.

The Gap – Town Planning

When all this has been said, and stock has been taken of the present situation, there remains one yawning and alarming chasm between technology and tradition, between operational lore and apparent intelligence – town planning. In a field too expensive for experiment, too full of practical minutiae for paper guesses or diagrammatic utopias to carry much conviction, the pull between the 'Two Cultures', as Sir Charles Snow has called them, results in a situation that would be tragic were it not more like the nihilistic farce of Ionesco and the Other theatre.

The idea of cities is an ineradicable part of the operational lore of civilization – a word which implies cities anyhow. The concepts we have of cities are as old as philosophy, and are so rooted in the language of cultured discourse that to say 'Cities should be compact' is to commit a tautology – we cannot conceive of a diffuse city, and have invented other words such as 'conurbation', 'subtopia', to underline our inability to conceive it.

Against this, the manifestations of apparent intelligence, in communications, traffic planning, services, industries, entertainment, sport, all dealing with the here and the now, preoccupied with current information, news and statistics, have no regard for the inherited traditions of urbanism by which towns are defined.

Yet most citizens – including those called upon to plan – are determined to have the best of both worlds. They expect to be able to drive straight down an Autoroute de l'Ouest, straight through the Arc de Triomphe, and into a Champs Elysées that still has the urbanity of a sequence from *Gigi*. They demand suburban expansiveness, and urban compactness, ancient monuments and tomorrow's mechanical aids simultaneously and in the same place.

They get neither, because on one side is a tradition which cannot be expanded to deal with new developments without disintegrating, and on the other hand a disorderly pressure of new developments whose effect – because they are competitive and lack an integrating discipline – is disruptive anyhow.

There may be any number of logical solutions to this problem – but the only one we have so far is the relatively desperate solution of handing over responsibility to the will of a dictator – Le Corbusier at Chandigarh, Lucio Costa at Brasilia – and we are entitled to ask whether this is an adequate solution for our most pressing problem in design.

1.8 A HOME IS NOT A HOUSE

In this piece for Art in America, *April 1965, Banham, with the help of François Dallegret and his succinct visualizations, playfully conjures up a house which is determined totally by its services – an 'anti-house' where absolute functionality dispels any thoughts of symbolic fulfilment. This, Banham feels, is the logical conclusion to the American architectural tradition which is not hung up on questions of aesthetics or style.*

hen your house contains such a complex of piping, flues, ducts, wires, lights, inlets, outlets, ovens, sinks, refuse disposers, hi-fi reverberators, antennae, conduits, freezers, heaters – when it contains so many services that the hardware could stand up by itself without any assistance from the house, why have a house to hold it up? When the cost of all this tackle is half of the total outlay (or more, as it often is) what is the house doing except concealing your mechanical pudenda from the stares of folks on the sidewalk? Once or twice recently there have been buildings where the public was genuinely confused about what was mechanical services, what was structure – many visitors to Philadelphia take quite a time to work out that the floors of Louis Kahn's laboratory towers are not supported by the flanking brick duct boxes, and when they have worked it out, they are inclined to wonder if it was worth all the trouble of giving them an independent supporting structure.

No doubt about it, a great deal of the attention captured by those labs derives from Kahn's attempt to put the drama of mechanical services on show – and if, in the end, it fails to do that convincingly, the psychological importance of the gesture remains, at least in the eyes of his fellow architects. Services are a topic on which architectural practice has alternated capriciously between the brazen and the coy – there was the grand old Let-it-dangle period, when every ceiling was a mess of gaily painted entrails, as in the council chambers of the UN building, and there have been fits of pudicity when even the most innocent anatomical details have been hurriedly veiled with a suspended ceiling.

Basically, there are two reasons for all this blowing hot and cold (if you will excuse the air-conditioning industry's oldest working pun). The first is that mechanical services are too new to have been absorbed into the proverbial wisdom of the profession: none of the great slogans – Form Follows Function, *accusez la structure*, Firmness Commodity and Delight, Truth to Materials, *Wenig ist Mehr* – is much use in coping with the mechanical invasion. The nearest thing, in a significantly negative way, is Le Corbusier's 'Pour Ledoux, c'était facile – pas de tubes', which seems to be gaining proverbial-type currency as the expression of a profound nostalgia for the golden age before piping set in.

The second reason is that the mechanical invasion is a fact, and architects – especially American architects – sense that it is a cultural threat to their position in the world. American architects are certainly right to feel this, because their professional speciality, the art of creating monumental spaces, has never been securely established on this continent. It remains a transplant from an older culture and architects in America are constantly harking back to that culture. The generation of Stanford White and Louis Sullivan were prone to behave like émigrés from France, Frank Lloyd Wright was apt to take cover behind sentimental Teutonicisms like *Lieber Meister*, the big boys of the thirties and forties came from Aachen and Berlin anyhow, the pacemakers of the fifties and sixties are men of international culture like Charles Eames and Philip Johnson, and so too, in many ways, are the coming men of today, like Myron Goldsmith.

Left to their own devices, Americans do not monumentalize or make architecture. From the Cape Cod cottage, through the balloon frame to the perfection of permanently pleated aluminum siding with embossed wood-graining, they have tended to build a brick chimney and lean a collection of shacks against it. When Groff Conklin wrote in *The Weather-Conditioned House* that 'A house is nothing but a hollow shell . . . a shell is all a house or any structure in which human beings live and work, really is. And most shells in nature are extraordinarily inefficient barriers to cold and heat . . .' he was expressing an extremely American view, backed by a long-established grass-roots tradition.

And since that tradition agrees with him that the American hollow shell is such an inefficient heat barrier, Americans have always been prepared to pump more heat, light and

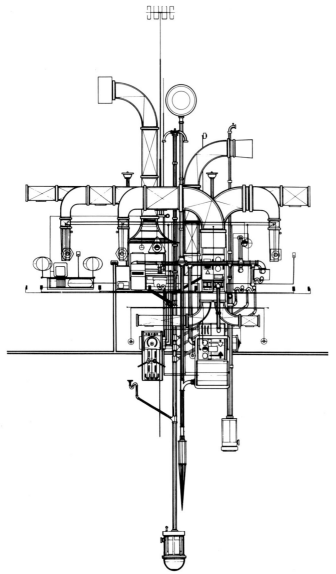

1 FRANÇOIS DALLEGRET, *Anatomy of a Dwelling.*

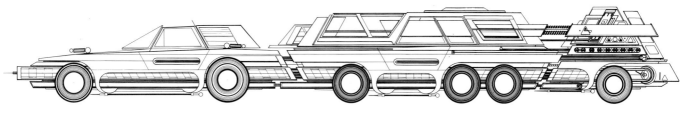

2 FRANÇOIS DALLEGRET, *Trailmaster GTO Transcontinental.*

3 FRANÇOIS DALLEGRET, *Super-Coupe de Long-Week-End*, 1927.

power into their shelters than have other peoples. America's monumental space is, I suppose, the great outdoors – the porch, the terrace, Whitman's rail-traced plains, Kerouac's infinite road, and now, the Great Up There. Even within the house, Americans rapidly learned to dispense with the partitions that Europeans need to keep space architectural and within bounds, and long before Wright began blundering through the walls that subdivided polite architecture into living-room, games-room, card-room, gun-room etc., humbler Americans had been slipping into a way of life adapted to informally planned interiors that were, effectively, large single spaces.

Now, large single volumes wrapped in flimsy shells have to be lighted and heated in a manner quite different and more generous than the cubicular interiors of the European tradition around which the concept of domestic architecture first crystallized. Right from the start, from the Franklin stove and the kerosene lamp, the American interior has had to be better serviced if it was to support a civilized culture, and this is one of the reasons that the US has been the forcing ground of mechanical services in buildings – so if services are to be felt anywhere as a threat to architecture, it should be in America.

'The plumber is the quartermaster of American culture', wrote Adolf Loos, father of all European platitudes about the superiority of US plumbing. He knew what he was talking about; his brief visit to the States in the nineties convinced him that the outstanding virtues of the American way of life were its informality (no need to wear a top hat to call on local officials) and its cleanliness – which was bound to be noticed by a Viennese with as highly developed a set of Freudian compulsions as he had. That obsession with clean (which can become one of the higher absurdities of America's lysol-breathing Kleenex-culture) was another psychological motive that drove the nation toward mechanical services. The early justifications of air-conditioning were not just that people had to breathe: Konrad Meier in *Reflections on Heating and Ventilating*, 1904, wrote fastidiously of ' . . . excessive amounts of water vapor, sickly odors from respiratory organs, unclean teeth, perspiration, untidy clothing, the presence of microbes due to various conditions, stuffy air from dusty carpets and draperies . . . cause greater discomfort and greater ill health.'

(Have a wash, and come back for the next paragraph.)

Most pioneer air-conditioning men seem to have been nose-obsessed in this way: best friends could just about force themselves to tell America of her national BO – and then, compulsive salesmen to a man, promptly prescribed

their own patent improved panacea for ventilating the hell out of her. Somewhere among these clustering concepts – cleanliness, the lightweight shell, the mechanical services, the informality and indifference to monumental architectural values, the passion for the outdoors – there always seemed to me to lurk some elusive master concept that would never quite come into focus. It finally came clear and legible to me in June 1964, in the most highly appropriate and symptomatic circumstances.

I was standing up to my chest-hair in water, making home movies (I get that NASA kick from taking expensive hardware into hostile environments) at the campus beach at Southern Illinois. This beach combines the outdoor and the clean in a highly American manner – scenically it is the ole swimmin' hole of Huckleberry Finn tradition, but it is properly policed (by sophomore lifeguards sitting on Eames chairs on poles in the water) and it's *chlorinated* too. From where I stood, I could see not only immensely elaborate family barbecues and picnics in progress on the sterilized sand, but also, through and above the trees, the basketry interlaces of one of Buckminster Fuller's experimental domes. And it hit me then, that if dirty old Nature could be kept under the proper degree of control (sex left in, streptococci taken out) by other means, the United States would be happy to dispense with architecture and buildings altogether.

Bucky Fuller, of course, is very big on this proposition: his famous non-rhetorical question, 'Madam, do you know what your house weighs?' articulates a subversive suspicion of the monumental. This suspicion is inarticulately shared by the untold thousands of Americans who have already shed the deadweight of domestic architecture and live in mobile homes which, though they may never actually be moved, still deliver rather better performance as shelter than do ground-anchored structures costing at least three times as much and weighing ten times more. If someone could devise a package that would effectively disconnect the mobile home from the dangling wires of the town electricity supply, the bottled gas containers insecurely perched on a packing case and the semi-unspeakable sanitary arrangements that stem from not being connected to the main sewer – then we should really see some changes. It may not be so far away either; defense cutbacks may send aerospace spin-off spinning in some new directions quite soon, and that kind of miniaturization-talent applied to a genuinely self-contained and regenerative standard-of-living package that could be towed behind a trailer home or clipped to it, could produce a sort of U-haul unit that might be picked up

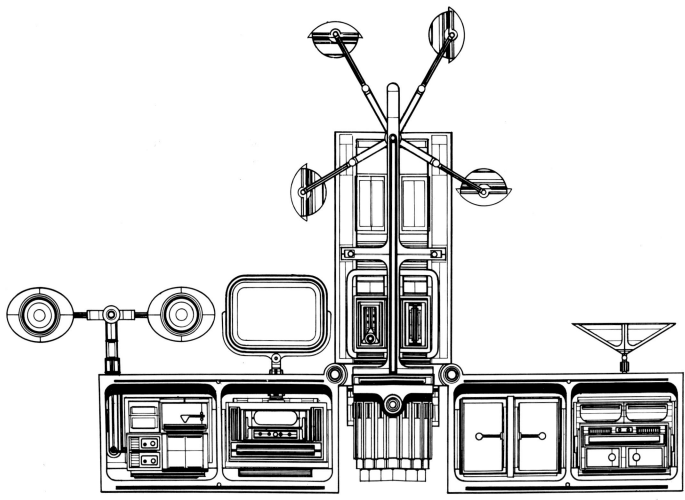

4 FRANÇOIS DALLEGRET, *Transportable Standard-of-Living Package.*

or dropped off at depots across the face of the nation. Avis might still become the first in U-Tility, even if they have to go on being a trying second in car hire.

Out of this might come a domestic revolution beside which Modern architecture would look like Kiddibrix, because you might be able to dispense with the trailer home as well. A standard-of-living package (the phrase and the concept are both Bucky Fuller's) that really worked might, like so many sophisticated inventions, return Man nearer to a natural state in spite of his complex culture (much as the supersession of the Morse telegraph by the Bell Telephone restored his power of speech nationwide). Man started with two basic ways of controlling environment: one by avoiding the issue and hiding under a rock, tree, tent or roof (this led ultimately to architecture as we know it) and the other by actually interfering with the local meteorology, usually by means of a camp-fire, which, in a more polished form, might lead to the kind of situation now under discussion. Unlike the living space trapped with our forebears under a rock or roof, the space around a camp-fire has many unique qualities which architecture cannot hope to equal, above all, its freedom and variability.

The direction and strength of the wind will decide the main shape and dimensions of that space, stretching the area of tolerable warmth into a long oval, but the output of light will not be affected by the wind, and the area of tolerable illumination will be a circle overlapping the oval of warmth. There will thus be a variety of environmental choices balancing light against warmth according to need and interest. If you want to do close work, like shrinking a human head, you sit in one place, but if you want to sleep

you curl up somewhere different; the floating knuckle-bones game would come to rest somewhere quite different to the environment that suited the meeting of the initiation rites steering committee ... and all this would be jim dandy if camp-fires were not so perishing inefficient, unreliable, smoky and the rest of it.

But a properly set-up standard-of-living package, breathing out warm air along the ground (instead of sucking in cold along the ground like a camp-fire), radiating soft light and Dionne Warwick in heart-warming stereo, with well-aged protein turning in an infra-red glow in the rotisserie, and the ice-maker discreetly coughing cubes into glasses on the swing-out bar – this could do something for a woodland glade or creek-side rock that *Playboy* could never do for its penthouse. But how are you going to manhandle this hunk of technology down to the creek? It doesn't have to be that massive; aerospace needs, for instance, have done wild things to solid-state technology, producing even tiny re-frigerating transistors. They don't as yet mop up any great quantity of heat, but what are you going to do in this glade anyhow; put a whole steer in deep-freeze? Nor do you have to manhandle it – it could ride on a cushion of air (its own air-conditioning output, for instance) like a hovercraft or dom-estic vacuum cleaner.

All this will eat up quite a lot of power, transistors notwithstanding. But one should remember that few Ameri-cans are ever far from a source of between 100 and 400 horsepower – the automobile. Beefed-up car batteries and a self-reeling cable drum could probably get this package breathing warm bourbon fumes o'er Eden long before micro-wave power transmission or miniaturized atomic

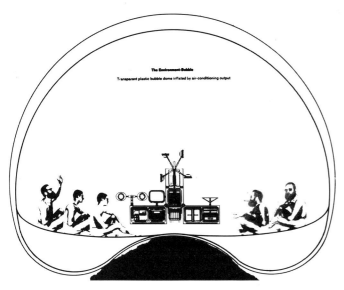

5 FRANÇOIS DALLEGRET, *The Environment-Bubble,* transparent plastic bubble dome inflated by air-conditioning output.

power plants come in. The car is already one of the strongest arms in America's environmental weaponry, and an essential component in one non-architectural anti-building that is already familiar to most of the nation – the drive-in movie house. Only, the word *house* is a manifest misnomer – just a flat piece of ground where the operating company provides visual images and piped sound, and the rest of the situation comes on wheels. You bring your own seat, heat and shelter as part of the car. You also bring Coke, cookies, Kleenex, Chesterfields, spare clothes, shoes, the Pill and god-wot else they don't provide at Radio City.

The car, in short, is already doing quite a lot of the standard-of-living package's job – the smoochy couple dancing to the music of the radio in their parked convertible have created a ballroom in the wilderness (dance floor by courtesy of the Highway Dept. of course) and all this is paradisal till it starts to rain. Even then, you're not licked – it takes very little air pressure to inflate a transparent Mylar airdome, the conditioned-air output of your mobile package might be able to do it, with or without a little boosting, and the dome itself, folded into a parachute pack, might be part of the package. From within your thirty-foot hemisphere of warm dry *lebensraum* you could have spectacular ringside views of the wind felling trees, snow swirling through the glade, the forest fire coming over the hill or Constance Chatterley running swiftly to you know whom through the downpour.

But ... surely this is not a home, you can't bring up a family in a polythene bag? This can never replace the time-honoured ranch-style tri-level standing proudly in a landscape of five defeated shrubs, flanked on one side by a ranch-style tri-level with six shrubs and on the other by a ranch-style tri-level with four small boys and a private dust bowl. If the countless Americans who are successfully raising nice children in trailers will excuse me for a moment, I have a few suggestions to make to the even more countless Americans who are so insecure that they have to hide inside fake monuments of Permastone and instant roofing. There are, admittedly, very sound day-to-day advantages to having warm broadloom on a firm floor underfoot, rather than pine needles and poison ivy. America's pioneer house builders recognized this by commonly building their brick chimneys on a brick floor slab. A transparent airdome could be anchored to such a slab just as easily as could a balloon frame, and the standard-of-living package could

hover busily in a sort of glorified barbecue pit in the middle of the slab. But an airdome is not the sort of thing that the kids, or a distracted Pumpkin-eater could run in and out of when the fit took them – believe me, fighting your way out of an airdome can be worse than trying to get out of a collapsed rain-soaked tent if you make the wrong first move.

But the relationship of the services-kit to the floor slab could be re-arranged to get over this difficulty; all the standard-of-living tackle (or most of it) could be re-deployed on the upper side of a sheltering membrane floating above the floor, radiating heat, light and what-not downwards and leaving the whole perimeter wide-open for random egress – and equally casual ingress, too, I guess. That crazy Modern Movement dream of the interpenetration of indoors and outdoors could become real at last by abolishing the doors. Technically, of course, it would be just about possible to make the power-membrane literally float, hovercraft style. Anyone who has had to stand in the ground-effect of a helicopter will know that this solution has little to recommend it apart from the instant disposal of waste paper. The noise, power consumption and physical discomfort would be really something wild. But if the power-membrane could be carried on a column or two, here and there, or even on a brick-built bathroom unit, then we are almost in sight of what might be technically possible before the Great Society is much older.

The basic proposition is simply that the power-membrane should blow down a curtain of warmed/cooled/conditioned air around the perimeter of the windward side of the un-house, and leave the surrounding weather to waft it through the living space, whose relationship in plan to the membrane above need not be a one-to-one relationship. The membrane would probably have to go beyond the limits of the floor slab, anyhow, in order to prevent rain blow-in, though the air-curtain will be active on precisely the side on which the rain is blowing and, being conditioned, will tend to mop up the moisture as it falls. The distribution of the air-curtain will be governed by various electronic light and weather sensors, and by that radical new invention, the weather-vane. For really foul weather automatic storm shutters would be required, but in all but the most wildly inconstant climates, it should be possible to design the conditioning kit to deal with most of the weather most of the time, without the power consumption becoming ridiculously greater than for an ordinary inefficient monumental type house.

Obviously, it would still be appreciably greater, but this whole argument hinges on the observation that it is the American Way to spend money on services and upkeep s and upkeep rather than on permanent structure as do the peasant cultures of the Old World. In any case, we don't know where we shall be with things like solar power in the next decade, and to anyone who wants to entertain an almost-possible vision of air-conditioning for absolutely free, let me recommend 'Shortstack' (another smart trick with a polythene tube) in the December 1964 issue of *Analog.* In fact, quite a number of the obvious common sense objections to the un-house may prove to be self-evaporating: for instance, noise may be no problem because there would be no surrounding wall to reflect it back into the living space, and, in any case, the constant whisper of the air-curtain would provide a fair threshold of loudness that sounds would have to beat before they began to be comprehensible and therefore disturbing. Bugs? Wild life? In summer they should be no worse than with the doors and windows of an ordinary house open; in winter all right-thinking creatures either migrate or hibernate; but, in any case, why not encourage the normal processes of Darwinian competition

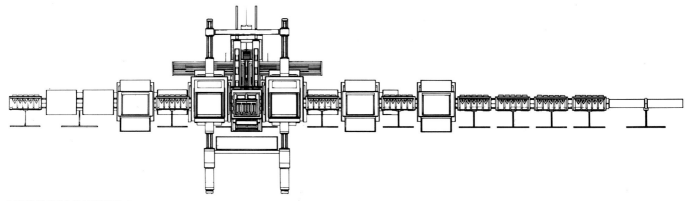

6 FRANÇOIS DALLEGRET, *Power-Membrane House*.

to tidy up the situation for you? All that is needed is to trigger the process by means of a general purpose lure; this would radiate mating calls and sexy scents and thus attract all sorts of mutually incompatible predators and prey into a compact pool of unspeakable carnage. A closed-circuit television camera could relay the state of play to a screen inside the dwelling and provide a twenty-four hour program that would make the ratings for *Bonanza* look like chicken feed.

And privacy? This seems to be such a nominal concept in American life as factually lived that it is difficult to believe that anyone is seriously worried. The answer, under the suburban conditions that this whole argument implies, is the same as for the glass houses architects were designing so busily a decade ago – more sophisticated landscaping. This, after all, is the homeland of the bulldozer and the transplantation of grown trees – why let the Parks Commissioner have all the fun?

As was said above, this argument implies suburbia which, for better or worse, is where America wants to live. It has nothing to say about the city, which, like architecture, is an insecure foreign growth on the continent. What is under discussion here is an extension of the Jeffersonian dream beyond the agrarian sentimentality of Frank Lloyd Wright's Usonian/Broadacre version – the dream of the good life in the clean countryside, power-point homesteading in a paradise garden of appliances. This dream of the un-house may sound very anti-architectural but it is so only in degree, and architecture deprived of its European roots but trying to strike new ones in an alien soil has come close to the anti-house once or twice already. Wright was not joking when he talked of the 'destruction of the box', even though the spatial promise of the phrase is rarely realized to the full in the all-too-solid fact. Grass-roots architects of the plains like Bruce Goff and Herb Greene have produced houses whose supposed monumental form is clearly of little consequence to the functional business of living in and around them.

But it is in one building that seems at first sight nothing but monumental form that the threat or promise of the un-house has been most clearly demonstrated – the Johnson House at New Canaan. So much has been misleadingly said (by Philip Johnson himself, as well as others) to prove this a work of architecture in the European tradition, that its many intensely American aspects are usually missed. Yet when you have dug through all the erudition about Ledoux and Malevitsch and Palladio and stuff that has been published, one very suggestive source or prototype remains less easily explained away – the admitted persistence in Johnson's mind of the visual image of a burned-out New England township, the insubstantial shells of the houses consumed by the fire, leaving the brick floor slabs and standing chimneys. The New Canaan glass-house consists essentially of just these two elements, a heated brick floor slab, and a standing unit which is a chimney/fireplace on one side and a bathroom on the other.

Around this has been draped precisely the kind of insubstantial shell that Conklin was discussing, only even less substantial than that. The roof, certainly, is solid, but psychologically it is dominated by the absence of visual enclosure all around. As many pilgrims to this site have noticed, the house does not stop at the glass, and the terrace, and even the trees beyond, are visually part of the living space in winter physically and operationally so in summer when the four doors are open. The 'house' is little more than a service core set in infinite space, or alternatively, a detached porch looking out in all directions at the Great Out There. In summer, indeed, the glass would be a bit of a nonsense if the trees did not shade it, and in the recent scorching fall, the sun reaching in through the bare trees created such a greenhouse effect that parts of the interior were acutely uncomfortable – the house would have been better off without its glass walls.

When Philip Johnson says that the place is not a controlled environment, however, it is not these aspects of undisciplined glazing he has in mind, but that 'when it gets cold I have to move toward the fire, and when it gets too hot I just move away'. In fact, he is simply exploiting the campfire phenomenon (he is also pretending that the floor-heating does not make the whole area habitable, which it does) and in any case, what does he mean by a controlled environment? It is not the same thing as a uniform environment, it is simply an environment suited to what you are going to do next, and whether you build a stone monument, move away from the fire or turn on the air-conditioning, it is the same basic human gesture you are making

Only, the monument is such a ponderous solution that it astounds me that Americans are still prepared to employ it, except out of some profound sense of insecurity, a persistent inability to rid themselves of those habits of mind they left Europe to escape. In the open-fronted society, with its social and personal mobility, its interchangeability of components and personnel, its gadgetry and almost universal expendability, the persistence of architecture-as-monumental-space must appear as evidence of the sentimentality of the tough.

1.9 TOWARDS A POP ARCHITECTURE

In this article, originally published in Architectural Review, *July 1962, Banham begins an inquiry which runs through much of his work in this period. He sets out to examine the relevance of the Pop aesthetic and ethic in architecture, searching for an architectural equivalent of the expendable, commercial objects that Pop artists admire. He finds it here in modern vernacular buildings like hamburger stalls, Odeon cinemas and in SPAN housing.*[1]

The presence of an article on Pop Art in a series devoted to architectural realizations of the potentials of technology, may appear to need some justification, but this is not so. Justification is needed only in the eyes of those who have tried to build up technology as a moral discipline, following a mistaken reading of the intentions of Mies van der Rohe, or an accurate reading of the mistaken conclusions of *Vers une Architecture*. Technology is morally, socially and politically neutral, though its exploitation may require adjustments of social and political structures, and its consequences may call moral attitudes in question. And the Pop Arts, being almost all of them inconceivable without a high level of mechanization and mass-production, are integral with technology, which does not discriminate between recordings of John Glenn heard through the ionosphere, and recordings of Cliff Richard heard through an echo-chamber. Technology is a commonwealth of techniques exploited to serve a disparity of human needs.

However, if this study needs no justification, the instance at which it has been written needs some explanation, since it depends on two circumstances that have no apparent connection, save a temporal coincidence. One circumstance is the continuing improvement in architectural quality of certain classes of speculative housing, which raises the question of the present state of popular taste. The other circumstance, which gives a precise time-mark for this study, is that certain types of fine art, notably painting, in which elements of Pop Art are employed, have recently attained a level of official success that marks a breakthrough for a kind of sensibility that takes fine and Pop equally in its stride. Since it is believed in some circles that any revolution or upheaval in the pure arts must, of some historical necessity, be followed by an equivalent upset in architecture, it is anticipated that the cordon-sanitaire between Pop Art and architecture is about to be breached like a metropolitan green belt, and a Pop architecture emerge about 1966.

This 'necessity' will not stand up to historical examination, however. The supposed causal connection between painting and architecture may have been true of the nineteen twenties, and it may be possible to reflect it back on the Renaissance, but it is far from a universal pattern. And in any case, it has been rendered vacuous by events of the past thirty years. On the painting side this development occupies only fifteen years at the maximum. Pioneer studies of Borax styling, such as those that appeared in *Architectural Review* in 1948, were resumed at the Institute of Contemporary Arts in the early fifties, but in an altered tone of voice – approval, not deprecation. This set in motion a series of repercussions among the painters under ICA influence (e.g. John McHale's cover for 'Machine Made America', *Architectural Review*, May 1957), created a school of Pop Art fanciers in the Royal College of Art, and led to awards and other recognitions for artists like Peter Blake and David Hockney – the latter's style can be seen in the illustrations of the 'Teenage Bar of the Canberra', *Architectural Review*, October 1961, and he received a John Moores award in 1962, as did Peter Blake.

That this was an extension, revolutionary and perhaps beneficial, of the iconography of the Fine Arts, is clear – but it is not clear how it might benefit architecture. The fundamental reason why it will have little to say to the arts of building and town-making is that architects and planners have got there already. For instance, the collage-effect of violent juxtaposition of advertising matter with older art forms, which appears in, say, Peter Blake's work as clusters of fan-club badges on realistic paintings of the human form, was being widely discussed in architectural circles around the time of the Festival of Britain and the Hoddesdon meeting of CIAM, or, in *Architectural Review*, as early as December 1952, when the editors took Professor Guyatt smartly to task for his 'aesthetically purist' views on advertising in the townscape.

The fact is that architecture, in a capitalist society, deals in real property and is therefore a branch of commerce. Furthermore, since it creates visible forms, it is apt to become a branch of advertising as well, and in this latter sense there has been a Pop architecture for some time now – Albert Kahn's Ford Pavilion at the New York World's Fair of 1939 is probably the true ancestor of the genre, and its progeny are in various ways widely diffused throughout the US in the form of exclamatory hamburger bars, and other roadside retail outlets. At this point some discriminations of style, method, intention and content are necessary, because it is still – alas – necessary to explain the difference between Pop Art and Folk Art. Many critics would clearly like to believe that a Pop architecture would turn out something like the towers of Simon Rodilla or the fantasy palace of 'Facteur' Cheval at Hauterive. But in spite of the good 'facteur's' mastery of Beaux-Arts façade composition, or Rodilla's intuitive genius in engineering, these are Folk Art. They lack the imagery of dreams that money can buy that characterizes Pop Art; desirable possessions and accessible gratifications, handily packaged, seductively displayed, mass-produced and ubiquitously available. Neither the palace at Hauterive nor the towers at Watts are marketable goods.

Clearly, the Royal College painters are handling Pop Art in their pictures much as if it were a particularly noisy form of Folk Art, and there is about them, quite frequently, a Marie-Antoinette air of Fine Art people dressed up hoi polloi (even though some of them privately *consume* Pop Art in the ordinary teenage way). But architecture can become involved in Pop Art at its own level and according to the same set of Madison Avenue rules. One way has already been discussed: it can serve as a selling point for some desirable standardized product that is too complex or too expensive to be dispensed from slot machines, and in this sense we have had a sort of Pop architecture in Britain since the beginnings of the Granada and Odeon chains of cinemas. Or, the other way in which architecture can be a part of the Pop world is in becoming, in itself, a desirable standardized product, and in this sense we have had a Pop architecture in Britain ever since the more progressive and aggressive speculative builders decided that it was time for housing to quit the eotechnic phase and to take over current advertising and marketing techniques, instead of methods that still smacked of the transfer of fiefs from one vassal to another. Since buildings, despite Buckminster Fuller, are still too heavy to be sent to supermarkets, the consumers instead must be

ALBERT KAHN, *Ford Motor Company Exhibition Pavilion*, New York World's Fair, 1939.

mobile and locally numerous, and these more modern merchandising techniques can only be employed in heavily motorized conurbations. We have had a Pop architecture in Britain, to be precise, ever since SPAN set up shop at Ham Common.

It will certainly be objected that buildings of the sort that have been discussed above are not architecture. The cordon-sanitaire between architecture and Pop Art, to which reference was made earlier, represents a very deep-seated desire, as old as the reformist sentiments of the Pioneers of Modern Architecture, that the profession should not be contaminated by commercialism, that architecture should remain a humane 'consultant' service to humanity, not styling in the interest of sales promotion. Yet SPAN housing is unquestionably accepted as architecture, for all that it is a nearly-standardized, almost mass-produced, accessible and attractively packaged product. The question of where to draw a line between architecture and commerce becomes almost unanswerable as soon as one tries to draw it, and even if it were to be drawn so far towards one extreme as to only *just* exclude, say, hamburger bars, it would still need an architect with a large capacity for self deception, or a very small practice, before he could say that, professionally, he had never stepped over that line. The preparation of rendered perspectives to present a scheme to clients is only one case in point.

In a capitalist society, every architect whose living depends on his work – even in public service – must operate at times within the terms, if not the financial structure, of commercial enterprise. Honesty should require the profession to admit that many of its virtues are commercial ones – such as CLASP's value-for-money operations in the component market – and that some of its most productive motivations are commercial too. But in some conspicuous examples of such motivations we appear to be drawing within the sphere of influence of the ICA's investigations of the Pop Arts. James Stirling, at a public meeting at the ICA, justified both the style and the constructional methods of his Langham House Close housing (*Architectural Review*, October 1958) in terms of 'the market.' The importance of this statement lies less in its truth as applied to this particular design by Stirling and Gowan (which may be arguable) than in another truth that was not to be known in 1958 – that elements of the Langham House Close type of architecture have become a viable spec-building style for which there is a real market among the sophisticated and mobile consumers of the London conurbation.

The question then arises, were Stirling and Gowan consciously influenced by these ICA discussions? Is this an early manifestation of a consequential connection between early Pop Art influenced painting, such as Richard Hamilton's and early Pop Art influenced architecture. Not only does the style of Langham House Close make this unlikely – Stirling and Gowan could have produced this particular and personal blend of the Maison Jaoul and *de Stijl* without Stirling ever visiting the ICA or seeing a Hamilton painting – but the dates make it pretty well impossible. 1958 as a completion date implies 1956 as a design date and throws the whole conception too far back in time. In the case of SPAN's pioneer development at Ham Common, which launched an even more viable and marketable housing style, the design dates go back to 1953–4, which would make any talk of ICA influence nonsensical, even if what one knows of the character of Eric Lyons, the architect, did not make it ridiculous.

The importance of SPAN as a landmark in British Housing needs no underlining here – it marks the point where the commercial operators at last began to dispute the leadership in housing design with architects in public authorities. But the dates given above have an added significance if one relates these pioneer schemes to their acceptance as stylistic exemplars by other speculative developers. Reference to the illustrations following Ian Nairn's article 'Spec Built' (*Architectural Review*, March 1961) will show that by the end of 1960 both the SPAN style and the Stirling and Gowan style had achieved a photographable degree of penetration into the market, and a number of different developers were involved. Both styles had, in fact, only become public property in 1960 – but the point is that one (Stirling's) is much tougher than the other, and had achieved its penetration in half the time. In other words, public taste was becoming sharper, quicker as the fifties ended – something that is all the more remarkable in view of the fact that public taste was not noticeably sharp at all when the fifties began.

A word of caution is necessary at this point. It is clearly true that where a moderately sophisticated and mobile market for housing exists, as in the London or Lancashire/Cheshire conurbations, public taste has become much keener, but stylistic taste is apt to operate in a negative sense. The *positive* selling point of a house at present is equipment and gadgetry (if we may leave location and price on one side for the moment), followed by space-standards and obvious factors of convenience. The aesthetics of the interior space appear to be of no consequence as a selling point, except where size and location of windows are concerned – a prospective buyer will often find himself pulled both ways by the contrary attractions of a fashionable picture window and a traditional British regard for privacy. But the style of the exterior seems more likely, at present, to discourage rather than promote sales. Buyers are more likely to be positively put off by a style that is too advanced than positively attracted to one that is familiar.

The fact that some developers in selected markets can use such styles indicates two things: one, already noted, that public taste in those areas is sufficiently advanced for the style to be no bar to sales; the other, that these developers are operating right at the limits of public acceptance. Though this New Frontier attitude to the market is more common in Pop Art than social Jeremiahs would have us believe (Braun radios and appliances are advertised in German teenage mass media like the magazine *Twen*) this is a fairly sensational situation in housing, and should prepare us for some unusual features in the firms behind it.

A degree of conscious, or – at any rate – *expressed*, pioneer-spirit is present. Even those who follow, rather than create the styles, are aware that they are still forcing the market, albeit the market is catching up fast. Consonant with this is the fact that most, probably all, are playing the market off the tops of their heads (in old-fashioned Madison Avenue cant) rather than on the basis of the considered examination of market research. The approach remains amateur – a developer works in an area that he knows, such as the southern suburbia of London, and works within margins of siting and cost that leave him little room for error. The accuracy with which the market has been assessed appears to depend on one simple factor – in the spear-head developments (mixed high rise and 2 storey estates, now becoming comparable with the LCC's Roehampton) the managing director, or partner in charge, is setting out to sell houses to the Zodiac-to-Jaguar income-groups – his own social class, who probably share his own *Observer*-reading sentiments about improving public taste and the need for better housing design. This is a unique and probably transient situation. It implies that the developer is a big enough firm to attract, or produce, executive talent of quality – but not so big that the executive talent cannot keep close personal control over a sizable segment of the enterprise. When the firms get bigger, this situation is pretty sure to change. When it changes, it may well prove to be the end of a honeymoon period in architect/developer relations. At present, the few significantly progressive developers do not ride their architects hard. In some cases, the architects make all the action, often locating and, in some cases, negotiating the purchase of the sites, and generally working very close to the limits of the code of professional conduct. In other cases, operators with their own architect's offices allow startling lee-way to their designers in all matters except costs, and, significantly, one of the biggest and most progressive developers, Wates, is proposing to establish a development section, comparable to the Development Groups in public offices.

But a big house-building company is not a big company compared even to, say, EMI, let alone BMC. Geography may keep the size of successful developers in check, but normal commercial expansionist pressures should begin to send some of them sprawling across the country – SPAN are already in Cambridge, and have their eyes on the profitable atom-scientist belt around Harwell. If they grow, then it seems likely that they may quite quickly pass beyond the critical size in which the present amateur and intuitive methods are considered safe. Since their expansion depends on their ability to play on forward taste, it is unlikely that they will revert to Tudorbethan and spray-on half-timbering in search of commercial safety, and they may then have to go out and get expert market advice.

At present, the service of keen Pop taste does not appear to interfere with accepted architectural practice at all – it is very nice work indeed for an architect with an eye for cost-control and residential densities. But once the market researchers come in, this situation will change. It has already become apparent that detailed user-research (purely functional) may play havoc with architects' preferences in planning and space-manipulation; market research is bound to bear largely on matters of style as well, and this will, inevitably, be even more painful. But that critical size has not yet been reached, and the situation remains, as they say, manipulative. It is up to architects to make what they can of conditions in which it is temporarily possible for them to mould the creation of a keen Pop taste in architecture without coming under the discipline of those commercial rituals that normally operate in the field of Pop merchandising, and to operate the amoral techniques of technology according to the morality of architecture. Of course, the alternative, to miss the opportunity, is always open to them.

1.10 ZOOM WAVE HITS ARCHITECTURE

Banham, in this article originally published in New Society, *3 March 1966, moves from the vernacular end of Pop architecture to the more self-conscious work of a group of architects who, like the Pop artists, deliberately include expendability, commercial imagery and humour in their architectural visions. Archigram and their contemporaries stimulate Banham's interest in the 'Clip-on', 'Plug-in' school of architecture which dominates his architectural criticism in the mid-60s.*

Wham! Zoom! Zing! Rave! – and it's not *Ready Steady Go,* even though it sometimes looks like it. The sound effects are produced by the erupting of underground architectural protest magazines. Architecture, staid queen-mother of the arts, is no longer courted by plush glossies and cool scientific journals alone but is having her skirts blown up and her bodice unzipped by irregular newcomers which are – typically – rhetorical, with-it, moralistic, mis-spelled, improvisatory, anti-smooth, funny-format, cliquey, art-oriented but stoned out of their minds with science-fiction images of an alternative architecture that would be perfectly possible tomorrow if only the Universe (and especially the Law of Gravity) were differently organized.

The Movement (and I think it deserves the name) began at the end of the fifties, with *Polygon,* emanating from the Regent Street Polytechnic, student-run, roneo'd but – for one memorable issue – adorned with genuine lipstick kisses by a real living bird.

The latest emanation, which appeared early in February, is *Clip-Kit,* student-published from the crisis-torn Architectural Association School. The crafty plastic binder into which later instalments of the kit can be clipped is a shade professional and smooth by the standards the Movement has established – beyond the resources of *Clip-Kit's* immediate predecessor *Megascope* (which also carried the burden of Bristol students' discontent) and outside the intentions of the reigning champion of protest mags, *Archigram.*

But *Clip-Kit's* title puts it right in the Movement: two more charisma-laiden words just don't exist in this context. 'Kit' is the emotive collective noun for Goodies (which are usually ideas, images, forms, documents, concepts raided from other disciplines) and 'clip' is how you put them together to make intellectual or physical structures. Alternatively, you can plug them in to existing structures or networks. But plug-in or clip-on, it's the same magpie world of keen artifacts, knock-out visuals and dazzling brainwaves assembled into structures whose primary aim seems to be to defy gravity, in any sense of the word.

The anti-gravity aspect, which delights students, makes the teaching establishment dead nervous. Even architects I would normally regard as far from square make worried noises, and the January issue of the Architectural Association's *Journal* devoted two pages to an attempt to put *Archigram* in the doghouse. Any prospective student reading this particular performance would probably decide to go somewhere else and study: paragraph by wooden paragraph it plods along, occasionally laying a genuine cardboard egg like, 'There are real dangers in living and designing up to the minute' (no kidding: page 171 if you can't believe me); stolidly listing all the standard objections of the Movement, like illiteracy; and winding up with a real coup-de-farce in a paragraph headed (incredibly enough) 'Lack of humour'.

This paragraph reads, in its entirety and with the *Journal's* punctuation:

> The zoom rave hits Bristol but with accompanying 'playboy' text and dead Dada photograph, e.g., '*lecture visit*' by 'Archigram' *editor* on Plug-In *scene* and *world* of zoom; it is neither with it nor sick but sad.

And anybody who can see the authors of this plastic pearl accusing *Archigram* of illiteracy and lack of humour will be inclined to sympathize with *Megascope* when it complained of 'the failures who teach in our schools' and of 'the mass of mediocrity seen in almost every field of architectural endeavour in this country. When faced with dreary projects and obsolete problems, it is no wonder that students are unable to produce anything but dreary solutions, balsa models and grey, grey drawings.'

The greatest value of these Opping-Popping mags is their insistence that even 'designing up to the minute' is barely good enough. Buildings still take a tidy time to make, cities even longer (Rome only *looks* as if it was built in a day). If you design right up to the minute, it will be many millions of minutes later before the human race can move in, and the buildings will be out of date by just that period of time. Hence the constant preoccupation of the Movement with far-out figures like Buckminster Fuller, Yona Friedman or (in Britain) Cedric Price, men who propose not only a more up-to-the-minute environment, but wild technological methods for getting it built quicker and in quantities more nearly commensurate with human needs.

Where the Movement dissipates its value is in its persistent sentimentality about bits of the past that seem to duplicate present student discontents and ambitions. It's a bit off for *Clip-Kit* to go on about 'The next Great Leap' in its

1 *Archigram 4,* 1964, cover illustration.

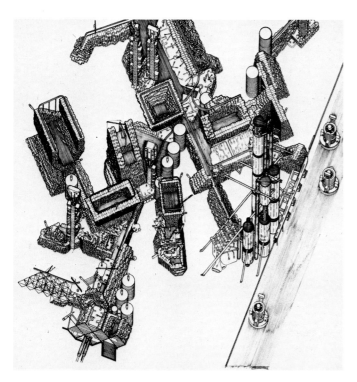

2 PETER COOK, *Plug-in City*, 1964, axonometric.

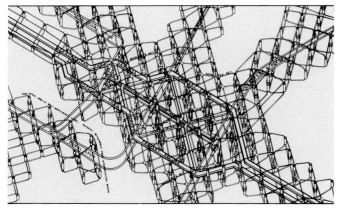

3 DENNIS CROMPTON, *Computer City*, 1964.

4 RON HERRON, *The Walking City in New York*, 1964.

editorial and then devote two giant fold-outs to Futurism, a pre-1914 leap that failed to get leaped. Being an Edwardian Futurist doesn't make a man relevant to *our* future.

For what matters, overall, about the Movement is its insistence on relevance. To quote *Megascope* again: 'The rounded corners, the hip, gay, synthetic colours, pop-culture props all combine to suggest an architecture of plastic, steel and aluminium, the juke box and the neon-lit street, the way a city environment should be.' An architecture relevant to the whole scene that's going; and if not, why not? We architectural pedagogues are prone to build architecture up into a higher discipline of abstractly ordering the masses about for their own good.

But the Movement is right in insisting that architecture must also touch the ground occasionally, and that it must also be relevant to what this week's dolly-girls are wearing, to ergonomics, inflatable air-houses, the voice of God as revealed by his one true prophet Bob Dylan, what's going on in Bradford and Hammersmith, the side elevation of the Ford GT-40, napalm down the neck, the Royal College of Art, caravan homes, Sealab, and like that.

Admittedly, the level of relevance is often only that of form-fondling, round-corner styling, art-work and paint-jobs. It is often more than that, but even if it *were* purely visual and superficial,. that would not in itself be contemptible. It does still matter to people what buildings look like. Indeed, it matters more than it did. From about 1830 onwards, architects designed for their fellow-professionals and a blind public. The telly and the proliferation of colour-journalism has altered all that by creating a more visually sophisticated public.

As the Architectural Association pomp-artists justly observed: 'There is no communication without conventions', and a one-glance comparison will show that the underground mags are in touch with the places where currently communicative conventions are being manufactured, and the Architectural Association's *Journal* is not. It could still turn out that the round-cornered zoom-styling of the Movement's page-layouts will have quite as much to do with the future architecture of democracy as any Architectural Association Symposium on Decision Making.

1.11 PUB-SHAPE AND LANDLUBBER FASHION

This article, originally published in New Society, *5 December 1968, is representative of Banham's interest in style-conscious, commercial architecture which sets out to communicate a linguistic message in a playful way. He locates, through the 1960s a number of new, public buildings, like the London Steak Houses, which set out to reject the dictates of the Modern Movement and appeal to the public imagination.*

Dropping anchor with the rousing splash of a beer cap falling in the sink, the Frigate has just hove-to at the corner of Upper St. Martin's Lane. It's the first of Watney-Mann's line of 'Schooner' pubs in the central London area. You know how it is with old nautical pubs – all that varnished plankwork, clippers in bottles, and group portraits of the crew of the Queenie S. Blenkinsop clustering sheepishly around the Prunier Trophy in sou'westers.

You do? Well forget it! The Frigate is no expression of the folkways of seamen ashore, but the fancy of Roy Wilson-Smith, architect, and Angela Maries who works in his office, and it can best be described as a Fantasy on British Sea Shambles. It's a landlubber's view of the old heart-of-oak Navy Lark, and however much ingenious research and designer's craft has gone into it, the result would doubtless make any ancient mariner, who served before the mast, just about splinter his bowsprit.

Still, the Seven Dials area of London isn't exactly crawling with Old Salts these days; the rest of us – tourists, fugitives from *Hair* and the *Mousetrap*, denizens of Covent Garden and Odham's Press – can rejoice that London at last has another pub of Pop fantasy to set alongside the legendary and too long unique Prince of Wales in Fortune Green, north London. The Frigate differs from the Prince, however, on two important counts: first, in being designed around this specific sailing-ship theme, whereas the Prince is total and unrestrained fantasy; and, secondly, in being a conversion, not a total rebuild.

The Frigate inhabits the shell of the old Cranbourne, an ornate Victorian boozer whose upper works make a nice foil for the plain dark slab of Thorn House behind. The lower floors have been punched out right through the cellars (hold?) and all the levels reshuffled, and everything restyled like the sort of dock-side scene that went out with Long John Silver's other leg.

Exterior view of *The Frigate* (now a Steak House).

And hardly a stick or string of all this is genuine. No, steady lads, the sticks *are* genuine – masts and spars from named ships, with brass plates recording what craft they were un-stepped from. But the rest is as cheerfully fakey as the Piltdown skull, the figureheads are fibreglass, the vast curving ships' timbers give back the resonance of genuine hardboard when tapped; the plankwork is covered in bubbled old tar that is moulded in one piece with the planks; and there's rigging that never was, afloat or ashore, even though it was all set up by a genuine old merchant seaman (who also gets his name on a commemorative plaque).

This rigging, though, is what it's all about really. It comes sprouting up from the cellars in a glorious tangle, through the open well where the ground floor used to be, either side of the catwalk that takes you across from the entrance to the Scuppers Bar, and reunites over your head in a double-acting balanced hoist (or something) that alternately raises and lowers slings of casks on either hand.

Now, the ropework of square-rigged ships was the acme of structural logic and organizational elegance in pre-stream technology. Provided you knew how it worked that is; to the lay eye it was always a lot of tangled string. The rigging of the Frigate is still a load of tangled string even when you have worked out what it thinks it is doing. Whoever actually tied its knots, whipped its rope-ends, sheaved its blocks and so forth, it remains a lay decorator's rigging, doing an interior decorator's job.

Doing it rather well, though, and a necessary job. These masts and rigging help to confuse the levels within, but also to unite them; they help to simplify the visual chaos by adding to its profusion. When you go in at external pavement level you aren't quite aligned with any of the internal levels; some visual fudging is obviously required. But the levels with which this fudge helps you to relate are the restaurant floors, revealed as decks seen in the cross-section of a ship's hull. The bilges of said ship are down at cellar level, and so is most of the drinking space; down below and out of sight. So it needs something to lead the eye down to where the elbow action is, and this – to judge from the crowds peering down from the pavement outside – the mess of rigging and the two hoists very effectively do.

But what happens when you get down there is, to my mind, more significant than all the nautical tat or the plaques recording which Olympic Golds were being won while this or that bit of plaster was being trowelled or floor laid. One of the reasons why the eye needs guidance down into the cellar is that it is very difficult to see the actual drinking going on – because it is mostly in the old brick vaults under the pavement. These vaults have been opened up after a fashion, but a fair amount of necessary structure (brick piers and the like) has to remain, and would make much of the area hard to see wherever the bar was placed.

But in the Frigate, the bar has been placed with its back to most of the drinking area, and the barmen can see hardly any of the goings on to speak of – or complain about. So the old routine of pub planning, whereby the bar – like the slavemaster's platform of a Roman galley – had to have direct line-of-sight command of the whole interior space has gone right overhead. It's a humane reform in pub design, and as much a contribution to the pleasure of drinking as all the jolly-tars type decoration. Sorry they didn't rip out the old Cranbourne entrance while they were at it, though, and put in a set of cargo doors. Nearly spoiled the pub for a hap'orth of tar.

1.12 ENCOUNTER WITH SUNSET BOULEVARD

A visit to Los Angeles in 1968 had a profound effect on Banham and inspired a set of talks for the radio which were then reprinted in The Listener. *'Encounter with Sunset Boulevard' is the first of the series, appearing in the 22 August 1968 issue of* The Listener; *in it Banham reflects, during a bus ride through the city, on the layout of LA and its similarity to London.*

The bus had broken down on the coast road, miles short of Los Angeles. The driver had thumbed a ride on a passing truck and gone for help. And we passengers sat on the rocks between the road and the surf, with the sun shining in our eyes and reflecting off the ocean in front of us, and off the aluminium flank of the bus behind us. We watched the perfect waves, exact as ruled lines from headland to headland, roll glittering towards us and break in un-mathematical profusion among the rocks below.

There was nothing else to do – except worry. I had an important date for dinner and a lecture by the Chancellor of the University of California in Los Angeles, for which I was to be collected from a hotel off Sunset Boulevard. I had never been in Los Angeles before, and I was anxious to get my arrangements sorted out in good time. But we were still sitting by the shore looking at that perfect – and perfectly boring – ocean, and my margins of time were ticking away.

Eventually, the relief bus arrived, and we were bowling along the highway again, through Malibu, through Pacific Palisades, and up through the tunnel into the bus-station at Santa Monica. There I sat, while the bus unloaded some of its passengers, in a fit of bewildered indecision; some way back along the highway, well beyond anything that could be called a built-up area, the bus had stopped at some traffic lights, and on a street name-board I had read the baffling words, 'Sunset Boulevard'.

Now Sunset Boulevard I knew, like any normal movie-goer, to be in Hollywood. Wasn't it? Could there be two parts of Greater Los Angeles with Sunset Boulevards, or did the same boulevard run on through the various parts of the town, and if so, which part did I need? Should I get out here and take a taxi or sit tight and get out of the bus at the terminal? I decided to sit tight, but rarely have the dictates of my natural caution been less trustworthy, for the bus rolled onto the elevated freeway, and from up there, Los Angeles seemed totally incomprehensible. Mile after mile of neat little houses, either the same bland colour as the gravel earth below, or the same bland colour as the late afternoon sky above, deeply bedded in lush greenery, overtopped by forests of ugly poles carrying utility wires, and even taller and uglier palm trees like rows of giant feather dusters. And it all looked the same, growing neither denser nor thinner; impossible to tell if we were approaching downtown or heading for some other suburban bus-station first. Then worry began to approach panic as the sun got lower in the sky and I realized I had no idea what downtown would look like when we finally got to it. I could summon up mental images of innumerable famous private houses in Los Angeles – by Charles Eames, Craig Ellwood, Frank Lloyd Wright, Greene and Greene, Pierre Koenig, Neutra, Schindler – but no public buildings or major office blocks at all could I call to mind, and thus watch out for.

I was late and I was lost – and bitterly humiliated. I had been saving up Los Angeles in the way that some travellers save up Venice or Kyoto, an experience to be anticipated and relished to the full. I was not going to be like namby-pamby

English architects and town planners who were terrified of Los Angeles and its sprawl – only I *was*. I could almost hear Ian Nairn chuckling 'I told you so!' on behalf of all those who hold Los Angeles to be an unmitigated disaster.

Anyhow, I got to the hotel, and to the lecture – but only just. I would have been right in abandoning the bus at Santa Monica, because it *was* the same Sunset Boulevard right through from downtown to the coast, and the hotel was much nearer the coast than downtown. But that is not the point of this story: the point is that I was out of my culture-shock and topograhical dismay within 24 hours and feeling perfectly at home in Los Angeles.

Now, at first sight, this is ridiculous. No city in the world could have been less like any of the cities I have called home. Los Angeles is spectacularly unique among the great cities of the world. It is vast in area, though not much vaster than the area defined by long-distance commuting into London. Within that area, the citizens live at conspicuously low densities, though not much lower, I suspect, than Oslo or Stockholm. And they live almost entirely in single storey houses surrounded by a style of horticulture which is a cross between the Anglo-Saxon tradition and the tropical, and like nothing on earth except possibly Perth in Western Australia. What is confusing is that the basic human habitat offered by house and garden is the same in exclusive Beverly Hills as it is in the ghettos like Watts. Equally confusing are the distances that the Angelenos are prepared to travel within their diffuse metropolis. To pick up some friends, bring them to your house for dinner, take them back afterwards and get home again, might involve you in 100 to 150 miles of motoring in one evening. Fortunately, it is no more difficult than ferrying dinner guests between Highgate and Fulham, say, because most of the distance will be done at 60 miles an hour on the freeway.

Under the general sunshine and exotic trees, with the Santa Monica Mountain for back-drop and the surfing beaches of the Pacific for foreground, nothing looks even remotely familiar in detail. Like all the truly great cities, Los Angeles is unique unto itself; but unique in a special way that makes it weirdly familiar to any mean sensual English academic of my generation and experience.

Let me begin to explain this backhandedly. Some months ago, one of our leading Americologues – Sir Denis Brogan, I think – complained of a callow cult of Los Angeles among the young. This just did not jibe with my own experience, which is that the cult of Los Angeles in England is strongest among persons of my own age – bluntly, the middle-aged. True affection for Los Angeles seems to come with the first grey hairs, or the second marriage, or the assumption of public responsibility. There is no greater enthusiast for the place among my near contemporaries than Peter Hall, who has just become Professor of Geography at Reading. The visionary closing pages of his book, *London 2000*, describe a city that is much nearer to Los Angeles now than to any London I expect to see by the end of this century.

And speaking of professors, my own – Lord Llewelyn Davies – has proposed for one of the new towns he is designing 'a modified type of Los Angeles plan'. This is an even more striking example of mature acceptance, because it implies that, far from being a total and disorderly shambles, Los Angeles has a comprehensible system that works, and can be applied elsewhere. Indeed, what seems to unite us greying Angelophiles is that we have been there and seen that it works in spite of the much-quoted complaints of some of its inhabitants.

But in being there and perceiving its virtues, all my generation have the help of a special kind of *déjà vu* – when we see it for the first time we know we have seen it before. We have been seeing it in the movies all our lives, and especially in the slapstick comedies of our impressionable youth. Far from being the city in all our futures, Los Angeles is the city in all our pasts. Those old Keystone Cops shorts, for instance, made on a shoestring and on available locations like empty building sites, remote street intersections, stretches of suburban railway line, have left our minds stocked with images of typical Los Angeles scenery. And they are still typical. If those movies have made the Los Angeles of the 1920s as visually familiar as Canaletto and Guardi have made Rococo Venice, most of Los Angeles has altered less since the time of Rudolph Valentino than Venice has changed since the time of Casanova; you would swear it's the same concrete road surface, the same little wooden houses, the same trees, even the same utility poles. The best possible study towards a basic understanding of the fabric of Los Angeles would be to sit again through that series of *Pause for Laughter* films that BBC-2 showed some months ago.

But there is another reason why so many Britons will feel at home in Los Angeles, and it is a very odd one. I couldn't quite put my finger on it myself, but Alan Forrest, one of my teaching colleagues, did. 'Los Angeles is just like London,' he said. As the visiting eye sees them, no two cities could look less alike, but as the resident uses and inhabits the place, it is profoundly true because, to finish what Forrest said, 'it's a collection of separate villages'.

Anybody who has read Rasmussen's famous book, *London, the Unique City*, will remember that it was this village structure of London that caused him to apply the adjective 'unique', but it must now share that title with Los Angeles. What he said about London will often fit Los Angeles word for word: 'Around every little village,' he said, 'the buildings crystallized into a borough and that development was to continue, so that London became a greater and still greater accumulation of towns, an immense colony of dwellings where the people still live in their own houses in small communities, with local governments.' That, with its emphasis on dwelling in one's own house in a small locally governed community, is probably more true of Los Angeles in 1968 than it is of London since the new giant boroughs were formed. In London, of course, the villages have been growing bigger, and growing together, since the Middle Ages. In Los Angeles it has all happened since about 1890, and the evidence of it is everywhere. There are bits of Wilshire Boulevard between the townships that still haven't been built on, and the house-numbering runs from both ends, out from downtown and back from Santa Monica on the coast. Neither London nor Los Angeles sprawled out from a single centre; both grew by filling in the spaces between a number of centres.

Perhaps because they are structurally similar, these two uniquely scattered cities exhibit a striking similarity in what I suppose must be called their psychological geography. New residents in London find their way about by entrusting themselves to the Underground, and the elegant abstract logic of its maps. When you tell them an address, they ask if it is anywhere near the Northern Line, or the Central. In exactly the same way, the new Angeleno clings to the almost equally elegant, abstract and logical diagram of the freeway network, and asks if an address is anywhere near the Harbor Freeway, or which off-ramp he should use on the San Bernadino. Both cities are illogical and haphazard in their street-plans – Los Angeles is nothing like the regular grid that a lot of people seem to imagine – and so one tries to short-circuit the ensuing navigational problems by replacing as much as possible of the chaos at ground level by the diagrammatic clarity of the railways below or the freeways above. This is a similarity that was mentioned to me by several ex-Londoners in Los Angeles. Perhaps it is the more striking, the more noticeable, because it is a similarity in the mind. The physical facts involved could hardly be more different: in London you rattle in a public vehicle through a tunnel that entirely cuts you off from the reality of the city. In Los Angeles you buzz along in your private car on an elevated highway that would give you excellent and revealing views of the city if you weren't so busy with driving.

The scale of everything is different, the style of life is different, almost everything is profoundly, disturbingly different. After my bad first experience in Los Angeles I can still see why others respond to it with immediate hostility and dismay. The cities of the Old World and the eastern United States run very much to a pattern – you don't realize how standardized they are beneath their much-vaunted individualities, until you come up against somewhere like Los Angeles.

London, as Rasmussen rightly observed, is something of a deviant from that pattern, but not such a deviant that London terminology like 'West End' can't be applied to the others. But it makes no sense if you try to apply it to Los Angeles – and Los Angeles makes nonsense of itself when it tries to see itself in terms of concepts borrowed from other cities, such as 'downtown'. The unique value of Los Angeles – what excites, intrigues and sometimes repels me – is that it offers radical alternatives to almost every urban concept in unquestioned currency. As they say in California, 'Los Angeles is so wild they should just let it swing and see what happens!'

1.13 COVENTRY CATHEDRAL

This adverse criticism of a piece of contemporary architecture centres on the failure of Spence's Coventry Cathedral, in Banham's opinion, to fit into the radical tradition of Modern architecture. He feels that the brief was unadventurous and that his solution conforms too strongly to Establishment pressures. This article originally appeared in New Statesman, 25 May 1962.

There can be little doubt that Coventry Cathedral is the worst set-back to English church architecture for a very long time. Its influence, unless sternly resisted, can only be confusing and diversionary. This is not a snap judgment: I have known the cathedral since it was a concrete foundation-slab, and followed all Sir Basil Spence's long series of modifications and revisions since the competition results were first published, and my conviction that something was fundamentally wrong with the whole operation has grown in parallel with my increasing admiration for the skill and astuteness with which Sir Basil has done what he set out to do.

In other words, it is the basic proposition that is adrift, not the architectural execution – there is only one fundamental point on which the architect is to be blamed, which is that (like every other architect in Britain fit enough, at the time, to lift a pencil) he accepted the competition conditions. It is

important, among all the rock-'n'-roll-crucifixion jazz currently being trumpeted up about 'a modern cathedral for a modern age', to remember that Coventry's original intention after the war was not to have a modern cathedral at all, but a Gothic-revival one, and that when this was abandoned after public outcry (largely from the architectural profession), the assessors chosen to judge the competition were about as square as could be found without going grave-robbing. The cards were effectively stacked to make a modern cathedral impossible: what was wanted, and what was got, was a traditional cathedral restyled. Not modern, because no radical reassessment of cathedral functions was undertaken before the conditions were issued.

Stories go round of heavy cerebration in the diocese during the preliminary stages of drawing up the conditions, but that must have been like the 'thinking' which goes on in the Conservative Central Office – mountains are in travail, and bring forth the status quo. Like the Tories, Coventry is trad, Dad, but has tried to give itself a new image – a medieval long plan with aisles and off-lying polygonal or circular chapels, but executed in non-medieval materials (in part) and adorned with devotional art-work in various non-medieval styles. A true Modernist, a radical Functionalist, would have rejected this basic proposition, seeing his obligation as Richard Llewelyn Davies sees it: 'To read

SIR BASIL SPENCE, *Coventry Cathedral*, 1962, plan.

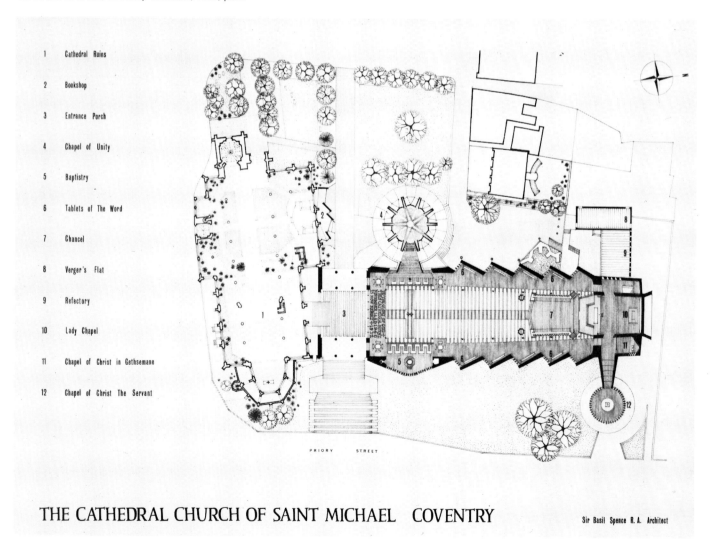

1	Cathedral Ruins
2	Bookshop
3	Entrance Porch
4	Chapel of Unity
5	Baptistry
6	Tablets of The Word
7	Chancel
8	Verger's Flat
9	Refectory
10	Lady Chapel
11	Chapel of Christ in Gethsemane
12	Chapel of Christ The Servant

THE CATHEDRAL CHURCH OF SAINT MICHAEL   COVENTRY

Sir Basil Spence R. A. Architect

carefully the client's statement of his needs, and to understand it fully – and then tear it up and find out what he really wants!' To accept the conditions of a competition is to by-pass this obligation, and, in spite of the very drastic modifications to some parts of the fabric, Sir Basil has still built something very close to his original sketch-plan.

This is not to object to that sketch because it does not exhibit the kind of centralized plan that has become fashionable, despite Peter Hammond's better intentions, since he published *Liturgy and Architecture*. To impose such a plan, as Archbishop (The Cruel See) Heenan did in the competition for Liverpool RC cathedral – again without radical analysis of cathedral functions – is worse, because merely fashionable. What was needed in both cases, and given in neither, was a fundamental and imaginative enquiry into those functions, engendered by the rites and responsibilities of episcopacy, that distinguish cathedrals from other churches. At Coventry, the emergence of certain genuinely new and progressive relationships between cathedral and town, cathedral and overseas Christendom, has resulted in no radical innovations, merely two clip-on chapels, one rejected by the guilds for whom it was intended, the other – the Chapel of Unity – a dramatic polygonal volume for which no one has yet devised a ritual function, other than lectures and readings for which its plan-form is unsuited.

Given, then, that Sir Basil may be blamed for not embarrassing the diocese into genuine thought by shock tactics after he had won the competition (such things have been done), what sort of job has he made of executing this brief that he ought not to have accepted? A real whizz! A ring-a-ding God-box that will go over big with the flat-bottomed latitudinarians who can't stand the quiet austerities of St Paul's, Bow Common (which remains the *pons asinorum* of genuinely modern church architecture in England). The sheer quality, and quantity, of detailing at Coventry, the mastery of dramatic effects, the richness of the art-work, the resplendent sonority with which the note of absolutely conventional piety has been struck, all combine in an image that will have to be fought to the death by everyone who believes, like Peter Hammond (and myself), that church architecture is part of the mainstream of the Modern Movement, not a picturesque backwater.

Only two things have gone wrong with Spence's scheme. The Sutherland tapestry is wrong in colour and in the scale of its elements – it dominates the east end, but chiefly because it *is* the east end; it fails to achieve the commanding presence of a Byzantine pantocrator, which is the nearest term of comparison. Clearly, in attempting this unprecedented scale in tapestry, architect and artist were biting off more than the artist could chew, and while failure was doubtless foreseen by professional told-you-sos, the detailed grounds of failure could not have been. But it is difficult to understand why the detailed grounds for the failure of the west window were not foreseen. Strictly, it is a screen of clear glass occupying the entire liturgical west wall of the cathedral, some of the panes engraved by John Hutton with life-sized figures of saint and angels in a forced

and arty style that one associates automatically with the Royal College of Art. However, the style of the applied art matters less than the amount of light that enters through it.

It was intended that the crowning movement of the entire design should be that when the communicant rises from the altar rail and turns to go back to his place, he sees, for the first time, the glowing ranks of stained-glass windows down either side of the nave. As it is, he is simply half-blinded by the glare of hard white light from the west. There are three reasons for this: liturgical west is, in fact, south, so that the window receives all day a level of illumination that a genuine west window does not begin to receive until evensong; the glass is clear, not stained, and therefore transmits vastly more light than, say, the west window at Norwich; and the successive raisings of the roof of the porch in search of a more monumental entrance since the first version of the design have lifted it to the point where it does not shade the window at all.

So, after the first blast of light, and the first disappointment with the tapestry, one avoids looking at either. The rest exhibits a level of sheer professionalism in the creation of visual effects and the manipulation of spaces that is rare in Britain (because the opportunities are rare, perhaps). The porch in particular, avowedly modelled on the exposed aisles of the unfinished nave at Siena, is masterly, creating with great economy of means the sense of soaring monumentality that has eluded both Scott at Liverpool and Maufe at Guildford. The general grouping of the exterior, with the two off-lying chapels seen against the long flank of the main building, is one of the few designs which preserves anything worth having of the South Bank aesthetics of 1951, but Spence has mated it with a manner of handling details that looks very like the smart modern churches of western Germany – which seems fair enough: what's good for Mercedesdorf should be good for Jaguarsville also.

The main ranks of stained-glass windows are so much at home with the whole conception that one is surprised to remember that they are not by Spence himself, but by Keith New and Geoffrey Clarke and Lawrence Lee. Similarly, Stephen Sykes's mosaic relief in the Gethsemane chapel, irrespective of its merits in its own right, is the perfect work of devotional art to catch and draw the eye at the end of the south aisle. This exact conjunction of architectural and artistic intentions becomes most obvious, but also most resoundingly successful, in John Piper's glass for the tall curved wall of the baptistery on the liturgical south side. The area covered is large, and largely, darkly glowing, but centrally placed and high up is a huge circular patch in much lighter golden colour. Seen, unexpectedly, on emerging from the Chapel of Unity opposite, it startlingly creates the impression of the Holy Ghost descending on the font in a ball of atomic fire.

Time after time, Sir Basil gives us, in this sense, masterstrokes of architectural religious drama. The pity is that the play itself should be by Eliot at his most Establishment, not Osborne at his most probing.

1.14 THE STYLE FOR THE JOB

Contrasting his disappointment with Spence's Establishment approach, Banham describes, in this article originally published in New Statesman, *February 14 1964, the much more radical solutions that are proposed by Stirling and Gowan in their Leicester University building. He admires their sophisticated combination of function with style that, he feels, results in a truly machine-age architecture.*

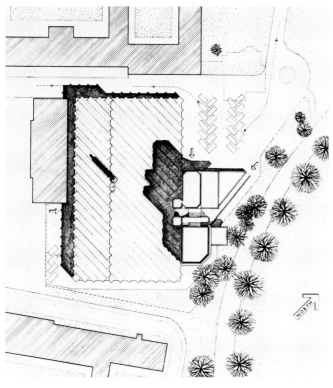

1 JAMES STIRLING and JAMES GOWAN, *Faculty of Engineering*, Leicester University, 1963, site plan.

2 JAMES STIRLING and JAMES GOWAN, *Faculty of Engineering*, Leicester University, 1963, elevation.

'Toasting,' said James Stirling, 'is a pretty primitive sort of conception. It just doesn't make sense in something rather smooth and elegant like the Braun toaster. I mean, you can burn bread all right in something crude and a bit old-fashioned like your Morphy Richards but not in the Braun. It's just not right!' There spoke again that hyper-sensitivity about appropriate character in design that has always needled the Stirling and Gowan partnership. Gowan's manner of expressing it may be less picturesque, but the phrase 'the Style for the Job' is his contribution to a debate that has spread to include the work of Eero Saarinen, and with them, as with Saarinen, this approach has had its pitfalls. But it has paid off in Saarinen's airports and it has paid off triumphantly for Stirling and Gowan in the new Engineering Building at Leicester University.

It succeeds because job and style are inseparable. In some earlier works, such as the housing at Preston, they seem to have decided the appropriate character subjectively, on the basis of arbitrary sociological decisions. But at Leicester, the first job complex enough to extend their talents to the full, they had neither time, money nor ground-space for disembodied speculation about style: the character emerges with stunning force from the bones of the structure and the functions it shelters. It is almost unique in Britain in having no detail, however extraordinary, that is overwrought or underdesigned by the standards set by the structure as a whole. Its character is not only appropriate but consistent in every part.

The building is in many ways as extraordinary as its details. At ground-floor level it confronts the visitor with a blank wall of hard-faced red brick, which is occasionally pierced with a rather private-looking doorway, except at the point where the glazed main entrance lobby splits this defensive podium into two parts: one a rectangle enclosing the teaching labs, the other a moderately irregular polygon forming the base of two towers housing research and administrative offices. Over the heavy teaching labs there foams, like suds from some cubist detergent, a good head

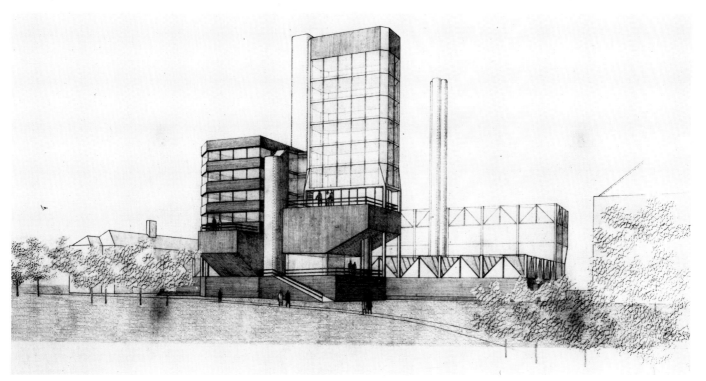

of angular north-light glazing, laid diagonally across the building. Down one side of the block, this pearly translucent glazing rises to four storeys, with the topmost floor of labs strutted well out over a service road that cannot, for the present, be eliminated: the whole complex has had to be crammed onto a site which by commonsense standards, ought to be about 25 per cent too small for it.

On the opposite flank of the main rectangle rise the towers, but they do not rise in any obvious or tidy-minded manner, since each rests on a lecture hall that cantilevers out beyond the limits of the podium below. The research tower rises only five storeys above the smaller auditorium, and is relatively conventional in appearance, except that it has one corner snubbed off to clear a legal building line, and its bands of windows are in the form of inverted hoppers, the glass sloping out to shelter flat bands of ventilators underneath. The admin tower, which carries a water-tank on top to give the hydraulics labs at ground level sufficient head of water, has all four corners snubbed off when it finally reaches its typical plan-form, and then rises clear above the research tower.

Between these two main towers rise three subsidiary shafts – a twinned pair for lifts and stairs rising the full height of the admin tower, a smaller one standing only high enough to serve the lower research tower. Where these five clustering towers do not touch – which is usually – the intervening spaces are filled by glazing that in only one case (between the twins) falls sheer and vertical to the ground. In the other gaps it descends in a sort of cascade, twisting to one side or the other, and angling forward to accommodate the ever larger landings that are needed in the lower and more populous parts of the building. This composition of towers and glass is a fantastic invention, the more so because it proceeds rigorously from structural and circulat-

3 JAMES STIRLING and JAMES GOWAN, *Faculty of Engineering*, Leicester University, 1963, detail with the roof of the teaching workshops behind.

4 JAMES STIRLING and JAMES GOWAN, *Faculty of Engineering*, Leicester University, 1963, view of the research laboratory tower on the right and the lecture theatres on the left.

ory considerations without frills or art-work. The solid walls are either of the same brick as the podium, or of the red tiling that covers nearly every square foot of concrete, even floors and ceilings. The glazing (like the tiling) is rock-bottom cheap industrial stuff, just glass and aluminium extrusions. It has no pretty details, just nuts, bolts, bars cut to length on site, and raggedy flashings left 'as found'.

By taking a thoroughly relaxed attitude to technology and letting the glazing system follow its own unpretentious logic, the architects achieved less a kind of anti-detailing (as some critics seem to suggest) than some form of un-detailing that would border on plain dereliction of duty were it not so patently right in this context. But, over and above the rectitude of the detailing, the stair-tower complex offers such bewildering visual effects that words are apt to fail. Both by day and by night (when the stairs are lit by pairs of plain industrial lamps, bracketed from the walls) the play of reflections in the variously angled glass surfaces can be as breathtaking as it is baffling. It really looks as if the grand old myths of Functionalism have come true for once, and that beauty, of a sort, has been given as a bonus for the honest service of need.

I say beauty 'of a sort' because the visual pleasures of this complex and rewarding building are neither those of classic regularity nor picturesque softness. Its aesthetic satisfactions stem from a tough-minded, blunt-spoken expertise that convinces even laymen that everything is right, proper and just so. It is one of those buildings that establishes its

own rules, convinces by the coherence of even markedly dissimilar parts, and stands upon no precedents. It rebuffs the attempts of art historians to identify its sources (unlike some of the other modern buildings on the Leicester campus, which provide a real feast for art-historical nit-pickers), though it has, in some obtuse way of its own, regained a good deal of the bloody-minded élan and sheer zing of the pioneer Modernism of the early twenties. Largely, I think, this is because it really does seem to be a natural machine-age architecture of the sort that must have been in the minds of the *Werkbund's* founding fathers or Antonio Sant'Elia.

If its attitude to technology is relaxed, its general quality is of a take-it-or-leave-it nonchalance, and this has undoubtedly contributed to the profound and niggling offence it has given in some creepy architectural circles. It is a fair measure of the collapse of self-confidence among students at certain British architectural schools that one of them could write:

> This is a worrying building. Formally it is one of the most exciting modern buildings in the country. Yet its very success ... calls into doubt the architects' motives and suggests that at times they were only concerned with human function in so far as it provided them with excuses for formal expression.

There follow a couple of paragraphs almost suggesting a hidden hope that it will turn out that the building doesn't work, so that little worries 'about the morality of it' (to quote two more frightened students) might turn out to be justified.

5 JAMES STIRLING and JAMES GOWAN, *Faculty of Engineering*, Leicester University, 1963, view of the spiral staircase leading to the upper floors in the research laboratory tower.

The whole proposition here, that a formally exciting building *cannot* be functionally correct, shows the kind of slough into which Functionalism deprived of ruthlessness can subside.

Fortunately, Stirling and Gowan applied the kind of radical ruthlessness that conjures convincing form out of the service of function, and receives as a bonus, not only the dizzy reflections in the stair-tower, but a nocturnal trans-formation scene when the building, glowing with its own internal and strictly functional illumination, assumes a mantle of light and mystery that is like no other architectural spectacle the world can offer. World – this is a world-class building, one of the very few that Britain has produced since the war, or ever. Its international fame does not rest on its being frightfully British, but on its being resolutely archi-tectural, and in a manner that would justify itself in any company.

The world is now beating a path to its door – where it is greeted by a badly lettered notice announcing that 'this building is not available to the public for visiting or photo-graphy'. Not to worry, effrontery or graft will get you in, and any trouble you provoke will help to hasten the day when the University authorities have to face their responsibilities and make proper arrangements for visitors. Architecture of this quality must be public property.

1.15 NATIONAL MONUMENT

Once again, unlike the conservative nationalism expressed by Spence in Coventry Cathedral, Lasdun has provided, according to Banham, a truly radical architecture in his National Theatre. By the 1970s Banham arrives at a neo-Modern definition of architecture which combines a complete re-working of the architectural language of architecture, both in form and technique. Lasdun's work operates, for Banham, within this tradition of radicalism. This article originally appeared in New Society, March 18 1976.

Here's the first of the National Theatre apocryphals to try on your friends. It seems that, at the beginning of the first of the acoustic test performances, Dinsdale Landen – or was it Albert Finney? – well, anyhow whoever it was came on with this other fella telling him some joke and the pair of them falling about and laughing, and nobody at the back of the house *could hear a single word...*

Pause craftily at this point, just long enough for your know-it-all friends to begin their wouldn't-you-know-it routines and then conclude with: 'and nobody at the front of the house heard a thing either because they weren't saying anything, just miming!'

The point of the story, alas, is not that Nicol Williamson – or was it Peter O'Toole? – is a great joker, but that anyone to whom you tell the yarn automatically assumes that there was an acoustic disaster of some sort, almost as if they *wanted* it so. No wonder Denys Lasdun, the architect of the National, has been so defensive about *all* criticism. In the present climate of conditioned reflex (I won't dignify it with the word 'opinion'), he knows he has hardly a hope in hell of getting a fair hearing. He's probably right in supposing that it may be five years before we know whether it's a good theatre of its kind.

Of its kind. That's part of the problem. Quite a lot of the shit that's been flying for the last five years or so is, quite simply, about it being a theatre at all, let alone national. Now every Dave Spart up the commune knows that basically, to his mind, the only, like, real theatre, man, is made by the people, you know, in the *street*, man, in the street. Only, when Lasdun was commissioned to design the National, it was back in the early sixties. Something like a shining new monumental version of the Royal Court was the most promising theatrical future generally current.

Whatever it was going to be a version of, it had to be a monument because a *national* anything has a job to be otherwise. A public building, a 'representational' building, a large object sitting there and offering statements on behalf of us generally to the rest of the world. Even within that currently nervous category of public architectural statements, the new National Theatre is a rather special case, like Coventry Cathedral.

Now I don't suppose Lasdun will thank me for comparing him to Sir Basil Spence (nor vice versa). But their careers as public architects are strikingly similar, and unlike the rest of their contemporaries. Their two major monuments are importantly alike in being key *post-war* buildings, symbolizing the values my generation went through mud blood and Naafi tea to make the world safe for. Coventry Cathedral was the retrospective symbol of the national determination to put back what the Hun had destroyed. The National Theatre is, belatedly, the prospective symbol of our determination to build a better future, the pinnacle of a cultural/political edifice which has somewhere been defined as 'the New Towns ... painless childbirth, modern art, decimal currency and free Shakespeare on demand'. Like the welfare state, a national theatre has been part of the progressive scenario for Britain since the Webbs were in rompers.

Completed, the NT pretty well finishes our likely set of major national monuments for the time being. Lasdun and Spence mopped up most of the major commissions between them: universities, a cathedral, a civic centre or two, the NT, even a learned society headquarters (Lasdun's College of Physicians in Regent's Park), which is a very rare kind of job these days. In spite of Lasdun's early success with housing in Bethnal Green, the housing-and-welfare jobs which are the backbone of most practices today, do not now bulk very large in the total output of Lasdun or Spence.

Beyond that register of jobs their outputs could hardly be more different.

Spence has tended to work at the Pop frontier of Modern architecture, exploiting the more accessible idioms of 'contemporary' with stunning skill, but somehow using them up, so that they can't be used again without looking cheap and cliché. At Coventry, with brilliant effect, he wiped out whole schools of Modern British Romanticism (Graham Sutherland's reputation has never recovered from that tapestry). At the Sussex University campus, he anglicized Le Corbusier's concrete-vault-and-shaggy-brickwork so prettily that not even an English architect would subsequently want to be seen dead with it.

Lasdun, contrariwise, has avoided these autodestructive soft options. He has preferred to work much nearer the cutting edge of Modernism. Even so, he is a hard man to place, falling generation-wise between the British pioneers like Maxwell Fry who made 'the white architecture of the thirties', and their followers-*révoltés* who made English Modern architecture a world-class affair in the sixties. If he has affinities, however, with anyone at all, it is with these last, who have mostly admired him and his work – especially in the mid-fifties when they would acclaim him as 'the only British architect with a real urban philosophy'. But his work never had the formal bloody-mindedness of James Stirling, nor his words the ethical high-falutin of the Smithsons.

Nor the free-form all-hung-out looseness of those who

1 DENYS LASDUN, *National Theatre on the South Bank*, London, 1976, site plan.

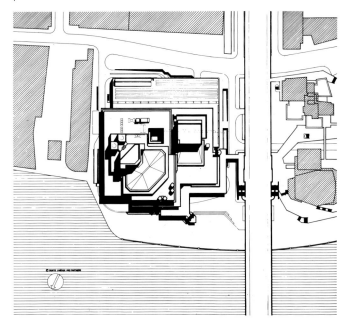

2 DENYS LASDUN, *National Theatre on the South Bank*, London, 1976, detail of the exterior by night.

3 DENYS LASDUN, *National Theatre on the South Bank*, London, 1976, Lyttleton foyer from the entrance.

4 DENYS LASDUN, *National Theatre on the South Bank*, London, 1976, the auditorium of the Olivier theatre.

later became the Archigram group. I say 'later' because the southward view over Waterloo Bridge allows one to compare the National on the left with an Archigram design 'before the fact', so to speak. The team who worked on the South Bank Arts Centre, to the right of the bridge, included several talents who helped to set the tone and style of Archigram's urban visions. Like those visions, the SBAC is informally assembled of separated components joined by footways, terraces, air-conditioning ducts and the like. Among the monuments of the South Bank, it is an extreme point of anti-monumentalism from which the National looks like a retreat.

In fact, it isn't. Lasdun never reached that point of loose organization, not even in the seemingly informal terracing of the residential parts of the University of East Anglia. The National's true affinity among the South Bank's earlier monuments is with the Royal Festival Hall. The first major post-war public building to go into service, the Festival Hall is really clear and together (as Dave Spart might say), with its auditorium box rising visibly from the layer of offices, foyers and etceteras wrapped around it. The National complicates matters by having two auditoria and their attendant fly-towers, and by having one of them turned through 45 degrees. But it is still basically the same architectural conception, as shows very clearly on the downstream side, with the upper works of the Olivier theatre standing proud of the terraced offices round the perimeter.

The 45 degree twist, however, gives some nice faceting and angled interceptions of surfaces where these upper works (and the lift-towers) break through the terracing. It all

gives some clear reminders of the angled intersections at East Anglia, and of the fact that this is really a building of the sixties, not the seventies. You can see that again in the massive sloping struts that support the downstream office-terraces from below. They are inevitably reminiscent of the similar usage on Stirling and Gowan's famous engineering laboratories at Leicester University – a work Lasdun cannot have failed to notice, since he was responsible for the next building of consequence on that campus, the Charles Wilson tower.

The time lag between the formulation of the design of the National and its final completion (ten years is a long time in Modern architecture!) makes it difficult to see how Lasdun has really developed as a maker of monumental statements, as a public architect. No doubt the exhibition of his drawings (all very sober and straightforward, no flashy perspectives) which will open at the Heinz Gallery in Portman Square on 7 April will help to make matters more clear. But even then you will still really need to visit the two public buildings by him in London which bracket the National on either side in time: the College of Physicians in the park, and the London University 'spine' building in Bedford Way.

From the Physicians at the very beginning of the sixties, Lasdun got what was once a literally 'textbook' commission, but almost unknown in post-war Britain. 'The headquarters of a learned society' was the kind of subject that used to be set for final-year architecture school exercises in the days when the Ecole des Beaux-Arts still ruled the world – buildings of almost purely ceremonial function. Because the College touched so many ancestral chords, but touched

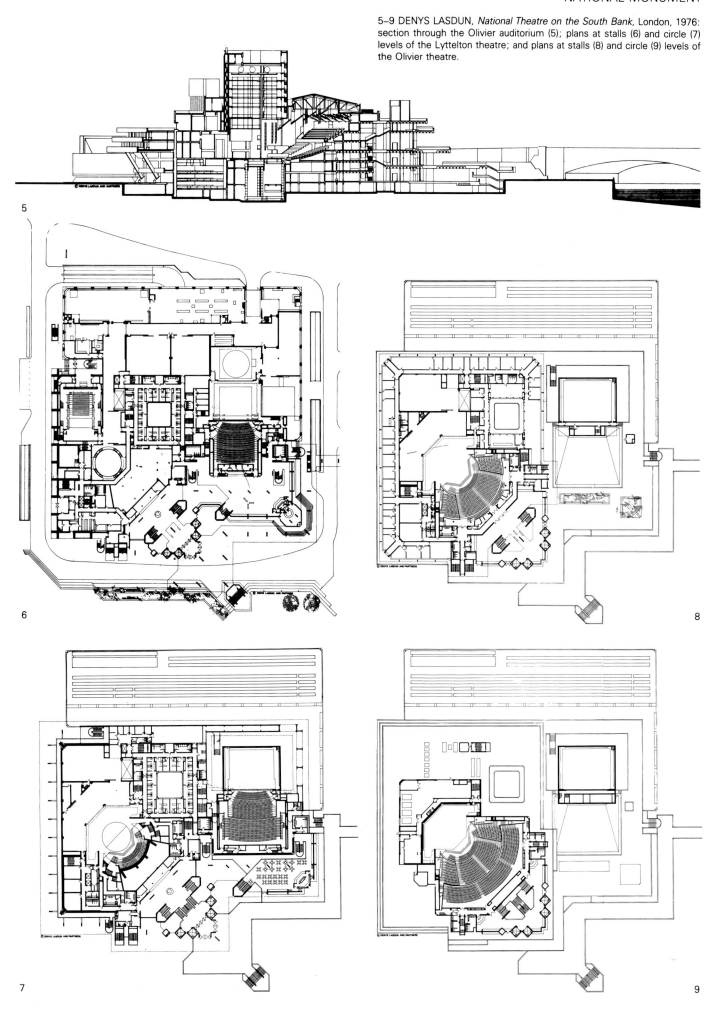

5–9 DENYS LASDUN, *National Theatre on the South Bank*, London, 1976: section through the Olivier auditorium (5); plans at stalls (6) and circle (7) levels of the Lyttelton theatre; and plans at stalls (8) and circle (9) levels of the Olivier theatre.

5

6

8

7

9

12 DENYS LASDUN, *Royal College of Physicians*, Regent's Park, London, 1960, general view from Regent's Park.

Opposite
10 and 11 DENYS LASDUN, *National Theatre on the South Bank*, London, 1976; general view from the north bank of the river Thames (*above*), and general view from Waterloo Bridge (*below*).

them without stylistic revivalism or sentimentality, it was one of Lasdun's greatest successes, bemedalled with awards and learnedly discussed by academics.

It gave them plenty to discuss. Though Edwardian in its ambitions and grandeur, its architectural vocabulary is entirely modern. When it adopts an ancient usage – such as the symmetrical planning of the façade towards the park – it then wittily thwarts the ancient expectation that you might enter on the axis of symmetry by placing three major structural columns around the ceremonial foundation stone which lies across the axis. By contrast to this extremely formal, if mildly perverse, composition, the auditorium alongside is a low and inscrutable brick pile, walled in warped and windowless planes of dark engineering brick, without visible symmetry in itself and only loosely attached to the ceremonial entrance block. This, probably, was Lasdun's farthest point along the road towards informalism, and it comes six or more years before he got the NT into shape.

Yet the National is closer to the Physicians than almost anything else he has done. The theatre generally has an easier relationship between its various geometries and their angled interceptions. But it repeats, more than once, the Physicians' device of splitting a corner by means of a deepset window inserted at 45 degrees. Throughout there is a feeling that Regent's Park is where he learned his stuff as a public architect, a designer of monuments.

That may be why the College has left its mark on those parts of the architectural profession that worry, intellectually and academically, about 'the public realm'. In places where they talk about High Architecture and prize it as an essential limb of Culture (places like the Ivy League schools in the US, or post-Frederic-Raphael Cambridge), they go on about the privatism of contemporary life because they see it as eroding the public realm which has been, traditionally, where the art of architecture flourishes.

Now there may or may not be any causal relation, but that curious device of the three columns obstructing the axial entrance is very like the (much more precious and contrived) devices that tend to turn up in the work of the Ivy-

Beleaguered New York Five architects. Only Lasdun got there at least five years ahead of them. At least one of the reasons why the National now looks so emphatically a building of the sixties could well be that its parent, the College of Physicians, was one of the crucial buildings in fixing the style of that decade for Modern public architecture. Historians may find themselves going back to it more often (after ignoring it for a decade) as a prime monument of the last period when monuments seemed publicly thinkable.

The London University 'spine' building (so called because it is the backbone of the grouping which also includes the new block for the School of Oriental and African Studies) is something that they will have to go back to for rather different historical reasons – the only public monumental building in anything like a style of the seventies.

When the model for it was first published, at about the same time as the first models for the NT, the 'spine' looked like a close relation to the National. Not any more; this was something of an optical illusion caused by the way the terraces on the back of the 'spine' looked in the model pics. As built, the architectural interest has moved round to the street front, which could *never* be mistaken for the National Theatre.

On this side, the 'spine' presents the lineaments of a single, immensely long and unmodulated dark-glass façade, not yet finished but ultimately running the whole length of one standard Bloomsbury block.

The forms are all huge, plain, and of very simple geometry, balancing the neutral blankness of smooth concrete against the dark reflectivity, or hollow transparency, of the 600 foot band of uninterrupted glazing. This is a sternly architectonic aesthetic that probably isn't going to have many admirers outside the profession for a long time to come. But historians will have to recognize in it the only completed realization, at anywhere near convincing scale, of the kind of heroically geometric megastructures that were proposed by the post-Archigram visionaries, particularly the Italian groups, Super-studio and Archizoom.

Again, Lasdun may not care for the comparison. But it looks as if what happened was that the hairies and weirdies, having rushed right past the point where architecture stops, started to pull back into more secure territory governed by the grand old rules of monumental form. They then discovered that Lasdun had, more warily, advanced into it from behind, following the logic of his own development. If there is, or has ever been, a convincing tradition of modern public building in the mid-20th century, a true line of monuments of our time, Lasdun may prove to be one of the men at the heart of it.

1.16 GRASS ABOVE, GLASS AROUND

An interest in the pluralistic language of architecture is developed in Banham's critique of Norman Foster's work which, for Banham, combines the vocabulary of architecture in an extremely competent way. Foster re-uses conventions in a new and surprising way, and represents for Banham the new architecture of the 1970s. This article originally appeared in New Society, *October 6, 1977.*

The Willis Faber and Dumas headquarters in Ipswich has taken just over two years to go from nine days' wonder to architectural respectability (RIBA Eastern Region award). But it remains almost as inscrutable as ever. It ought not to be. Most of us by now can 'read' a glass-walled office tower without difficulty. Many of us, indeed, are demonstratively bored by *having* to read them as often as we do. But then, what Foster Associates have designed in Ipswich is not a conventional rectangular tower, but a seemingly free-form four storey plan, waving about as it pursues the outlines of its site, slickly clad in dark, unmodulated glass from eaves to pavement.

The decision to build in this way in the historic heart of downtown Ipswich can be defended – and has been – on purely functional and economic grounds, as architects are wont to do. But when you have said that, you have said nothing about why it is a controversial, important and (possibly) extremely good building to have on that particular site. All that part of the argument must turn about purely visual, formal and symbolic aspects of the design, because what Norman Foster has done is to mix, without apology, two completely different (some would insist, utterly opposed) sets of architectural approaches, expectations and customary usages.

In the traditions of the Modern Movement in architecture, glass is of the party of order and hygiene. It stands for the replacement of the slums of the huddled poor by clean crystal towers. It stands for the illumination of the dark places of vernacular superstition by the pure light of rationality. World-wide, it has become the symbolic material of clarity, literal and phenomenal. As such it is – or was – universally delivered in crisp rectangular formats, pure and absolute, impervious to local accidents and customs. It was therefore appropriate to all the aspirations of the founders of the United Nations, who gave it canonical form in their headquarters tower in New York. Less felicitously it proved equally apt to the ambitions of great multinational corporations. Worse yet, to the avarice of downtown developers the world over.

In Ipswich, this last manifestation is represented, just across the street from Willis Faber and Dumas, by the Franciscan Centre development. But the glass vision is there bowdlerized by the sixties' most favoured substitute for architectural thought, *beton brut* – off-the-form concrete, here so poorly detailed, so neglected and unloved, that it is already growing moss! The architecture of rationality runs down into the architecture of profit and loss; and being without profit, is accounted the deadest of losses.

Against this kind of design is normally set a different Modern tradition which has had many names at different times, but is most fully represented by the doctrine of 'Townscape', advanced by *Architectural Review* in 1950, and elaborately developed over the years by the *Review*'s two brilliant draughtsmen, Gordon Cullen and Kenneth Browne. It has had its triumphs – notably the Festival of Britain – and, in spite of attempts by writers in the *Review*'s arch-rival, *Architectural Design*, to prove the contrary, continues in the 'Contextualism' of sundry German, Dutch and Belgian gurus that AD is pushing at the present time. Essentially, it is an amalgam of picturesque contrast and surprise, with circumspect (and usually sentimental) respect for what the Italian phase of the movement would have called the 'ambiente pre-esistente', plus recycling, rehabilitation and so forth. Above all, *not* putting up standardized glass boxes all over the world.

1 NORMAN FOSTER, *Willis Faber Head Office*, Ipswich, 1975, exterior by day.

That is the latter tradition that Foster's acquiescent pursuit of the boundaries of his given site appears to support. It's not what he usually does: his nearly complete Arts Hangar at the University of East Anglia pays no visible respect to anything at all in its surroundings. So he seems to have made even his faithful fan club uncomfortable, as well as making the opposition feel they are being got at. Yet he has, indeed, made his glazed perimeter follow the soggy curve of a post-war traffic improvement on one side, the irregular joggles of existing medieval streets on two others; and only on the fourth has he imposed a rationalized straight line on an irregular sequence of property boundaries – and that is the least seen of all the elevations.

But then to hang (literally) an uninterrupted and unaccented sinuous curtain of glass all round this 'historic' perimeter... For many good souls it's too much to take, even at the purely conceptual level. No, *especially* at the conceptual level, since, given the tendency of good-guy ideas to cluster, even when they have no logical connection, the Contextual, 'herbivore' approach has lately taken on board the moral load of energy conservation as well.

Now 'everybody knows' that glass is an energy-wasteful material. Yet Foster Associates have the gall and (tough luck, herbivores) the figures to show that this is a reasonably energy-efficient structure – partly because its very deep-plan four storey format gives a low ratio of glass to internal volume (and the glass is deeply bronzed as well), and partly because much of its roof is clad in one of the oldest and most reliable insulating materials known to vernacular wisdom – growing turf!

But: turf on top of a high-technology building full of air-conditioning, escalators, computers and stuff? Once again, separated expectations, different architectural languages, have been shotgun-married without apology or regard for the niceties of academic discourse, where turf is perfectly acceptable as long as it is on small-windowed, irregular technologically low-profile buildings. Academic polemicists might do well to remember that the man who reminded the present century of the roofing virtues of growing turf was none other than the true and only begetter of the universal, damn-local-traditions, glass-skinned, pure rectangular office block, Le Corbusier himself.

And so on. The pity of it is that so much of this academic debate is about matters which are marginal and trivial to the important business of seeing the world better housed, better serviced, better symbolized – but are matters suitable for academic debate. And Willis Faber and Dumas makes fools of them all. For what really hurts is that the building delivers precisely those anecdotal and serendipitous pleasures to the trained eye that *Architectural Review* campaigned for 30 years ago and that the Contextualists have now rediscovered via linguistics and a kind of populist neo-Marxism ... delivers all that by doing exactly the kind of architecture they would unobservantly claim couldn't do it.

As I recall, it is since Theo Crosby's rather Radical Chic *Environment Game* show at the Hayward four years ago, that the cry has been for more craftsmanship, more detail, more decoration, more incident. All those qualities that the standard, off-the-peg, minimalist glass wall could never give, and was therefore deemed uncultured and dehumanizing. Foster's wavy wall, with its storey-high sheets of glass butted edge to edge without framing, is even more detail-free than glass walls usually are. Yet when you look at the building you see almost nothing but craftsmanship, detailing, incidents, decoration, historical values – all reflected from the buildings on the other side of the street.

Look upon its featureless façades, and you shall see every period of East Anglian urban architecture from Low Gothic to High Brutalist, and almost every catalogued historical detail from *abacus* to *zygus*. Spire and dome are there, chimney and gable, column and pilaster, arches round, ogival and pointed. Better still, by choosing your viewpoints with creative care, you can manoeuvre an artisan-mannerist gable (reflected) on top of a modern matt-black metal ventilating grille (real), and make them fit together exactly. Indeed, you need to keep your eyes peeled and your wits about you, because the façade can deliver sequences of this sort of effect quicker than you can keep up with at normal walking pace.

2 NORMAN FOSTER, *Willis Faber Head Office*, Ipswich, 1975, exterior by night.

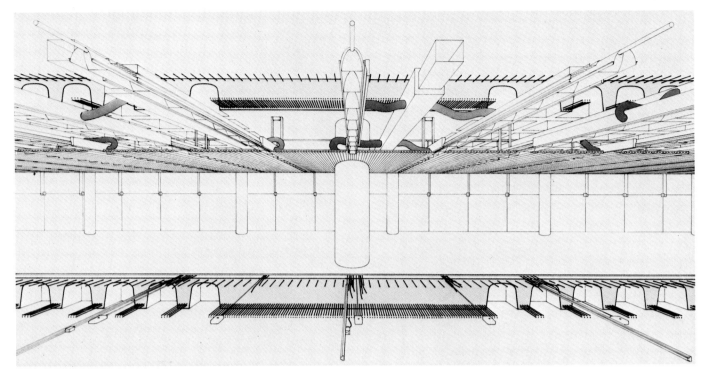

3 and 4 NORMAN FOSTER, *Willis Faber Head Office*, Ipswich, 1975, perspective sections.

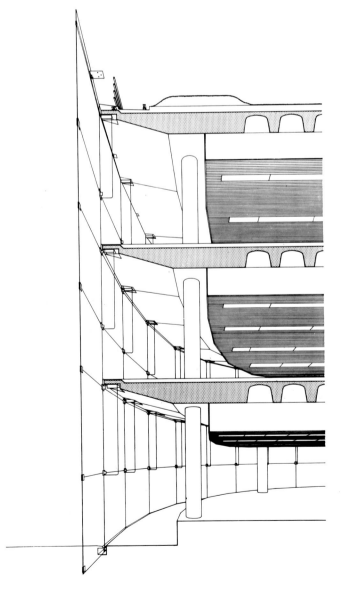

The reason for this quick-change display of visual puns, oxymorons, metaphors and other tropes, is that the façades are curved but the glass is flat. So no two adjoining facets are in the same plane and thus reflect non-adjoining subject matter. Everything is reflected in tall vertical slices, with violent visual discontinuities between the content of one slice and the next. You may, for instance, on the incurved side toward Friars Street, observe the same facing building reflected (in part) twice, several panes apart. The intervening facets are taken up with a quotation from a totally different building opposite, a short length of Willis Faber reflected at right angles to itself, and a tree apparently in a different part of Ipswich altogether.

These are exactly the kind of visual effects – surprise, truncation, concealment, confrontation – for which Townscape always campaigned. Looking back now on the discomfiture *Architectural Review* clearly experienced when confronted with this building (that did so many things *Architectural Review* held dear by architectural means the magazine's editors affected to abominate), it would be difficult not to smile, but for the contemptible intellectual contortions the editors went through to find something definitively bad with which to damn it. After two pages of praising with faint damns, they finally produced their polemical masterstroke (sic): the possibility of *two* such buildings: 'One Willis Faber and Dumas building may be a revelation, but two facing one another make a prison.'

Come off it! Two such façades facing one another would not (just) reflect a lack of craftsmanly detail on both sides of the street, but also – as in all facing-mirror situations – the viewer repeated to infinity in both directions. Not only does that flatter the viewer, but it is a form of ego massage which the editors of *Architectural Review* enjoy all over their editorial offices every day of the working week, for their premises are notoriously the most bemirrored in the business. Perhaps they're just jealous. Perhaps it is not flattering to see a bankrupt ideological position reflected to infinity. Perhaps they should put turf on their heads and see if that looks any better.

2
POP CULTURE

THEORY AND DESIGN

2.1 THE ATAVISM OF THE SHORT-DISTANCE MINI-CYCLIST

In this paper, originally published in Living Arts 3, *1964, and transcribed almost verbatim as delivered in the first Terry Hamilton Memorial Lecture, Banham presents an autobiographical picture of his upbringing in Norfolk, showing how it prepared him for an alliance with Pop culture in later years. He explains that one can enjoy Pop culture without repudiating left-wing politics.*

Those who are familiar with the recent professional literature will know that I now ride a mini-cycle. The most illuminating comment on this came from that south-of-the-Thames social critic, R. R. Langford, who said to me when he heard the news, 'that is your bike outside I take it?' And I said 'yes'. He looked at me and said, 'cycling, that's a bit atavistic isn't it?' The point went home because I have had one or two accusations of atavism recently. I've had for

Reyner Banham riding his mini-cycle in London.

what I thought the best reasons in the world to describe myself in print as a 'scholarship boy', to define my position for people who don't know the English social scene, but this is regarded by my wife as both atavism and (apparently) showing off. But the thing remains true, the working class is where I come from. I come from a cycling community. Anybody who knows Norwich knows that the cyclist is still the king of the road there, and all other traffic has to stand aside when the cyclists get loose.

I don't know that I'm particularly proud of this working class, cloth-cap bit in my background, but I think it gives me a right to speak on certain subjects. It's a funny thing being back on a bike after twelve years. The reflexes don't disappear; you put your leg over it and sit on the saddle and you make off straight away, and everything you learned with such great pain, more or less at your father's knee, comes back absolutely instantaneously, it's there, bred in the bone and blood. It's got to be a really weird bike, much weirder than the mini, before you come on a situation where you can't just sit on it and pedal off. And similar reflexes work also at the cultural level, for other things that take you back to where you came in.

It gives those of us who come from that part of the world a certain right to speak on subjects like Pop. We are not, as Basil Taylor said at the time of *This is Tomorrow*, 'sophisticated people meddling in unsophisticated matters'. I would in any case dispute that Pop Art is an unsophisticated matter, or that any other part of Pop culture is particularly unsophisticated. We were very much at home with this material, it was return-of-the-native stuff, we were in our own culture, sub-culture, or whatever you like to call it. We were natives back home again. But at home in a what? Not a working-class culture à la Hoggart, not a working-class culture as it has been heavily documented of late by a number of people who have fought their way 'up' from a proletarian background. What I mean is working-class culture in the sense that an anthropologist would normally describe it and understand it; the way that working-class people live, the kind of cultural standards they hold, enjoy, respond to. Thinking back, the cultural background against which I grew up was a very curious one indeed, if one is to believe the sort of things in Hoggart. The area had a certain amount of 'real' culture with a capital C, like the local Philharmonic Society, which could never even play Beethoven right, an occasional concert by someone like Muriel Brunskill, and the local operatic society in *The Mikado*. This was the capital C culture background against which I grew up, and which really meant nothing to any of us. The live culture, the culture in which we were involved, was American pulps, things like *Mechanix Illustrated* and the comic books (we were all great Betty Boop fans), and the penny pictures on Saturday mornings; I know the entire Chaplin canon back to front and most of the early Buster Keatons, not through having seen them at the National Film Theatre under 'cultural' circumstances with perfect air-conditioning, but at a 1d or 2d a whack, in a converted garage (practically next to Nelson Street Primary School which was the rest of my cultural background, not to mention the speedway. I was a bob-ender in the days when a bob-ender meant a certain class of person doing a particular kind of thing on a Saturday night). Now the thing about this background is that it really was the live culture of a place like Norwich at that time in the thirties. The emphasis and most of the content of this culture was American because there was nothing else. Once when we couldn't get American comics we bought a copy of *Punch* by mistake and never again, do you blame us? This was our scene. And I think this is true for a great many of us, especially those who made up the Independent Group, who were the pacemakers of the early and middle fifties in London. Now if this is where we came from, it left many of us in a very peculiar position, vis-à-vis the normal divisions of English culture, because we had this American leaning and yet most of us are in some way Left-oriented, even protest-oriented. This was why I picked this subject to discuss in the first Terry Hamilton Memorial Lecture, because Terry in many ways pinpointed this peculiar situation; people whose lightweight culture was American in derivation, and yet, in spite of that, were and are, of the Left, of the protesting sections of the public.

It gives us a curious set of divided loyalties. We dig Pop which is acceptance-culture, capitalistic, and yet in our formal politics, if I may use the phrase, most of us belong very firmly on the other side. I remember John McHale saying to Magda Cordell once, 'If we go on voting Labour like this we shall destroy our own livelihood,' – it was during their advertising period, and that's the way this particular split of loyalties struck many people. But equally it struck a lot of people outside our group and they genuinely believed that we didn't know where we were going, or had got into a contradictory position.

To some extent I think we were the victims of the Cold War. Something very weird happened around 1946–1947 when the lines were being drawn for the Cold War. Suddenly there came a moment when it was very difficult to read *Time* or any American magazine at all, simply because of one's political loyalties. In that period there arose a situation where one's natural leanings in the world of entertainment, and so on, were to the States, but one's political philosophy seemed to require one to turn one's back to the States. I remember the curiously divided mind in which one listened to Pop records on Radio Luxembourg in the evenings and wondered just whose side you were on. And, as I say, this Cold War distinction made, in the forties, a division which runs right through English thinking, and indeed much American thinking (people like Dwight McDonald): that to accept, to enjoy, the products of Pop, the products of the entertainment industry, Detroit-styling and such things, was to betray one's political position. We left ourselves with one foot on either side of the dividing line that had been drawn through the culture of the West. And we were blamed from this very platform. Five or six years ago I gave a talk at the ICA which was simply a descriptive attempt to sort out the way the Pop and fine art cultures were related, but I got a tremendous hammering during the questions afterwards from people who genuinely felt that I was deluding myself, confusing the public, misleading everybody, simply by being prepared to regard Pop as something which might be merely described. Apparently it was something which had to be rejected.

So what's wrong? Well first of all there is this diagrammatic division of current culture into commercial and non-commercial. This is very strongly felt by a lot of Left people, but by many non-Left people it is merely accepted. The charming gentleman from *The Observer* who came and conned me into doing an article for them, kept interrrupting his discourse with 'Of course, it is just commercialism, isn't it? Pop is all whipped up by commercial interests isn't it?' This is widely believed, without anyone stopping to think. There is a great deal of evidence available to suggest that whatever the intentions of the entertainment industry, the public is not being, and apparently *cannot* be, manipulated to that extent. Take the Twist. A major cultural phenomenon, and apparently a fairly durable one. Some very astute articles full of inside information about Denmark Street, were written about the Twist (particularly in *New Statesman*) at the time it was starting. The degree to which the Twist was an exercise in commercial manipulation was made abundantly clear, with the assumption that the Twist had simply been dreamed up as a commercial exploit.

Now one can compare what happened with the Twist, an uncontrollable craze which penetrated even the Iron Curtain, with what happened to another dance which was equally heavily promoted, and didn't take; the Madison. The first attempt to sell the Madison on the English market pre-dates the appearance of the Twist. Nothing happened. Then after the Twist, when it seemed you could sell any new dance, the Madison came back. Another tremendous attempt to sell it, because all the sheet-music, all the instruction books and so on, were there still waiting to be used. We had about six months of two-up-two-down-and-hit-it agony, and it *still* didn't take. Despite the fact that the whole ballroom industry was behind it and pushing it, it still didn't go. The evidence seems to me to show that the Twist stands for something real which might have happened even without commercial exploitation. Indeed, it grew far quicker than the English industry could cope, that's clear. The Twist seems to stand for something real, and the Madison – as far as the British public was concerned – did not stand for anything real and so didn't take. That there is commercial exploitation in Pop culture nobody in his right mind would deny, but there has to be something else underneath, some sub-stratum of genuine feeling, a genuine desire for the thing, which has to be touched off before the market will really move. The commercial worry runs all through the attempts of serious social critics to say something sensible, intelligible and explanatory about a whole series of Pop manifestations. It has been particularly interesting to watch my fellow columnists on *New Statesman* trying to deal with the Beatle phenomenon. John Morgan was in print on the subject as far back as October 18th – very with it, John Morgan. He wrote a long piece on the Liverpool Sound, which I might add, was not triggered off by the Beatles but by a joint autobiography of the Braddocks. It says, among other things: 'not that there is fighting at the Cavern. Indeed there is less than there used to be in the golden days – as they seem in retrospect – when the best traditional jazz bands in the land played at the club, and when old men of thirty would come and sit and listen to a music that was relatively adult and civilised. What there is now is a kind of hell.' It goes on later about the Mersey Sound: 'this "sound" owes nothing musically to Liverpool. It echoes American rhythms rather than songs like "Walking by the Liverpool Strand" or "Nelly Gray". But that it should have originated on Merseyside, subsequently dominated the interest of young people throughout Britain is – to follow the argument of bar-room students – of more than trivial interest. The tentative notion is that it could mark a breakthrough; the asphalt jungle has a British drum beat for the first time.'

Now these two quotes come from the same piece. And if the Beatles owe anything musically to Liverpool it is precisely to trad jazz. Liverpool is the Nashville of Great Britain because there, as in Nashville, the sound comes out of holes – I mean *literally* – comes out of holes in the ground. The beat has been growing in Liverpool since even before the war. Trad jazz there has a very long history that goes back to the days when trad jazz was alive, before it became a sort of Gaitskellite affectation of the Labour middle. And when you have a town where men have been blowing as good as they used to blow in Liverpool, and beating things, and indeed using electric amplifiers on their guitars, then the Beatles derive from something which is real – there is a long tradition there of making, roughly speaking, this kind of noise. It's not a new imposition, nor is it the product of that character who has been worked so hard in Left Wing journalism since the Beatles appeared – the entrepreneur. Liverpool has been for years the town with the wildest Pop culture in England and to suppose the Beatles owe nothing to this seems to me to miss the point: to miss it for purely diagrammatic political reasons; that trad jazz was not commercially successful, and could be represented as a music of protest. The Beatles visibly *are* commercially successful, and are rather cheerful and affirmative, and not at all protest-type music.

More recently the gentleman who masquerades under the name of Francis Newton in order to write about jazz for the *New Statesman* observed 'They are probably just about to begin their slow descent: the moment when someone thinks of making a film with a pop idol normally marks the peak of his curve. In twenty years' time nothing of them will survive.' Hard luck, they'll be forty or so by then. 'This is where products like the Beatles differ from the ancestor of their "beat music" – the urban blues, an historical cross-section of which we were lucky to hear recently in the unexpected environment of Croydon.' I know it's not fair to lift these pieces out of context, but they make you think. 'Nothing will be left of them in twenty years' time, unlike the urban blues.' Well, what is left of the urban blues? It's preserved as a minority cult like, say, reed thatching or horn dancing. This hit me very forcibly when I was in St. Louis – we actually went to hear real Dixieland jazz being played within a long sniff of the Mississippi, if not within sight and sound of the father of the waters. Marvellous; for anybody who grew up with scratchy 78 r.p.m. records of King Oliver and so on, this was a fantastic moment, to be in the place and hear the sound being made live without the gramophone industry between you and the instruments. It's quite a moment to be in St. Louis and hear the sound being played by respectable grey-haired gentlemen who were obviously there at the time the records were made in the twenties – solid citizens, all veterans of WPA music projects, playing the real sound – the big rich full trombone noise, and fine wailing clarinet and that kind of thing. But it was only history. It had nothing to do with the St. Louis of the MacDonnell Aircraft Corporation, the St. Louis of the free-ways, of the Climatron, the Planetarium and so on. It was as real or unreal, as genuine or as phoney as all the rest of the Gaslight Square bit. Because Gaslight Square has been made up out of old panelling and light fittings salvaged from the Mill Creek area when it was pulled down to make way for re-development, and you get a strong feeling these old gentlemen were also salvaged from the area at the same time. The sound was perfectly accurate, rich and full, and a bit like Colonial Williamsburg – it has been very carefully put together brick by brick, note by note, and it is not in any sense anything to do with the way we live now. It is a survival under the very specialized circumstances of a continuing minority fan club or vintage car support.

But there are more serious objections, not merely from the Left but from progressive opinion generally. Particularly from the adult education movement. It's also part of my background – I've been both a consumer and then a producer of adult education, and I've seen this situation from both sides. At Bawdeswell, out in the sticks in Norfolk, I had a marvellous class with whom I did a course on the principles of basic design – we looked at pictures and we did abstracts and that kind of thing; we had a great time. They were really loyal, they even stuck through potato-setting, which is quite something. And, at the end, one of the girls in the class said to me: 'It has been very very interesting, Mr. Banham, but I still like Giles better'.

This quite simply is a situation where Pop competes directly with what has been one of the main instruments of social improvement in this country. Pop competes directly with the adult education movement for the *time* of the consumers. Say you're reading Spanish or doing Italian or something like that, and you accidentally win two tickets for the Beatles, how would you choose? That would be one week when the Italian class had had it. Pop competes directly for the time of the potential adult educatees, or whatever the word is. It also competes very heavily for their loyalties. Most of the people who teach adult education are anti-Pop because of this competitive situation, and most of them are not prepared to go even half-way to meet it; they would rather talk about Dostoevsky than science fiction. And above all I believe Pop competes with the middle-class aims of adult education, since the historical function of adult education as part of the progressive movement in England was to equip the working-classes with middle-class responses. The rise of the working classes to political power has rested upon someone equipping them with the right kind of responses to social and political situations, manipulative responses. The desire to do something about the situation had to be attuned to basically middle-class systems of government, both at the national and even more at the local level, in order to give the working class, not the automatically defeatist response of regarding government as 'they', but the traditional 'we own the joint' middle-class response of regarding government as 'us'. And it runs right through. Nowadays the adult education movement particularly as it applies in urban areas, is the adjunct of a middle-class, not a working-class, culture. It lays on language lessons, it lays on art appreciation, music appreciation, literature classes and so on, which are aimed at an urban middle-class funny-hat-wearing, female clientele.

This, of course, makes the movement extremely nervous and insecure. I have heard one of the organizers of the London District describe science fiction as 'this furtive underground literature'. He made the mistake of describing it so in the presence of Lawrence Alloway, who put him straight back in his box. But this is typical; it's a classic situation where the Workers' Education Association which for better or worse is a class-oriented body, is faced with an unclassed and largely unclassifiable cultural phenomenon. Science fiction is a literature not enshrined in great monuments. The expendability of SF is as high as the expendability of Pop music – a few tunes become Pop 'classics' or Pop 'standards', like 'Black Magic' and 'Smoke' and stay current for ever and ever, and one or two great SF stories become classics, standards, and remain current for ever and ever. But most of the field is just a wash of pulp which passes over you month by month and week by week in *Venture* and *Analog* and so on, and disappears and is forgotten, and justifiably so. It is high turnover entertainment stuff. And that is something very difficult for a movement like this to take seriously, because so much of the Left is culturally still in the grip of traditional conservative institutions such as universities and above all, Eng. Lit. If there's one thing that the adult education movement would do well to get shot of, it is Eng. Lit, both as something taught and as a general cultural background against which its studies are to be seen. For this movement Pop is a real threat, and will I think remain one for a long time. It's impossible for people in this situation to regard it in the classic way of *jolly fun*. This is the traditional upper-class English response to this sort of situation – it's the squire-who-can-make-jokes-with-the-dairy-maid bit. He's not taking her seriously, his relationship with her is not the same as his relationship with the lady of the manor. And it is on a strictly *jolly fun* level that a certain number of fine art people have made their peace – some kind of jokey relationship – with Pop design and Pop Art. This again was a phrase that was thrown about a good deal during the period of *This Is Tomorrow*. You know – these are sophisticated people mucking about with unsophisticated things because they regard it all as jolly fun. But, jolly fun or deadly serious, it seems to me that the adult education movement, and a number of other bodies of the progressive Middle and Left, need to redefine their relationship to the live culture of the working classes as it exists. There seems to be some call for a decent humility in the face of something which, simply in terms of the response it gets, appears to stand for something real. When something is so largely consumed and with such enthusiasm and such passion, as many aspects of Pop culture are, then I don't think any social critic in his right mind should simply reject it as being a load of rubbish or even the opium of the people. It's something which would bear serious enquiry of a sort that it's not really received so far.

Nor do I think you will ever make stand up a view of Pop as a compensation for some social deprivation or lack which would disappear if society was organized on other lines. One of the shattering aspects of Pop for a lot of people has been its universality, the response it has elicited in countries with all kinds of political régimes. Whether your country is a nominal Western democracy or a nominal People's democracy, the Twist has been there, and Rock before it and jeans survive through thick and thin as the badge of some kind of international teenage culture which is apparently as widespread as industrialization. No one has yet thought of a kind of social organization for a country which will make jeans unthinkable.

It is fairly clear that most hostile reponses to Pop culture stem from an ingrained, built-in, previous commitment. But this is not *only* for political reasons; the response of architects to Pop culture has been – to a person like myself, watching from close-in on the side-lines – continuously fascinating, frustrating and in the end disappointing. There are certain aspects of Pop culture which architects find extremely hard to take. The most obvious one is expendability; the new President of the AA is already on record against expendability on a fairly well-taken, purely mechanical point, that if you make a building which will stand twelve months of English weather it will need to have sufficiently high safety factors to stand for twenty cycles of the English seasons. (I'm surprised he put the figure as low as twenty.) But, as I say, expendability is difficult to take because you're dealing with a body of men who, for good reasons or ill, are traditionally involved with the erection of long term permanent structures. The autumn issue of *Archigram*, admittedly, is devoted entirely to expendability in architecture, and I think it does great credit to Peter Cook and the boys who did the *Living City* exhibition here at the ICA that they are trying to grapple with the problem. I'm not quite sure where they have got with it so far, but this is still a minority reaction within the general body of architecture, which remains extremely cautious in its response to Pop because of the expendability aspect. But there are more things than just the time-span problems involved here. Pop

is economically linked to what, for architects, is an alien culture. Pop puts the ultimate command in the hands, if not of the consumer, then at least of the consumer's appointed agents. And architects cannot really manoeuvre themselves into this position. Some architects have good personal relationships with their clients but it's a different matter when you come to the social relationships of town planning and other large scale matters. You could put it like this: could architects accept the position of being designers of a technological infrastructure, but not be responsible for its eventual appearance? There have been lots of schemes recently in which parts of the building are expendable or are at the whim of the individual occupant, or consumer, or whatever you like to call him, but it's always been arranged so that the big frame dominates visually over the individual private unit. As far back as the apparently permissive aesthetics of the Tecton schemes for Finsbury, where you had a big façade full of little windows, and each window a carefully framed working-class still-life with Nottingham lace curtains and a plaster dog and a pot plant, the whole proposition still called for a *carefully framed* working-class still-life. It kept such firm quotation marks round the inhabitants that they were not deciding the aesthetic of their own dwelling or anything of the sort, the big frame dominated and the working-class inhabitant was simply allowed to peep out through carefully-framed holes on every floor.

This is something which has been a live worry right from the very beginning of the fifties, and the early days of arguments about whether one could create a neutral technological frame which was simply a support of structure and services within which people could express themselves freely. It has become a live subject again at the moment because of the Cedric Price/Joan Littlewood Fun Palace project. But it's something which still hasn't quite come off, and because of all sorts of things, but chiefly because in the end architects are still committed to some kind of hieratic culture in which command comes from the few experts at the top and not from the mass of consumers at the bottom. And even so, one wonders how well-founded the difficulties with the time-scale are. The motor industry takes four years to work up a new car, which is longer on the average than it takes to design and build a significant new building, so that the Pop industry, the styling industry, works on a longer time-base. But they're working for four years to produce a product with a life, aesthetically and generally, of one year; they're working for four years to design one year's model. There is a constantly expanding and contracting time-scale in designing different parts of the product but it still means that a vast amount of effort goes into producing a design which will be scrapped at twelve monthly intervals.

Could the building industry, architects, and everybody involved in it, support an equivalent mass of research and development for a new model every year? They might be able to do it but I don't know whether they'd want to know the answer, even if this research and development could produce it. Basically they're not interested in the state of the working-class here and now because it is in their terms of reference also to be concerned with the state of the working class in twenty-five years' or fifty years' time. This is a forward-looking problem which becomes a backward-looking problem. You try to isolate durable and continuous aspects of popular life but things have happened so fast that, say, the planning of all the new towns is already hopelessly out of date. Harlow has traffic problems which really need Colin Buchanan already; for one very simple reason; that Harlow was designed for those long term permanent working-class things like riding bicycles. Only, of course, the working class don't ride bicycles any more. Radicals like me ride bicycles, and the working class have got Populars and Cortinas and Minis – there's nowhere to park them in Harlow, and they leave them all over the grass verges. It's a fair chance that private cars will be banned from Harlow before they're banned from the centre of London.

In the end, to accept the Pop situation is to let the whole *uomo universale* mythology of architecture go slide. The *uomo universale*, the man who is omnicompetent, will always demand to be omnipotent. If he *can* do everything in sight then by God he'll *want* to – among other things, just to prove that he can. And therefore in most architect's worlds there is no real room for a contribution from the consumers because it would get in the way of his determination to do everything himself.

It's interesting to see how many architects who at one time were with the Pop scene, have in their various ways resigned or withdrawn from it. Peter Smithson in his House of the Future was designing a fully styled-up house *intended* to be styled-up, in order to make it desirable. The House of the Future had token chrome strips painted round it, and so on. It was to be a fully Pop product so that it would move realistically on the Pop market – it had the sort of gimmicks that were thought necessary then in order to make it viable on the Pop scene. But, more recently, the Smithsons and Eduardo Paolozzi and people like that, have been calling rather necrophilic revivalist meetings of the Independent Group to try and clear their names of being responsible for the present Pop Art movement in England. It's now become necessary for them to revise their own immediate back-history and autobiography, almost in the Le Corbusier manner. And people like Sir Hugh Casson, for instance, who were very keen and with it when Pop was new and jolly fun are pulling back rather cautiously now because they feel they've opened Pandora's Box and are not quite sure what's coming out. I think David Hockney's hair-do's were enough of a shock to make the Royal College of Art terrified that Pop might spread to industrial design and areas like that where it would cease to be jolly fun. Again, among other people who were never consciously in Pop but are now officially out of it is Misha Black. I find this very weird because a sizeable portion of Design Research Unit's income at one time came from some very keen Pop design indeed, done for Ilford Cameras by Ken Lamble, who is one of the best Pop designers, if anybody would let him. He's outstandingly good at making a small cheap camera look like a small cheap camera with ideas above its station. But at these DRU self-criticism sessions to which I am occasionally invited, people are pretty weird about these Ken Lamble designs. In some cases the designs are brilliant – not as they reach the shops but as they come in model stage to the table, for criticism – but the knocking they get at these sessions is quite remarkable.

So these self-criticism sessions are fascinating and revealing simply because one can see an absolutely basic crisis of orientation running through design. What it comes to in the end is that for good reasons or bad, with or without political predilections, education gives people a sort of slant or twist of mind which means they can accept or not accept Pop. This is the real determinant-that the English educational system, as you get towards the top of the academic pyramid, cuts certain people off from their origins, their ability to remember what they were like. I am not talking about people who don't have Pop origins – I'm talking about people like myself who have come up the educational ladder hand over hand. They can either accept, or not accept – and

slumming is no substitute for being able to accept. Too many progressive people are not with it, they don't dig the scene, they are slumming. They think they're enjoying it but they don't really understand what it is they're with, what it is that they're exposing themselves to, and the result produces false expectations. But the basic and crucial false expectation is concerned less with Pop directly than with the aims and the products of universal education, of universal literacy. It appears to have been assumed by the generation of men who built the board-schools and launched the great adventure of giving the three Rs to everybody, that education-plus-the-masses equals a nation of Shakespeare lovers. But the joke is in Shakespeare: if you read Caliban's observations on having been taught Eng. Lit.: 'You taught me language, and my profit on't is, I know how to curse.' The cultural proposition in universal literacy was sent up before it even started.

This quite clearly was (and still is) the expectation of our educators: that if you educate everybody the result will be the same as educating a privileged minority. It's something I don't dig at all, because the sort of people who appear to believe this are mostly from the Left and they ought to be good enough at Hegel (or any rate at Marx) to know about the thesis/antithesis/synthesis relationship, in which what comes out from thesis and antithesis is different from what went in at the beginning.

The effect of universal literacy on language appears to have been to produce a nation of dead men. But where education hasn't been laid on so thick, in music and in visual design, something real seems to have come out. All right, so the Beatles aren't Beethoven, but they are a live music, and there's a lot of other live Pop music which has been coming on ever since the skiffle craze began. On the visual side, what people go for is not Michelangelo, they prefer Giles, but at least they begin to know what they're looking at and can put a name to it, which is a very considerable improvement on the condition of mass taste even twenty years ago. And for this one has television to thank. We are faced with the unprecedented situation of the mass distribution of sophistication. It may not be profound art appreciation, it may not be profound learning in music, but it is an ability to discriminate. To know whether music is with it or whether it's old and square, to recognize something as being keenly styled, to be able to distinguish a mod from a rocker – this introduces a degree of popular sophistication which is a genuine cultural innovation, and we really don't know a damned thing about it yet. In many cases the rejection to which it's been subjected is simply a rejection of the unknown, the rejection of a situation for which the traditional theories of democracy and education have not prepared people – it's very new and unknown territory, particularly to people who come up with a traditional dead languages education of the normal European sort.

Progressive people, the people who are going to have to make social action, have got, somehow, to learn to ride with the real culture of the working classes as it exists now. It's no good these well-meaning people deluding themselves with trad jazz and Morris dancing and reed thatching and all that. It is time for them to try and face up to Pop as the basic cultural stream of mechanized urban culture. For guidance on how to do it one is driven back (as so often) to quotation from Panofsky's famous, but alas very little read, essay on the movies. It's one of those documents you go back to again and again, because it's written from a great and Olympian height and by a man with no axe to grind, yet it contains some of the best common sense ever written about the Pop culture of our time. I want simply to quote one passage which touches the heart of the subject. It's about the movies, but what he says here will apply to Pop culture generally.

Today there is no denying that narrative films are not only 'art', – not often good art, to be sure, but this applies to other media as well – but also, besides architecture, cartooning and 'commercial design', the only visual art entirely alive. The 'movies' have re-established that dynamic contact between art pro-duction and art consumption which, for reasons too complex to be considered here, is sorely attentuated, if not entirely interrupted, in many other fields of artistic endeavour. Whether we like it or not, it is the movies that mould, more than any other single force, the opinions, the taste, the language, the dress, the be-haviour, and even the physical appearance of a public comprising more than 60 per cent of the population of the earth. If all the serious lyrical poets, composers, painters and sculptors were forced by law to stop their activities, a rather small fraction of the general public would become aware of the fact and a still smaller fraction would seriously regret it. If the same thing were to happen with the movies the social consequences would be catastrophic.

I think one can safely read 'Pop culture' for 'movies' throughout that; because the live stream of contemporary culture is Pop, and that is one of the reasons why so many of the live manifestations of other branches of culture all round us derive from Pop. Pop is now so basic to the way we live, and the world we live in, that to be with it, to dig the Pop scene, does not commit anyone to Left or Right, nor to protest or acceptance of the society we live in. It has become the common language, musical, visual and (increas-ingly) literary, by which members of the mechanized urban culture of the Westernized countries can communicate with one another in the most direct, lively and meaningful manner.

2.2 A THROW-AWAY AESTHETIC

This article, written originally in 1955 and published in Industrial Design, *March 1960, under the title of 'Industrial Design and Popular Art', parallels similar inquiries by John McHale and Lawrence Alloway. In it Banham is searching for a way of describing popular aesthetics, for a set of criteria with which to discuss expendable consumer goods. He comes to the conclusion that urban popular culture studies must start with an analysis of content rather than form, and with the relationship between styling, symbolism and the consumer. This provides a methodological framework for many of his later studies.*

It is still little more than a century since the idea arose that the design of consumer goods should be the care and responsibility of practitioners and critics of fine arts. This conviction was part of the 19th-century democratic dream of creating a universal élite, in which every literate voter was to be his own aristocratic connoisseur and arbiter of taste – the assumption being that the gap between the fine arts and the popular arts was due only to the inadequate education of the 'masses'. This view of popular taste drew much of its strength from a romantic misconception of the Middle Ages: it assumed that because only well-designed and artist-decorated artifacts had survived from Gothic times, then all medieval men, from prince to peasant, must have possessed natural good taste. (Actually, all the evidence suggests is that only the expensive objects warranting elaborate decoration were sufficiently well-made to last five or six centuries, and we know practically nothing of the inexpensive artifacts of the period because few have survived.)

Nevertheless, this view of medieval goods did not entirely perish even after Art Nouveau's floridity had been rejected by the generation of designers and theorists who established themselves after 1905. Adolf Loos, rejecting all ornament, read the evidence to mean that later generations, with debased taste, had allowed all undecorated medieval craftwork to be destroyed, while carefully conserving the depraved and untypical ornamented examples. Loos, while an extremist, is fairly typical of his contemporaries who rejected all forms of ornament because they could find no meaning in it, and turned to the concept of 'pure form' because it offered proof against fallible human taste. This and other attitudes of their generation were synthesized after World War One by Gropius and Le Corbusier, in writings that postulated a sovereign hierarchy of the arts under the dominance of architecture, and a common dependence on laws of form that were objective, absolute, universal and eternally valid. The illusion of a common 'objectivity' residing in the concept of function, and in the laws of Platonic aesthetics, has been a stumbling block to product-criticism ever since.

In the century of fine art product-criticism now finishing, every school of thought, every climate of opinion, has had to formulate its attitude toward industrial production. In contrast to all earlier formulations, the 'neo-academic' synthesis just described – a mystique of form and function under the dominance of architecture - has won enthusiastic acceptance. It is the result of telescoping the Loosian ideas of pure, undecorated machine forms and Futurist ideas of the mechanized urban environment as the natural habitat of 20th-century man. But this telescoping, which brought machine products within the orbit of pure aesthetics, was achieved at the cost of ignoring three fundamental fallacies, which may be labelled: simplicity, objectivity, and standardization.

Geometrical *simplicity* has been identified as a basic preference of Platonic aesthetics since the end of the last century, and Plato's celebrated quotation that absolute beauty is found in 'forms such as are produced by the lathe, the potters' wheel, the compass and the rule' has been one of the most frequently quoted justifications for abstract art, and for supposing that product design should follow its laws. Neo-academic critics of 1900–30 could see in such fields as bridge-building and vehicle design, quite accidentally, the same sort of rule-and-compass geometry of which Plato approved.

Although these resemblances are obviously a mere coincidence depending on the aesthetic atmosphere of the period and the primitive condition of vehicle design, the neo-academic critics took them as proof of the *objectivity* of their attitude. Engineers were believed to be working without aesthetic contamination and according to immutable physical laws. To this misconception, they added a confusion between the meaning of objectivity in mechanical engineering laws and in the laws of aesthetics (the latter meaning that their logic is impeccable, not that their factual basis has been subjected to scientific evaluation). The neo-academics then succeeded in circulating the belief that all mechanically-produced articles should be simple in form, and answer to abstract and supposedly permanent laws based on architectural practice. The final absurdity of this view is found in Herbert Read's influential book, *Art and Industry*, epitomized in two quotations. The first draws an unwarranted conclusion from an impeccable observation: 'The engineer's and the architect's designs approach one another in aesthetic effect. Entirely different problems are being solved, but the same absolute sense of order and harmony presides over each.' The aesthetic prejudice suggested in this conclusion reveals itself in another, quite meaningless as a statement of fact but instructive as a rhetorical flourish: 'The machine has rejected ornament.'

Somewhere in this confusion lies the third of the concealed difficulties – *standardization*. This word has been used in a muddled way by many 'machine aesthetes' in a manner that suggests a mark, an ideal, at which to aim. But in engineering, a standardized product is essentially a norm stabilized only for the moment, the very opposite of an ideal because it is a compromise between possible production and possible further development into a new and more desirable norm. This double expendability, which involves not only the object itself but also the norm or type to which it belongs, is actually what excludes mass-produced goods from the categories of Platonic philosophy.

We live in a throw-away economy, a culture in which the most fundamental classification of our ideas and worldly possessions is in terms of their relative expendability. Our buildings may stand for a millennium, but their mechanical equipment must be replaced in fifty years, their furniture in twenty. A mathematical model may last long enough to solve a particular problem, which may be as long as it takes to read a newspaper, but newspaper and model will be forgotten together in the morning, and a research rocket – apex of our technological adventure – may be burned out and wrecked in a matter of minutes.

It is clearly absurd to demand that objects designed for a short useful life should exhibit qualities signifying eternal validity – such qualities as 'divine' proportion, 'pure' form or

1 *Bugatti Royale Type 41*, designed by Jean Bugatti, c.1931.

'harmony' of colours. In fairness to Le Corbusier, it should be remembered that he was the first to raise the problem of permanence and expendability in engineering: 'Ephemeral beauty so quickly becomes ridiculous. The smoking steam engine that spurred Huysmann to spontaneous lyricism is now only rust among locomotives; the automobile of next year's show will be the death of the Citroën body that arouses such excitement today.' Yet, recognizing this much, he declined to accept the consequences. He singled out the work of Ettore Bugatti for special praise, using components from his cars as examples of engineering design that supported his fine art view of product aesthetics.

As a result, the engines of the Bugatti cars have been regarded as models of the highest flights of engineering imagination – *except* by some of the most distinguished automobile designers. Jean Gregoire, for example, on whose work in the field of front-wheel drive all subsequent vehicles of this type depend, has refused to find the Bugatti engine admirable. He speaks from inside engineering: 'In a particular component, mechanical beauty corresponds to the best use of materials according to the current state of technique. It follows that beauty can vary, because the technique, upon which the utilization of material depends, is progressive.' He goes on to develop a type of product criticism that is unique and instructive:

> As might be expected, Bugatti was proud of his eyes. He loved engines that had straight sides and polished surfaces behind which manifolds and accessories lay hidden.... At the risk of making the reader jump six feet in the air, I consider many American engines, surrounded as they are by forests of wire and bits and pieces, and designed without thought for line, to be nearer to beauty than the elegant Bugatti engines. An engine in which the manifolds are hidden in the cylinder-head, the wiring concealed under the covers, and the accessories lurk under the crankcase – all for

the sake of 'beauty' – is less good-looking than the motor where the manifolds are clearly seen.

This deliberate rebuttal of neo-academic standards must make us ask by what standards he judges what he sees. A comparison between the Bugatti engine and an American V-8 will serve for study. The Bugatti offers a rectangular silhouette with a neutral, unvaried handicraft surface, compartmented into forms that answer closely the Platonic ideals of the circle and square. (With these words one might also describe, say, a relief by Ben Nicholson, and we should remember that Bugatti had been an art student of the same generation as the pioneers of abstract art.) The Buick V-8 of 1955, on the other hand, presents a great variety of surface materials, none of them handwrought, in complex, curving, three-dimensional forms composed into a block with an irregular and asymmetrical silhouette. No doubt impeccable functional reasons could be found for these differences, but one should also note that both engines show considerable care in their visual presentation.

The Bugatti, riding high between the sides of a narrow bonnet, is meant to be seen (as well as serviced) from the side. The Buick, spreading wide under a low 'alligator hood', has its components grouped on top, not only for easy access but also to make an exciting display. The Bugatti, as Gregoire noted, conceals many components and presents an almost two-dimensional picture to the eye, while the Buick flaunts as many accessories as possible in a rich three-dimensional composition, countering Bugatti's fine art reticence with a wild rhetoric of power. This difference – basically the preference of a topological organization to a geometrical one – might be likened to the difference between a Mondriaan painting and a Jackson Pollock, but this would be no answer to our present problem because it merely substitutes one fine art aesthetic for another.

If we examine the qualities that give the Buick engine its unmistakable and exciting character, we find glitter, a sense

2 *Buick Century de Luxe Riviera Sedan*, 1956.

of bulk, a sense of three-dimensionality, a deliberate exposure of technical means, all building up to signify power and make an immediate impact on whoever sees it. Now these are not the qualities of the fine arts: glitter went out with the gold skies of Gothic painting, Platonic and neo-academic aesthetics belong to the two-dimensional world of the drawing board. But if they are not the qualities of the fine arts, they are conspicuously those of the popular arts.

The words 'popular arts' do not mean the naive or debased arts practised by primitives and peasants, since they inhabit cultures in which such artifacts as Buicks have no part. The popular arts of motorized, mechanized cultures are manifestations like the cinema, picture magazines, science fiction, comic books, radio, television, dance music, sport. The Buick engine, with its glitter, technical bravura, sophistication and lack of reticence admirably fulfils the definition of 'Pop Art' of Leslie Fiedler: 'Contemporary popular culture, which is a function of an industrialized society, is distinguished from other folk art by its refusal to be shabby or second rate in appearance, by a refusal to know its place. Yet the articles of popular culture are made, not to be treasured, but to be thrown away.' This short passage (from an essay on comic books) brings together practically all the cultural facts that are relevant to the Buick.

We have discussed the absurdity of requiring durable aesthetic qualities in expendable products, but we should note that aesthetic qualities are themselves expendable, or liable to *consumo* or wastage of effect, in the words of Dorfles and Paci; and this using up of aesthetic effect in everyday objects is due, precisely, to that daily use. We can see the correctness of this in communications jargon: the 'signal strength' of many aesthetic effects is very low; and

being unable to compete with the 'random noise' aroused in situations of practical use, any low-strength signal (fine arts or otherwise) will be debased, distorted or rendered meaningless where use is the dominant factor. Such situations require an aesthetic effect with high immediate signal strength; it will not matter if the signal strength is liable to taper off suddenly, if the object itself is expendable, since the signal strength can always be kept up if the signal itself is so designed that use acts on it as an *amplifier*, rather than as random noise.

In other words, if one opens the Bugatti hood and finds that motor covered with oil, one's aesthetic displeasure at seeing a work of fine art disfigured would be deepened by the difficulty of repair work when the ailing component proves to be hidden away inside the block 'for the sake of beauty'. In similar circumstances, the Buick would probably be far less disfigured by an oil leak, and its display of components makes for much easier repairs, so that visual gratification is reinforced by the quality of the motor as an object of use.

More than this, the close link between the technical and aesthetic qualities of the Buick ensures that both sets of qualities have the same useful life, and that when the product is technically outmoded it will be so aesthetically. It will not linger on, as does the Bugatti, making forlorn claims to be a perennial monument of abstract art. This, in fact, is the solution to Le Corbusier's dilemma about the imminent death of the 'body that now causes excitement'. If these products have been designed specifically for transitory beauty according to an expendable aesthetic, then they will fall not into ridicule, but into a calculated oblivion where they can no longer embarrass their designers. It is the Bugatti that becomes ridiculous as an object of use, by making aesthetic claims that persist long after its functional utility is exhausted.

We may now advance as a working hypothesis for a design philosophy this proposition: 'The aesthetics of consumer goods are those of the popular arts'. But this still leaves us with the problem of how such an hypothesis may be put into a working methodology.

Unlike criticism of fine arts, the criticism of popular arts depends on an analysis of content, an appreciation of superficial rather than abstract qualities, and an outward orientation that sees the history of the product as an interaction between the sources of the symbols and the consumer's understanding of them. To quote Bruno Alfieri about the 1947 Studebaker, 'The power of the motor seems to correspond to an aerial hood, an irresistible sensation of speed'. He sees a symbolic link between the power of the motor and the appearance of its housing, and this is made explicit by the use of an iconography based on the forms of jet aircraft. Thus we are dealing with a *content* (idea of power), a *source* of symbols (aircraft), and a *popular culture* (whose members recognize these symbols and their meaning). The connecting element between them is the industrial designer, with his ability to deploy the elements of his iconography – his command and understanding of popular symbolism.

The function of these symbol systems is always to link the product to something that is popularly recognized as good, desirable or exciting – they link the dreams that money can buy to the ultimate dreams of popular culture. In this they are not, as many European critics suppose, specific to America. They can be found in any progressive industrialized society. An example in Italian design is the Alfa Giulietta whose diminutive tail fins might be defended in terms of body fabrication, the need to carry the tail-lights, or the abstract composition of the side elevation. But how much more effective they are in evoking the world of sports-cars and aerodynamic research that is one of the ultimate dreams of automobilism. Not all iconographies are so specific; such concepts as the good life in the open air, the pleasures of sex, and conspicuous consumption are other sources of symbols, and it is clear that the more specific any symbol is, the more discretion must be used in its application.

These trends, which become more pronounced as a culture becomes more mechanized and the mass-market is taken over by middle-class employees of increasing education, indicate the function of the product critic in the field of design as popular art: Not to disdain what sells but to help answer the now important question, 'What *will* sell?' Both designer and critic, by their command of market statistics and their imaginative skill in using them to predict, introduce an element of control that feeds back information into industry. Their interest in the field of design-as-popular-symbolism is in the pattern of the market as the crystallization of popular dreams and desire – the pattern as it is about to occur. Both designer and critic must be in close touch with the dynamics of mass-communication. The critic, especially, must have the ability to sell the public to the manufacturer, the courage to speak out in the face of academic hostility, the knowledge to decide where, when and to what extent the standards of the popular arts are preferable to those of the fine arts. He must project the future dreams and desires of people as one who speaks from within their ranks. It is only thus that he can participate in the extraordinary adventure of mass-production, which counters the old aristocratic and defeatist 19th-century slogan, 'Few, but roses', and its implied corollary, 'Multitudes are weeds', with a new slogan that cuts across all academic categories: 'Many, because orchids.'

2.3 WHO IS THIS 'POP'?

Banham explores, in this article, originally published in Motif 10, *1963, some of the main areas of Pop culture, pointing out the importance of the mass media. He isolates transport styling, sci-fi, film stars, comics and consumer gadgets – all of them categories which he goes on to describe in greater depth in his magazine articles.*

What right has he to call himself by a name that is now sacred, accepted in those stratospheric realms of art where prizes are awarded, gallery reputations made. A scrutiny of his vocabulary may give us some insight into this 'Pop'. *Vidiots*, for a start, is hardly an endearing term by which to address one's offspring...

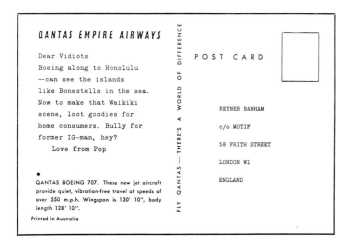

Pop's vocabulary

Vidiots: formerly a term of pejoration, now purely descriptive – one trained in the use of the mass media, originally TV (*Video* in US usage). The word 'trained' is vital to the present meaning of *Vidiot*. At first it meant 'trained' in the Pavlovian sense of 'equipped with reliably conditioned reflexes' – people who developed uncontrollable leg-actions whenever a commercial said '... don't walk, *Run*, NOW to your dealer for a giant family sized pack.' Then followed a subtle change of meaning to pick up the sense of 'one so conditioned to the medium that she can eat, knit, smoke, talk and read a book, all at the same time as watching the screen'. From this only a further shift of emphasis was required to make 'trained' carry the sense of 'one skilled in the use of the medium' and thus, by extension to anyone trained to extract every subtlety, marginal meaning, overtone or technical nicety from any of the mass media. A Pop Art connoisseur, as opposed to a fine art connoisseur. The opposition, however, is only one of taste, otherwise the training required to become a connoisseur is the same. Thus the Fine Art connoisseur starts by acquiring a Pavlovian conditioning that causes him to run, not walk, to the Tate Gallery every time he reads the art column in *The Observer*; later he becomes so thoroughly at home with the medium that he can flirt, drink sherry and make smarty-pants conversation while looking at the pictures; and finally he acquires sufficient skill to distinguish between abstract and representational art, and begins to get something out of what he is looking at. Neither the Pop Art fancier nor the fine art connoisseur will be able to get anything much out of Royal College Pop Art painting however: both will be convinced that they are being taken for a ride.

Pop's transports of delight

Boeing: one of the things that have changed since we first began the systematic study of Pop Art is the status of transports of delight. Even fairly square bodies of opinion, such as the Council of Industrial Design, have now caught up with the idea that car-styling makes some kind of reference to the forms of jet aircraft. This was certainly true once – Pop needs must love the highest when it sees it, and the 'highest' in Pop means the summit in any related field. Thus, in the early fifties, cars, as a form of transport, took their style from the summit of transportation, which in those days was jet flying. (As symbols of sex, power and wealth, of course, cars looked to other summits – that is why the Rolls Royce has a radiator shaped like the portico of the Royal Exchange.) But styling deals – as all Pop Art deals – with dreams that money can *just* buy (it is axiomatic that any Pop product looks as if it come out of one drawer higher than its price would suggest) while the summits are, by definition, dreams that money just *can't* buy – Bunny Girls, membership of the Clan, lunch at the Palace – and now that a broad section of consumers can expect to fly jet to next year's holiday, if not this one, jet travel is purchasable and no longer a summit – car-styling has visibly gone off the jet kick. Supersonic flight remains, but has no definitive and instantly recognizable forms for the stylists to ape; space travel has such forms, but try to imagine a car in the shape of a Mercury capsule. In any case, car-styling is a dead Pop Art at present; the Minis and the compacts buried an epoch, and cars ceased to be Number One status symbol. Only a few types of transportation gather any stardust now – big hairy motorbikes; small boats with two very large outboard motors on them; private or chartered aircraft, preferably with French jet engines.

Pop's imagery of space-flight

Bonestell: only rarely can the creators of basic Pop imagery be identified, but Chesley Bonestell is certainly one of those who have issued fundamental coinage for the stylists and entertainers to trade with. In collaboration with space-brains like Willy Ley and Werner von Braun, and information sources like the Hayden Planetarium, he has created the bulk of the accessible imagery of space-flight, from our common image of moonscape, to the un-streamlined, orbitally-built spaceship. Most of this was in *Life, Colliers*, etc, but there were also two notable films, *Destination Moon* and *Conquest of Space*, on which he advised. Period pieces by the high-discard standards of Pop Art today, yet the archetypal visions survive everywhere you look. But electronic 'space-music', which is the aural equivalent of Bonestell, seems to have no single inventor. Rather, it seems to have sprung, like a number of Pop Art phenomena, from the sudden collison of a keen, far-out taste and the technical means to satisfy it. Space-music did not audibly exist before *The Forbidden Planet*, when it emerged fully-blown as a new sound to dig.

Pop never has to go and get

Make the scene: something wrong here – the whole point about the product culture of which Pop Art is part, is that you don't have to go and get anything, it comes to you, processed and pre-packed, reliable and standardized. So you don't go to Honolulu, Rome, Tahiti, because you can't make these scenes as you make the coffee-bar or Palais scenes. The reasons are curious, but obvious, if you stop to think. In

The Forbidden Planet, 1956.

the real, these exotic places have alien cultures (even Rome is profoundly alien to most Anglo-Saxon consumers) and they have dead or embarrassing patches between the accepted high spots – slums, factories, beggars, humdrum people in humdrum houses. So the only scenes that can be made are either completely artificial ones (Butlin's, but also Miami) or small enough to keep under control (Cheddar Gorge, but also Capri) or both (Venice). The other places, as they function in Pop Art, are abstractions, visual images made by condensing the whole into a few select views. Thus, Rome is the Spanish Steps, Trevi, the colonnade of St. Peter's, Moravia interviewing Claudia Cardinale in his penthouse, three cafés on the Corso and Anita Eckberg; portable and transmissible images that are truer than the facts. To make the scene and observe the facts firsthand is to transgress against the Consumptuary Laws, and those who do so must accept their responsibilities and package their memories carefully before they say a word about their trip, back home in Scranton, Penge or Duisburg-Ruhrort.

Pop's goodies tricky for squares

Goodies: most vital new concept in Pop since *gimmick,* and still very tricky for squares to handle; not yet capable of definition, it must be described circumferentially. When Yogi Bear scents 'goodies' in someone's picnic spread he identifies fancy food, a relish his diet does not normally afford.

When a teacher at a mid-Western university asks 'What goodies did you bring back from Chicago?' he means wit, funnies, frivols, like genuine Brand-X cigarettes, Japanese wrestling magazines, foreign paperbacks from Krogh and Brentano's – in sum, things the drug store doesn't stock. But when a hot-rodder advertises, say, 'a real cherry Dodge '56 V-8 stroker with Jahns, Iskenderian speed goodies', he means nothing inessential or functionless. He is talking about special camshafts, pistons, pipe-work and other etceteras all meant to make that rod really go. But these are all optional extras that you don't get FOB Detroit when you buy the heap in the first place. Like, all goodies are *extra,* clip-on improvements that make the eyes pop by promising a better diet, life, car. But there is also a sense in which goodies must come in a fairly compact package – the pistons, cams and pipes are a 'speed kit' for instance, Yogi's bonanza of tasty snacks is normally found all together in a picnic basket or on a table, the Chicago loot will be found crammed into the academic brief-case – and there is good reason to suspect that the original goodies were the plastic give-aways in cereal packets. Peter Blake's Pop Art paintings are a mass of goodies, usually, so are most of the New American Dreamer paintings and objects, such as Oldenburg's *Cakes,* described by Sidney Tillim as among 'the booty' recently acquired by the Museum of Modern Art – goodies for egg-heads.

Pop can take it and throw it away

Consumer: Pop culture is about things to use and throw away. Only an economist could conceive such a flat contradiction in terms as 'consumer durables' – there is no Pop architecture to speak of, and never will be in any ultimate sense, because buildings are too damn permanent. The aesthetics of Pop depend on a massive initial impact and small sustaining power, and are therefore at their poppiest in products whose sole object is to be consumed, that *must* be consumed, whether physically, like soft serve ices, or symbolically, like daily papers that can only last twenty-four hours by definition. In fact, physical and symbolic consumability are equal in Pop culture, equal in status and meaning – something that Nabokov dimly perceived in that celebrated passage from *Lolita*.

> In the gay town of Lepingville I bought her four books of comics, a box of candy, a box of sanitary pads, two cokes, a manicure set ... a portable radio, chewing gum, a transparent rain-coat, sun-glasses, some more garments....

All this pile of goodies are consumable, and on this scale of values books and disposable sanitary towels are equally periodical. It is this that really galls fine art people about the Pop Arts; printed words are the sacred tablets of their culture; they build libraries, universities and literary supplements to maintain their permanency, while Pop consumers treat them like coke and chewing gum. The addition of the word *expendable* to the vocabulary of criticism was essential before Pop Art could be faced honestly, since this is the first quality of an object to be consumed. Unfortunately, expendability is also one of the qualities of everything made by man – not even the Pyramids are proof against wear – and once the principle had been enunciated it looked like yet another way in which Pop Art was taking the mickey out of the fine arts. Sure enough, the boys were soon to be heard talking about 'fine art consumers', which brings us to ...

Pop's fine art egg-heads

IG: the boys in question were the Independent Group at the ICA, whose activities around 1953–5 are at the bottom of all conscious Pop Art activities in fine art circles. The basic vocabulary, including the words Pop Art themselves (analogy with Pop music), came into circulation via the IG, even if they weren't invented by them; so did the systematic study of the iconography of car-styling, science fiction, Westerns, the rock-'n'-roll industry, advertising. It has been a source of the greatest grim humour to IG veterans like the present author to watch those who were quick to damn the IG as frivolous, conformist, etc., and its manifestations as 'sophisticated meddling with unsophisticated tastes', to watch all these Basil Taylors and John Bergers and Francis Newtons, trying to catch up, taking over our vocabulary and trying not to adopt our attitude. There is one very good reason why the IG was with it so long before anyone else, something that was clearly never understood by Basil Taylor, who actually produced that bit about 'sophisticated meddling'. The key figures of the IG – Lawrence Alloway, John McHale, Eduardo Paolozzi, Richard Hamilton, Frank Cordell, even myself – were all brought up in the Pop belt somewhere. American films and magazines were the only live culture we knew as kids – I have a crystal clear memory of myself, aged sixteen, reading a copy of *Fantastic Stories* while waiting to go on in the school play, which was Fielding's *Tom Thumb the Great*, and deriving equal relish from the recherché literature I should shortly be performing, and the equally far out pulp in my hand. We returned to Pop in the early fifties like Behans going to Dublin or Thomases to Llaregub, back to our native literature, our native arts.

Is 'Pop' really with it, then? He is too much with it! Far from being a normal consumer of expendable goods he knows about origins and sources; worse, he was a member of the dreaded Independent Group. He is of one of those who have helped to create the mental climate in which the Pop Art painters have been able to flourish in England (there is a direct line from the Independent Group to Peter Blake and the Royal College) and the New American Dreamers in the USA. Like them, he knows too much to believe that there is anything such as an 'unsophisticated consumer', knows that all consumers are experts, have back-stage knowledge of something or other, be it the record charts or the correct valve timing for doing the ton, and that all experts are consumers at some time, if only of English detective novels, the most completely standardized, pre-digested, pre-packed and universally available product on the market. Like all Pop Art consumers he is *knowing*, Pop Art is sophistication for all. *Vidiot* is no term for abuse.

2.4 DESIGN BY CHOICE

The main emphasis of this article, originally published in Architectural Review, *July 1961, is upon the crisis that Banham sees happening in design values. He describes the way that, in the present admass society, styling and the psychological significance of objects have superseded function as a criterion of acceptability. He examines a cross-section of consumer objects which display the values – the Olivetti typewriter, the VW car, the Japanese camera, the Braun radio, etc. – many of which receive closer attention in other articles written around this time.*

The last extensive surveys of industrial design by *Architectural Review* were published ten years ago around the time of the Festival of Britain, including an essay enquiring into the progress of the newly-formed Council of Industrial Design by Nikolaus Pevsner, and a critique of the designs selected for the Festival, both in December 1951. Any reader looking back at these articles today will be struck by the apparent calm and certainty with which judgment was passed on individual products, a situation bespeaking settled and widely-held standards such as conspicuously do not exist today, when different sections of 'informed opinion' (who were allies and firm friends ten years ago) not only differ in their judgments on individual products, but differ even more fundamentally on methods of criticism. The article which follows examines the position of the architect in these changed circumstances accompanied by a marginal chronicle of the new men and new concepts that have emerged in the decade just past, the coincidence of the IUA Congress with the tenth anniversary of the Festival providing a compelling occasion for their review.

It is said that Industrial Design has altered out of recognition in the last ten years. Alternatively, it is said that only fashions have changed, and that Industrial Design is what it always was. It would be as well, therefore, to start by setting out what is unchanged, and what has been transformed. Firstly, the *subject matter* of Industrial Design has not changed; it is still concerned with (*a*) quality (materials and workmanship); (*b*) performance (functional and human) and (*c*) style (of appearance and use). Secondly, the *problem* of Industrial Design has not changed; it is still a problem of affluent democracy, where the purchasing power of the masses is in conflict with the preferences of the élite. In a subsistence economy there is no problem (though progressive Indians are just beginning to be aware of it) and in a controlled society there is no problem – a couple of jovial interruptions, larded with Ukrainian proverbs, at the relevant annual congress will put things right.

But, in the affluent democracies where the problem exists, the whole manner of squaring up to the subject matter of Industrial Design has changed, because the foundation stone of the previous intellectual structure of Design Theory has crumbled – there is no longer universal acceptance of architecture as the universal analogy of design. When the Modern Movement was young, there were obvious and valid reasons for giving architects hegemony over the training of designers and the formulation of theory: architects alone of arts men had any technical training even remotely applicable to product design; alone of tech-men they had a sufficiently liberal education to be able. to relate their designs to the general environment of human life; they alone had been doing anything consciously to further the practice and theory of Industrial Design.

Almost everything of interest written, said or done in this field between 1900 and 1930 is the work of an architect or someone closely connected with architecture – Voysey, Lethaby, Muthesius, Gropius, Wright, Le Corbusier, Moholy-Nagy, all heirs of the polymath attitude of the Morris/Webb circle of the previous century. In the next twenty years to 1950 the architectural claim was accepted by writers like Edgar Kaufmann and Herbert Read as the natural basis for argument – the latter announcing in his *Art and Industry* of 1934 'I have no other desire in this book than to support and propagate the ideals ... expressed by Doctor Gropius.' The only novelty of even apparent consequence in this line of thought did not appear until 1954, when G. C. Argon, at that year's Triennale Congress proposed that urbanism, rather than architecture, should be at the head of the design hierarchy.

But even at that date, alternative estimates of the nature and principles of Industrial Design had begun to appear. Paradoxically, while most of these favoured the kind of design associated with the architectural dispensation – spare, neat, unadorned, etc. – they defended it by arguments that could equally well have been used to favour completely different styles of design. The classic instance is Hayakawa's essay, memorably entitled 'Your Car Reveals your Sex Fears', which assailed Detroit styling by means of semantic and iconographic arguments that could equally well have been used to demonstrate, say, how the London taxi, acclaimed by Charles Eames as the best industrial design in the world, reveals the communal death-wish of the English ruling classes.

Eames must be saluted at this point as the last figure from the architectural side to make a significant contribution – with his *Ahmedabad Report* – to design thinking. Otherwise, architects have relinquished control of the mind of design to theorists and critics from practically any other field under the sun. The new men in the USA, for instance, are typically, liberal sociologists like David Reisman or Eric Larrabee; in Germany, the new men at Ulm are mathematicians, like Horst Rittel, or experimental psychologists like Mervyn Perrine; in Britain they tend to come from an industrial background, like Peter Sharp, John Chris Jones or Bruce Archer, or from the Pop Art polemics at the ICA like Richard Hamilton. In most Western Countries, the appearance of consumer-defence organizations has added yet another voice, another viewpoint, though no very positive philosophy.

In these circumstances, where no single viewpoint is sufficiently widely held to make effective communication possible, arguments tend to be conducted in an eclectic framework of postulates gathered from a variety of disciplines; the basis of selection may be unscrupulously slanted to justify some point of view to which the speaker is committed (this is true of most arguments on aesthetics or styling) or, more honestly, to give directions through a field that needs to be explored – hence the preoccupation with information theory at Ulm, where it is felt that many pieces of equipment are insufficiently explicit about their functions and mode of use. Lash-up formulations of this sort are, of course, only ad hoc intellectual structures and should be neatly put away when they have done the job for which they were assembled. Thus, a narrowly Stalinist frame of reference, rigidly maintained beyond its last point of utility, has resulted in the sterility and subsequent disappearance of radical left-wing design criticism in Western democracies, and leaves intelligent socialists, like Richard Hoggart, apparently sharing the opinions of an 'Establishment' that they otherwise despise.

For those who are not too rigid, however, the situation is, as the saying goes, manipulative – it is possible to discuss anything, even the validity of the architectural claim. Not on the basis of right or wrong – Industrial Design can use a short rest from exclusive moralities – but on the basis of what contribution architects could reasonably be expected to make, and the needs they might reasonably hope to see satisfied.

Looking back, one sees that in truth large parts of the architectural claim have never been seriously pressed – aircraft design, for instance, has cheerfully been left to aerodynamicists, architects retaining only the right to criticize the results. There are other areas where architects have persistently intervened – pleasure boats are an example – without contributing anything very interesting to their design; clearly, architects have extra-curricular activities where they put their professional skills on one side. But, where, then, is the architect's real area of painful or profitable involvement with industrial design? It is easiest to define convincingly by considering questions of scale and propinquity – how big things are, and how near to buildings. A survey of architectural communications such as conversations, letters to editors, and other daily small-talk will show that architects are hypersensitive to the design of objects roughly comparable in scale to building components. Some of this sensitivity is simply an atavistic relic from the days when the architectural claim was universal in its coverage, but if it is trimmed down to include only objects in or near buildings, then it makes operational sense. Architects are clearly right to be concerned over the design of things like automobiles, lamp-posts, refrigerators and crockery, since these are classes of objects that commonly inhabit the same view, occupy the same space, supplement the functions of their buildings and no one in his right mind will deny their right to be heard on such subjects.

To say this is not to revive inflationary or imperialistic claims that architects are 'total designers' or 'responsible for the whole human environment,' but simply to say that even if the practice of architecture is viewed in quite a narrow and conventional professional sense, there is a wide variety of equipment which is not structurally part of their buildings nor mentioned in the specification, but is, nevertheless, their concern and ought to be much more their concern than it is at present. Even if we no longer regard the architect as the universal analogy for the designer, a large area of the architectural claim is rightly his. But if this is an area where he has rights, then he also has responsibilities. If he is to be heard, then his utterance must carry weight – howls of 'I won't have that ugly trash in my building' will no longer serve, reasons must be given, improvements suggested.

But how? If architects have lost their original dominance over the field – a dominance always more de jure than de facto – what is their standing now? It is precisely at the level of objects comparable in scale to building components that the average architect's capacity as a designer begins to taper off, and this diminished capacity is due far less to technical ignorance of, say, electronics or gas technology, than to the training, experience and habits of mind that fit a man to be an architect. This combination of intellectual factors tends to make an architect not only unfit to design free-standing appliances, but even the interiors of his own buildings – as *Architectural Review* pointed out in justification of its 'Interior Design' features in April 1958.

As was also pointed out then, the fundamental difficulty is incompatible rates of obsolescence; architects, for entirely valid reasons, are habituated to think in terms of a time-scale whose basic unit is about half a century. Industrial design works on a variety of time-scales, roughly proportional to the bulk of the objects being designed, and none of them phased in units one fifth the size of the architect's. This situation is not the product of an evil economic situation, as professional alarmists like Vance Packard maintain (though there is a constant pressure towards hastened obsolescence in capitalist countries) but exists because industrial designers are creating objects in which the opposing forces of stabilized investment and technical improvement are in a different equilibrium to that governing the design of a building. A building-structure will not be disastrously out of date for some centuries in many cases, and there are lifts at work in London that saw the century in, but are still mechanically sound and have not been rendered noticeably obsolete by sixty years of technical improvement.

But a sixty year old car, even if in perfect mechanical condition, would nowadays cause traffic jams and invite accidents if it were let loose among the nimbler products of more recent decades – as witness the elaborate policing and marshalling required to isolate the carefully maintained veterans on the Brighton Run from real traffic. This is an extreme case of rapid mechanical obsolescence, no doubt (only by an architect's standards, by those of aeronautics or electronics, automotive technology has been sluggish) but it can easily be paralleled inside buildings – consider the history of electric lighting from carbon filament to colour corrected cathode, from the concentrated light source of a bare bulb in an exposed socket, that even Brutalists tolerate only as a gesture, to the even glow from a lumenated ceiling that psychologists and physiologists are already beginning to question for going too far the other way.

The design of light fittings is very much a case in point. On the basis of scale and propinquity, they lie firmly within the architectural area of concern. Over the years, a number of leading Modern architects, from Rietveld to Utzon, have made forays into the field of lighting design, and – the product being mechanically simple – they have been able to produce equipment that was workable as well as handsome. But, reviewing the period covered by this development, one cannot help feeling that an excess of aesthetic and emotional capital has been squandered on ephemera. There is hardly any important Modern Movement interior that is still lit as the architect originally designed it – not only the equipment but the whole installation has been rendered obsolete by later events.

In other fields, where their technical inadequacies are more obtrusive, architects can only do what they affect to despise in other designers – style up the outside of machinery that has been designed by somebody else. The polite name for this, of course, is 'built-in equipment' in which everything the architect is incapable of designing is bundled into cupboards that he *can* design. But this solution, too, is subject to the effects of technical obsolescence, as cookers, radios, and so forth, change their bulk, performance, power needs and relationship to the surrounding space, and entirely new equipment such as TV enters the domestic scene. Built-in equipment is little more than an attempt to impose a veneer of totalitarian order in a situation where something like democratic give and take may have been more to the point.

This, again, is not to ask the architect to abandon responsibility for the equipment in the buildings he is called upon to design, for it is possible to abandon the position of autocratic dominance implicit in Bauhaus theory without losing control of the over-all design. Very small powers of

1 *Eames Chair and Ottoman*, designer Charles Eames, 1956.

2 *Braun Model SK2 Radio*, designers Artur Braun and Fritz Eichler, c. 1955.

accommodation enable an architect to do what Le Corbusier anticipated as long ago as 1925, that is, to exercise creative choice. His Pavillon de l'Esprit Nouveau was entirely furnished and equipped from manufacturers' catalogues, without the architect himself having to design a thing.[1] Although the convincing unity of the total effect was doubtless helped by the fact that the rooms themselves had been designed in what he conceived to be the style of the objects that were to furnish them (and in this there is a lesson to be pondered), the whole operation was a triumph of disciplined and adventurous selection from what was at hand.

This, in practice, is how most architects and interior designers work anyhow. In the 1960s an architect knows he will be able to equip his interiors with Eames chairs, Noguchi lamps, Braun radios, Saarinen tables and so forth from stock, and the knowledge of their availability probably

3 *Bertoia Chair*, designer Harry Bertoia, c. 1952.

colours his designing, unconsciously, from the very beginning. Coloured, but not inhibited – the catalogues also offer him Bertoia chairs, Jacobsen chairs, Robin Day chairs; Utzon lamps, Rotaflex lamps, Atlas lamps. . . . The range of choice is so broad that the equipment of the building by objects that were not designed by the architect may not diminish the value of the finished work by one material or aesthetic particular. Indeed, the prestige inherent in knowing that the chairs are by one of the world's greatest industrial designers and the radios by another adds a peculiar lustre to the whole operation.

However, the very breadth of choice increases the architect's responsibility – he must resist the temptation to hand over the interior to Jacobsen, Noguchi, Bertoia and Co. His choice must be disciplined by a clear idea of what the building has to do, and if there is nothing just right in the catalogues at hand, then he must go to other catalogues, his choice must be adventurous – *none* of the furniture in the Pavillon de l'Esprit Nouveau came from the catalogues of 'domestic' furniture manufacturers, it was all office and factory equipment.

Here, indeed, is one of the points where the architectural profession has a job to do in industrial design. By way of contract furnishing, architects are among the most articulate and most powerful sections of consumers, in some fields the most powerful absolutely. They have power economically in the market, they also have experience that far outstrips that of any domestic consumer who perhaps buys a dozen chairs in a lifetime, they are trained to study functional problems and human requirements. Simply by the exercise of their market influence, architects may find that they are in a position to kill a poor design, encourage a good one, and embolden a manufacturer to tool up for a new product. Further, by their experience and training they should be in a position to advise and assist manufacturers and designers to produce better goods, even where mechanical complexity puts them (as in the case of communications, ventilating systems, etc.) right outside their technical competence as architects.

This proposition may not be news, but it is worth saying again because it still needs to be acted upon; it is a field where positive action can be taken. However, there will be large fields of activity where the architect's careful design will be filled with equipment not chosen by an architect or a sympathetic interior designer, but by an ordinary domestic occupier. Here is a classic instance of a conflict between mass taste and the preferences of an elite – or, in the form of words used to describe the situation when the Unité at Marseilles was ready for occupation, 'What will happen when the bourgeoisie move in with their inherited prejudices and imitation Louis Quinze wardrobes?' Le Corbusier's solution, to build in so much built-in furniture that there was no room for wardrobes and barely room to voice a prejudice, was, in fact, the result of unforeseeable circumstances,[2] and not even he would normally advocate so undemocratic a procedure.

For the architect simply to 'retire hurt' when faced with this situation, is no solution, and the idea of designing 'background architecture' of studied neutrality is an unconvincing attempt to make a thin virtue from a pressing necessity – there is no way of disposing a door and a window in a rectangular space without setting up a relationship that can be wrecked by an ill-placed TV set. The need is some sort of reasonably permissive architecture with built-in directions about where to put things. The so-called Appliance-House solution to this problem has tended, so far, either to take too much for granted, or to make heavy weather of the directions. Either it assumes too readily a community of taste between architect and occupier (Kikutake's Sky House is occupied by Kikutake himself, so the problem disappears, but what happens when someone else moves in?) or else – as in most of the Smithson projects in this genre – the whole house tends to degenerate into a series of display niches for ever-changing relays of hire-purchased status symbols.

But there is no need for such elaborate controls, nor for hidden persuaders hopefully contrived out of plays of colour and lighting – though these have never yet proven sufficiently reliable to direct a Louis Quinze wardrobe or seven cubic foot refrigerator to the point where the architect hopes to find it. On the contrary, the traditional location of a fifteen-amp plug next to the traditional British fireplace has done much to keep the TV set within the traditional area of focused attention in the traditional British sitting-room. With this approach, the architect no longer attempts to impersonate all the characters in the drama of design, as in the days of the universal analogy, but becomes the producer of the play, handling a mixed cast of metropolitan professionals and local talent.

This is a workable situation, provided the producer knows his players well enough to gauge the effect of ad-libbing and playing off the cuff – what happens in the architectural dialogue between dressing-table and light source, how far the eternal triangle of the three-piece suite can be expected to share the stage with a picture window opposite the fireplace. To handle these problems effectively – so effectively that he need not regret that the objects involved are not designed as he would have designed them – an architect needs to know just how, and how strongly, some desirable and visually fascinating piece of equipment like a tape recorder or a coffee-percolator focuses attention and thence organizes the visual and functional space around it. This must be known and thoroughly understood, if only at the intuitive level of knowing instinctively that a poster will always have a more galvanic effect than an abstract painting, that the real landmark in the length of the Grande Galérie of the Louvre is not the Mona Lisa but the view out of the window into the traffic of the Place du Carrousel.

It might appear, on the strength of a broad survey of present purely technical trends in design, that this problem is about to disappear. A really desirable and sophisticated (in the engineer's sense of the term) central heating system deals with the problem of the well-designed radiator by abolishing radiators and disappearing into the floor-slab or under the carpet. A man who looked at a TV set of 'Britain Can Make It' vintage saw a lot of cabinet work as well as a small screen, but a head-on view of a modern twenty-one incher is apt to consist simply of the screen itself. Nothing has shrunk faster than stereophonic gramophones, except sound radio, where transistors have produced such rapid miniaturization that there is a sort of regretful vacuum round the source of sound. And just when architects were despairing of ever making much visual and spatial sense of domestic exteriors lumbered with *two* status-boasting, jet-styled Detroitniks, suddenly there were compacts and Mini-Minors.

Miniaturization appears to be a consistent tendency at present, that must be agreed, but the chances are that the objects concerned will become more concentratedly desirable as they become smaller, or more functionally important as the systems they control vanish from sight. When the heat-source is invisible, its controls must be more visible than in the days when the tap accompanied a large, conspicuous radiator; when the radio becomes no bigger than an ashtray, then there is clearly a chance that it will become the equivalent of art-pottery – on a table in the office of the US Ambassador to London there was recently a transistor radio in an elaborately hand-chased brass box, like an eighteenth-century clock mechanism.

The chances are, then, that the miniaturized product is going to demand attention with a hard, gem-like insistence, and focus attention as surely as the red button on which our atomic fate depends. And if it works by batteries, it may not be possible to fix its place on the domestic scene by a crafty location of power outlets. But the world of the miniaturized product is also the world of the visually sophisticated consumer, who may be susceptible to other forms of persuasion, may even, before long, be in a mental condition to seek architectural advice.

To sum up, the passing of the architect's claim to be the absolute master of the visual environment has not greatly reduced the area of his real responsibility at both the visual and functional levels. In fact, his responsibilities have increased – the stakes mark out a smaller claim, but he now has to dig all of it. The manner of implementing these responsibilities is not simply to assume control of the schools and expect everyone to accept architectural standards as the norm of judgment, as the theorists of the thirties supposed, but to exercise choice and background control over the choice of others, to advise, suggest and demand on the basis of knowledge and understanding. Conceivably there may be less glory involved than in being able to sign one's name to everything as 'designer' but there may be more useful work done and better service rendered to the public. If that is so, then ten years of uncertainty and dispute will not have been in vain.

An Alphabetical Chronicle of Landmarks and Influences, 1951–1961

Alarmist Literature

In the 1950s the shortcomings of some aspects of product design became a subject for sensational journalism which – in some cases – contained an element of serious warning. The most prolific of these professional Jeremiahs was the American writer, Vance Packard, whose book *The Hidden Persuaders* drew attention to the social consequences of motivation research (q.v.). His subsequent works *The Status Seekers* and *The Waste Makers* continued variations of the same theme of social enquiry into design, but began to suggest that he had fallen victim to the very situation against which he was protesting: his elevation to the best-seller class involved him in the dynamics of the mass market and more or less committed him to bring out a 'new model' every other year. At a less sensational level, warnings to consumers were transmitted in Great Britain by way of the editorials in *Which?* and *Shoppers' Guide*.

Appliance

The increasing mechanization of households in the Western world, and the beginning of mechanization of households in other continents, gave a special status to electrical and other power-operated tools in the eyes of manufacturers, designers and consumers. The rise of 'do-it-yourself' acquainted many householders with small power tools for the first time, but also introduced a degree of mechanization into the creative work of painters, sculptors and designers, thus giving them an increased first-hand knowledge and sympathy for the world of appliance design – the whole output of Charles Eames (q.v.) can be related in one way or another to the mechanization of the designers' workshop, but appliances also claimed a widely recognized function as indicators of the social status of their owners. The diversification of different types of refrigerators and washing-machines, not to mention the almost annual increase in the screen size of television sets, became a recognized method of indicating or claiming improved social and financial status, and was duly damned by puritanical critics and sociologists. At the same time, however, certain less grandiose appliances became the accepted symbols of intellectual status – the possession of an Olivetti typewriter (q.v.) or a Braun gramophone or radio became one of the standard ploys in the world of intellectual snobbery.

Aspen Congress

One of the major international centres of discussion of industrial design was established at the mountain resort of Aspen, Colorado, which had been built up by the late Walter Paepke, President of Container Corporation of America, as a species of secular retreat for meditation and discussion among business executives. The Annual Design Congress there, of which there have been now twelve, confronted the leading opinion-makers of the American business world with designers, manufacturers, critics and theorists from Europe, South America and Japan. While the findings of these congresses don't constitute a body of literature comparable with that of CIAM, the reports made annually by speakers returning to their native countries and customary business, have provided a running survey of the preoccupations and troubles of thinking designers all over the world. Aspen has, to some extent, replaced the Triennale (q.v.) as a world centre of opinion and debate.

Brand Image (or House Style)

During the 1950s it became the practice in all large industrial concerns to inculcate into the minds of the public a recognizable style to identify their products or services. In many cases this was a process of necessary rationalization where a large firm found itself with a number of different styles and a number of different designers. Where unification of style was undertaken as a form of rationalization and in good taste, this process was known as 'creating a house style,' but where it was undertaken as part of an advertising campaign it was called 'fixing the brand image.' Examples of both processes can be seen in the stabilization of the design of filling-stations and filling-station equipment by such companies as Shell/BP or Esso, both of whom developed international styles in the period; in the restyling programmes undertaken by brewery companies like Courage in the earlier 1950s, and Watney towards the end of the decade; and in the restyling of chain stores.

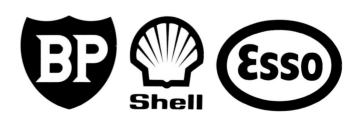

4 *BP, Shell and Esso brand images.*

5 *Citroen DS 19 Saloon*, 1960.

British Railways

Though it is the largest industrial concern in Britain, and probably in Europe, British Railways did not set the universally high standards of design that were hoped for at the time of nationalization. Nevertheless, valiant efforts were made, in spite of the progressive dismemberment of British Railways into independent regions, and as nationalized concerns go, it has probably done as much as any, except the Post Office, to promote a lively attitude to design. The change-over to diesel traction has had industrial designers built into the contract as consultants almost from the beginning, and although there have been technical difficulties, the influence of Design Research Unit and of Jack Howe has been noticeably beneficial. Other British Railways adventures in design include experimental carriage interiors designed by various architects; the setting up of a Design Advisory Panel in an attempt to improve the style of station equipment; and the activities of Eastern Region's development group in improved ticket-office design; and in commissioning waiting-room furniture by Robin Day which should become standard for all regions.

Citroën

Like the Volkswagon (q.v.) the Citroën was one of the two fixed points in a world of rapidly changing car design – until 1957 when the familiar Tractionavant of 1934 vintage was dramatically replaced by the DS 19. Although few found it possible to admire the DS's apparent mixture of different automotive styles, brand-loyalty coupled with something like awe at its technical specification served to establish the DS, almost at once, in the same position of esteem as was enjoyed by the preceding model, and by the end of the decade its radical appearance no longer excited the same alarm as before.

Consumer Research

The formal recognition of a specific consumer viewpoint in relation to industrial design is one of the more important new factors that has emerged in the 1950s. Viewed broadly, it covers market research into consumer preferences and human engineering or ergonomics (q.v.) as well as what is more specifically regarded as the defence of consumers' interests. Organizations for this latter purpose have emerged both at an official and unofficial level; thus most of the nationalized industries have some form of Consumers' Consultative Committee built into their administrative structure, and the British Standards Institute sponsors a Consumers' Advisory Council which publishes a periodical – *Shoppers' Guide*. However, there are also Consumer organizations whose attitude embodies an element of social protest, viz.: The Consumers' Councils in the USA and the Consumers' Association in England, which publishes a periodical called *Which?*, and whose leading figure, Michael Young, has even proposed the formation of a Consumers political party (see his pamphlet *The Chipped White Cups of Dover*).

Design Centre

The foundation of the Design Centre in the Haymarket, London, gave the Council of Industrial Design an opportunity to give tangible form to its views on design by placing on show a constantly changing selection of products, chosen by Committees appointed by the Council. Although the selections have constantly been a subject of dispute throughout the subsequent five years of the Centre's existence, they have undoubtedly performed an important function, if only in putting before the public alternatives to the normal commercial selections undertaken by buyers for even the most progressive shops. It was only towards the end of this five-year period that doubts began to be expressed that the Centre might be driving the Council of Industrial Design into something like a commercial position itself, when it was observed that the rents recovered from exhibitors at the Centre amounted to a sizeable proportion of the Council's income.

Detroit

If the most suspect aspects of commercial design were symbolized by any one object or class of objects in the 1950s it was by the American automobile and by Detroit, the centre of the United States automobile industry – the phrase 'Detroit-Macchiavellismus' was coined in Germany to describe everything that was felt to be hateful about US design. At the same time, there was a visible tendency to admire Detroit products for their unconventionality and boldness, and even in some circles serious attempts to discuss objectively their social and moral implications. In

6 *Ford Mercury Comet,* 1962.

many ways Detroit was a symbol also for the War of the Generations, and the language of American automobile advertising became the language of revolt among the young. The hard core of any admiration for Detroit, however, was the belief that here was a language of visual design, no longer based on subjective standards like 'good taste,' but on objective research into consumers' preference and motivations. The phrase 'an objective aesthetic' could be taken to refer either to the absolute logic of pure form or to absolute subjection to market research statistics.

Eames, Charles

Although a number of substantial figures in the world of design emerged in or around the decade following the Festival of Britain, none has made so great an impact on the world, both by his products and his personality, as Charles Eames. By 1951 his first chairs in moulded plywood on steel frames, were becoming known outside the United States of America, and were the inspiration of innumerable copies all over Europe, and in most other continents. It was generally recognized that the Eames Chair constituted the first major development in chair design since the Breuer chairs of 1928. After this there followed, in a bewildering succession, toys, films, scientific researches, lecture tours, special exhibits, three further generations of chairs, the celebrated *Ahmedabad Report* on design in development countries, and a great number of awards and citations, culminating in the Kaufmann award to himself and his wife Ray in recognition of their work together for the progress of industrial design.

Ergonomics

The most important branch of design science by the end of the 1950s was undoubtedly ergonomics, which seemed likely to push matters of taste and aesthetics well into the background. As the derivation of the word suggests, the earliest studies to receive the name were concerned with economy of human effort in the operation of mechanical equipment, notably complicated electronic and aeronautical equipment developed towards the end of the War, some of which taxed the mental and physical capacity of its operators beyond the limits of efficiency. By the end of the decade, however, the term had been expanded by thinkers and readers in many parts of the world to cover all forms of relationships between man and equipment, including purely physical studies of human engineering and the communicative studies of control systems and others, in which matters of mental capacity and perception of vision were involved. Unlike most words or phrases, which are promoted to the level of slogans or catchwords, Ergonomics has generated little facile optimism, except for a faith that by patient and painstaking research the relationship between men and their tools can be improved. At one level this has meant quite simply the reshaping of the handles of traditional tools, but at other levels it has meant exercises as abstract as the devising of new sets of symbols for the keys on the control panels of computers.

Festival of Britain

Great hopes were entertained for the influence that the Festival of Britain would have on the arts of design, and the level of public taste. At first sight, the whole exercise was a failure in these terms: its influence, as Sir Gerald Barry (its Director) more or less admitted in a 10th Anniversary lecture, has been practically negligible in the field of design – the 'Festival Style' has practically disappeared from the face of the land and left only a few travesties behind. But it is clear that for reasons that are not altogether coincidental, the Festival marks a turning point in the history of public taste in Britain. Public taste may not have improved, but it has become infinitely more sophisticated in the ten years since the Festival. This development must be attributed to the influence of the mass media such as television and illustrated magazines, but the Festival played a vital part in setting before the public an image of a brighter, smarter and more colourful world of design. This may not have been what the originators of the Festival set out to do, but in this they undoubtedly secured a lasting success.

Italian Craze

One of the most remarkable developments of the 1950s was the craze for Italian design which galvanized the smarter elements of all classes of British Society. The Scooter, the Olivetti typewriter, furniture by Gio Ponti, hairstyling by Richard Henry, Espresso coffee and its attendant machinery, certain tricks of shape, design and display,

7 BOAC 707 jetliner.

and even certain type faces from the Nebiolo foundry, helped to stamp the image of Italy as the home of good design at all levels of consumption. The reasons for this development have baffled critics and sociologists from the time of its first appearance in 1953 to its waning around 1960. The Triennale (q.v.) was a major contributing influence at the level of conscious design. The cinema and motor-racing also played their part, but explanations based simply on good taste and engineering cannot explain the whole Italian mania. Espresso machines, as several critics pointed out, usually had a strong flavour of Detroit or 'Paris 1925'. There is little doubt that the rise of teenage affluence and the improved quality of inexpensive, fashionable clothes, had also a large part in the phenomenon.

Japan

In 1960 it was discovered that Italian manufacturers were plagiarizing Japanese designs for transistor radios – a situation that symbolized, as well as anything could, the change of exotic influences on Western design. Everything in the way of studied elegance and rare qualities in the handling of materials that had been true of Italian design, was found to be yet more true of Japanese, with the added incentives of the abstract power of Japanese calligraphy, the philosophical prestige of Zen Buddhism, and the technical aptitude of the Japanese for miniaturization (q.v.). At the architectural level these developments were supported by the growing reputation of men like Kenzo Tange and Mackawa, and the final seal of Western acceptance of Japanese dominance was set by the enthusiasm with which Western designers, critics and theorists participated in the World Design Congress in Tokyo in 1960.

Jet Liners

The successful establishment of the Jet Passenger Liner in air transportation marked the first major break-through in air-line operation since the introduction of the first Boeings and Douglases early in the 1930s. They also marked a phase of increasing sophistication in air travel, and nearly all had their interiors designed by well-known industrial design offices, rather than by the aircraft designers. Whether French, American or British, all tended towards a grey and tan international style with aluminium trim, except for the Russians who resolutely maintained their traditional Victorian Rococo with cut-glass and flowers even on the TU104.

Magazines

Late in the 1950s one of the pioneer industrial design magazines passed away in one of those fits of financial cannibalism which currently overtake the British Press. However, Art and Industry had been displaced long before its death by the CoID magazine Design which – though born before the beginning of the decade under review – had gone from strength to strength in circulation, in breadth of vision (under the editorship of Michael Farr) and in international prestige. It was in particular one of the organs that made known the science of ergonomics (q.v.) to working de-signers all over the world. Its most distinguished foreign contemporaries by the end of the decade, though of varying influence in Britain, were Industrial Design (New York), the most professional of design magazines under the editorship of Jane Fiske McCullough who finally retired from the paper in 1960, and the other was Stile Industria, an offshoot of the Domus publishing house, under the editorship of Alberto Rosselli, which consistently maintained the Italian view-point, both on matters of practice and theoretical approach.

Medals and Awards

It was justifiably observed by an Italian critic that the ever-increasing supply of medals, certificates, prizes and other awards for designers, were signs of an inflationary epoch in design. As far as Britain is concerned the most important awards were those given by the CoID under a variety of names, finally stabilized as the 'Design Centre Awards'. These were supplemented in 1959 by the 'Duke of Edin-burgh's Award for Elegant Design', a clear indication of the vastly increased prestige of industrial design in the eyes of British governing classes. Perhaps the most hotly discussed of all awards in the 1950s was the 'Compasso d'Oro,' sponsored by the Rinascente store in Milan as a kind of annual supplement to the Triennale. Awarded on an interna-tional basis by an international jury, the Compasso d'Oro reflected a growing crisis in design criticism by being awarded in 1960 and 1961 to the CoID, and to MIT, thus showing a clear lack of any confidence in the jury's ability to select an individual design or individual designer for a premiation; in contrast, the jury of the Kaufmann award (founded in 1960) clearly had no difficulty in awarding their substantial money prize to Charles and Ray Eames.

Miniaturization

The transistor radio has become the most obvious symbol of miniaturization in practice, and is the culminating develop-ment of a train of thinking in electronics which has been proceeding since the first airborne radar during the Second World War. However, it is not the only trend in electronics, as witness the growing size of television screens, and it is not restricted to the electronic field. There has been a

8 *Olivetti Lettera 32*, 1963.

conspicuous and growing development of miniaturization in the world of personal transport, made possible by accumulated mechanical improvements over the previous 20 years. Italian motor-scooters at the beginning of the 1950s were succeeded by German bubble-cars in the middle of the decade, and by the BMC Ado 150 (Mini-Minor or Austin 7) at the end of the decade. At the same time, Detroit reversed its own committed policy and introduced a flock of compact cars which, like the European miniatures, were distinguished by radical technical improvements as well as their diminished size.

Motivation Research
The branch of advertising regarded with the gravest suspicion in alarmist literature (q.v.) was Motivation Research, which formed the theme of Packard's first book *The Hidden Persuaders*. The object of this rather dubious science was to establish the 'real' or subconscious reasons for buying one product or another. It is thus, in a sense, a sub-branch of ergonomics since it deals with a particular, though short-lived, relationship between man and equipment, and was cautiously welcomed by broad-minded ergonomists as an extension of our precise knowledge of man. Conversely, the manipulative intentions of its practitioners were clearly liable to anti-social perversion, but any mass take-over of consumers' minds seems to have been prevented by the imprecision of MR techniques of investigation. From the designer's point of view, MR was most suspect as yet another restriction on his freedom to design and his freedom to serve the public as he felt best. Yet it should be noted that one of the major triumphs of MR's High-Priest, Dr. Ernest

Dichter, was to make a suggestion that any competent designer should have been able to make before he appeared on the scene, that is, the fitting of rear-view mirrors to farm tractors so that those who set their hands to the plough need not look back.

Olivetti
The place of the Olivetti typewriter, both in the Italian craze and in the wider design sense, was best illustrated by the violent reaction to its threatened demise in 1960. The original design for the small portable (which has always been the hinge of the argument) was the work of Marcello Nizzoli, who is, of course, still the designer responsible for all Olivetti products. The neat, squarish case he devised was constantly being held up as an example of pure straightforward design in contrast to American 'styling,' but was in fact itself a styling job, since Nizzoli was in no way responsible for the machinery inside. This point was avoided in discussion until Diaspron, a larger typewriter, appeared in late 1959. This had faceted side and front panels, no doubt for quite sound constructional reasons, but immediately brought down the wrath of the critics on Nizzoli's head, because it was (apparently) 'irresponsible styling.' The reasons for the change of style, apart from any technical considerations, were clearly commercial, but Olivetti, probably because of his enlightened social policy, has always been treated as if he were nothing to do with commerce. What will happen under the new style and the new management, which has succeeded since Adriano Olivetti's early death, remains to be seen.

Organizations

The profession of designer became more heavily organized as well as more heavily bemedalled as the idea of design as an independent profession took hold and established itself. No longer content to proceed under the aegis of other professional bodies, such as those devoted to architecture, designers established or took control of new organizations in order to speak with their own voice. In Britain a major attempt was made to give the SIA (Society of Industrial Artists) a status and function equivalent almost to that of the RIBA, and, at a wider level, ICSID (International Council of Societies for Industrial Design) founded in 1957, began to assume functions broadly analogous to those of the IUA, though it has, so far, met more frequently. One of the major professional problems of both bodies has been the stabilization or establishment of effective copyright in design – a matter in which they are professionally ahead of architects.

Packaging

New ways of selling, summed up in the ambiguous phrase 'merchandising' centred attention on the way in which goods were presented at the point of sale, but they also brought new classes of goods within the field covered by the package-designer's art. If frozen foods were the classic example of the new merchandising and the new packaging techniques, it should also be observed that long-playing gramophone records in their smartly designed sleeves, and reprints of best-sellers in exclamatory paperback bindings, brought music and literature into the realm of general merchandising, both being sold through general stores, tobacconists and other non-specialist outlets. The actual design of such packages became one of the most flourishing departments of the graphic arts during this decade and like TV (q.v.) brought the latest and most sophisticated types of design into domestic environments which had hitherto been immune to them.

Pop Art

Alongside ergonomics (q.v.) one of the emergent concepts, though a bitterly disputed one, of the 1950s, was that of Pop Art. This was distinguished from earlier vernacular arts by the professionalism and expertise of its practitioners (i.e. rock-'n'-roll singers, TV stars, etc.). The concept was widely discussed in Europe and the United States, and impinges on industrial design at two points – two points which are not altogether independent of one another. Firstly, its visual manifestations, as in advertising or Detroit car-styling, were often endowed with a vitality (not always bogus) that seemed absent from the fine arts and from 'good' design. Secondly, the protagonists of Pop Art at an intellectual level, i.e. those who insisted that it should be taken seriously and discussed rationally, maintained that there was no such thing as good and bad taste, but that each identifiable group or stratum of society had it own characteristic taste and style of design – a proposition which clearly undermines the argument on which nearly all previous writing about taste in design had been based. This position was not adopted by any established authority in design, but was given serious discussion at some schools and was certainly accepted by a large part of the student body in *most* schools.

Television

The great increase in popular sophistication about all visual matters, including design, in the 1950s must be largely attributed to television, even more than to magazines or educational bodies. For the first time, almost, in the history of man, a great part of the population was introduced to a

9 *Sony Television*, 1960.

constant stream of smart visual images, was shown new products and Old Masters, either in their own right or as the backgrounds to drama and discussion. In so far as well-designed products are smart in appearance, they have undoubtedly benefited from this trend whose influence had hardly been anticipated at the beginning of the 1950s. Television companies themselves seemed only half aware of the genie they had conjured out of the electronic lamp, but programmes dealing specifically with design and visual arts, became a little more common as the 1960s began, on both the BBC and commercial networks.

Triennale

Four Triennali di Milano fall within the scope of this survey and of these, only the 11th in 1957 can be dismissed as trivial, partly because of the poor quality of the exhibits, and partly because of its failure to pull in an influental audience – neither the trend-setters, nor their followers took much notice of it. The 9th and 10th (1951 and 1954), however, probably did more to establish the image of Italian design in the public mind than any other equivalent manifestation, and the 10th was followed by a Congress on Industrial Design that marks the beginning of a new self-consciousness among Italian designers, and sense of international solidarity amongst designers at large. The disappointing results of the

11th were to some extent a consequence of Italian self-satisfaction with the preceding two, and a degree of international boredom with Italian design that was already becoming apparent among the leaders of taste, if not among the mass followers. The 12th in 1960 was at cross-purposes with its audience. Intended as a serious revival of the best standards of the Triennale, it was unfortunately attended largely by those who had only now caught up with Italian design at a purely fashionable level, and its exhibits did not really receive the discussion that was their due. Among those exhibits was, of course, the complete Nottingham school which marks probably Britain's greatest impact on the international world of design.

Ulm

The Hochschule für Gestaltung at Ulm was certainly among the most important design organizations to emerge in the last ten years. Originally founded in memorial piety as a successor to the Bauhaus at the time that most of the American descendants of the Bauhaus were going into decline, it had a functional plan in its buildings (designed by Max Bill) and a teaching programme (also directed by Max Bill) that both strongly recalled the original Bauhaus. In 1956 and 1957, however, there was something of a 'Palace Revolution' and a new order effectively headed by Tomas Maldonado took over the running of the school. An innovation of considerable importance made on this point was the disappearance of the Fine Art or Graphics department such as one normally finds in a school of this sort and their replacement by a division of verbal and visual communication. Ulm was thus the first school to withdraw completely and programmatically from the earlier dispensation dominated by architecture (here replaced by industrialized building) and by the Fine Arts. Although small, the school proved extremely influential in the world of design, at least at the level of ideas. Its manner of designing is best known through the cabinet work of Braun electrical appliances, but it has so far produced no characteristic style of design. Rather it has become a cool training ground for a technocratic élite.

Volkswagen

Since the end of the Second World War, the design of motor-cars has been in constant revolution, but the standard against which most cars have been judged and found wanting (not always justifiably) has been the Volkswagen. Clearly it is a car that has meant different things to different men, but the points on which its reputation is based, are primarily these: that it had, until recently and with very few exceptions, a more advanced technical specification than any other vehicle produced in quantity, and that spares and after-sales service set a standard of practical involvement with users, and their problems, that few other manufacturers could equal. But the overwhelming virtue in the eyes of men of liberal conscience was that in a world of automotive flux its appearance remained constant and that in a period when cars grew larger year by year, it remained the same size. In other words, it was a symbol of protest against standards of Detroit, the mass media and the Pop Arts.

2.5 THE GREAT GIZMO

Banham describes in this article, originally published in Industrial Design, *September 1965, the growth of the electronic and mechanical gadget and its place within the American culture that has sponsored it. He makes a plea at the end for a methodology with which to approach these often anonymous mass-produced objects and implies that it will have to be interdisciplinary and wide-ranging in its terms of reference.*

'The purpose of technology is to make the dream a fact... The end is to make the Earth a garden, Paradise; to make the mountain speak.' – Arthur Drexler

The man who changed the face of America had a gizmo, a gadget, a gimmick – in his hand, in his back pocket, across the saddle, on his hip, in the trailer, round his neck, on his head, deep in a hardened silo. From the Franklin Stove, and the Stetson Hat, through the Evinrude outboard to the walkie-talkie, the spray can and the cordless shaver, the most typical American way of improving the human situation has been by means of crafty and usually compact little packages, either papered with patent numbers, or bearing their inventor's name to a grateful posterity. Other nations, such as Japan may now be setting a crushingly competitive pace in portable gadgetry, but their prime market is still the US and other Americanized cultures, while America herself is so prone to clasp other cultures' key gadgets to her acquisitive bosom that their original inventors and discoverers are forgotten – 'Big Kahuna' mysticism aside, even the Australians seem to have forgotten that they were the first White Anglo-Saxon Protestants to steal the surfboard from the Polynesians, so thoroughly has surfing been Americanized. So ingrained is the belief in a device like a surfboard as the proper way to make sense of an unorganized situation like a wave, that when Homo Americanus finally sets foot on the moon it will be just as well the gravity is only one sixth of earth's for he is likely to be so hung about with packages, kits, black boxes and waldos that he would have a job to stand under any heavier 'g'.

Landscape with figures with gadgets

True sons of Archimedes, the Americans have gone one better than the old grand-daddy of mechanics. To move the earth he required a lever long enough and somewhere to rest it – a gizmo and an infrastructure – but the great American gizmo can get by without any infrastructure. Had it needed one, it would never have won the West or opened up the transcontinental trails. The quintessential gadgetry of the pioneering frontiersman had to be carried across trackless country, set down in a wild place, and left to transform that hostile environment without skilled attention. Its function was to bring instant order or human comfort into a situation which had previously been an undifferentiated mess, and for this reason it is so deeply involved with the American mythology of the wilderness that its philosophy will bear looking into, both for its American consequences, and for the consequences of its introduction into other landscapes, other scenes.

Underneath lies that basic confusion about the American landscape – is it a wilderness or a paradise? – that has bedevilled American thought from Walden Pond to the barbecue pit in the backyard, a confusion on which Leo Marx's recent book *The Machine in the Garden* is so illuminating on every aspect except industrial design. Marx

observes that the early settlers brought with them from Europe 'the pastoral ideal of a rural nation exhibiting a happy balance of art and nature', and continues 'In this sentimental guise the pastoral ideal remained of service long after the machine's appearance in the landscape. It enabled the nation to continue defining its purpose as the pursuit of rural happiness while devoting itself to productivity, wealth and power. It remained for our serious writers to discover the meaning inherent in the contradiction.'

Now, from a less bookish standpoint, it might appear that the contradiction between industry and garden is only a local disturbance – local in time as well as space – in a more widespread process of employing machinery to make the pastoral garden-ideal available to the whole nation. Local in time, because one of the surest ways to convert the American wilderness into the American paradise is to let agronomy or industry pass across it and then vanish – as witness the second growth woodlands of Connecticut that have supplanted a vanished agriculture and produced perhaps the most paradisal suburban landscape in the world (or, again, I know areas in the Middle West where the mere mowing and brush-cutting of an abandoned farm will produce a landscape that could have come from the brush of Claude Lorraine). Local in space because the ground permanently occupied or permanently blighted by US industry is still infinitesimal compared with the vast acreage opened up to human settlement by industry's products.

Portable technology closes Leo Marx's contradiction as surely as do the meanings discovered by serious writers: industrial productivity was perhaps the only means of converting the disorderly wilderness into an humane garden. For, if there is rural happiness in America that is in any way comparable with the European pastoral dream – whether noble, as in Palladio's villas, or ridiculous, as in Marie-Antoinette's spoof dairymaiding – it depends on technology rather than serfdom or chattel-slavery as it did in the Old World. Yes, agreed – the American pastorale probably did start in slave-owning Virginia (through Monticello was full of mechanical ingenuities) but the dream's proliferation beyond the Appalachians, beyond the Mississippi, beyond the Rockies, increasingly depended at every stage upon the products of industry and the local application of mechanisms. For the first time, a civilization with a flourishing industry encountered a landscape that was entirely virgin or, at worst, inhabited by scattered tribes of noble (or preferably, dead) savages.

In Europe and the Orient, industry has had to worm its ways into the interstices of an already crowded pattern of social strata and landownership: over most of the US there was neither society nor landownership until mechanization came puffing in on railroads that were often the first and only geographical fixes the Plains afforded. In Europe, the pastoral ideal is the heir of the medieval *hortus clusus* or walled garden – from the landscape parks of the eighteenth century to the nudist colonies of the twentieth, the pastoral dream has meant withdrawal behind protective barriers to keep out the pressure of the hoi polloi. In America the pastoral ideal is available to the hoi polloi as well, and if he wants wilderness the average man rarely has to drive for more than an hour to find unimproved ground – remember, pockets of undisturbed prairie ecology survive even in Gary, Indiana. The pastoral ideal in the USA is an extraverted vision, and while Manhattan-based Jeremiahs moan over the disappearance of the wilderness, Europeans (who really

1 The Franklin Stove.

3 OLE EVINRUDE, *Outboard Motor*, 1909.

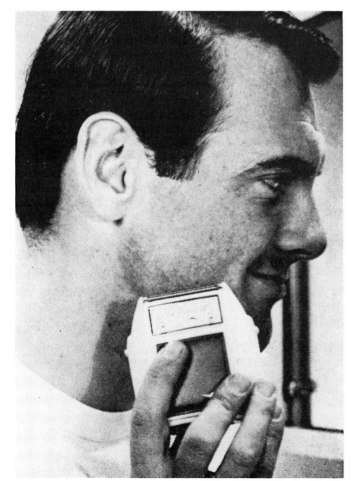

2 Remington's cordless shaver.

4 The Evinrude powers a Viking Engineering Whirl-O-Bird.

5 E. F. Johnson Company's Walkie-Talkie.

6 Illustration for Catherine Beecher's *The American Woman's Home.*

know about intensive occupation of land) goggle unbelievingly still at the empty acres beyond the filling stations and hamburger stands along the freeway.

The technologist on the back porch

Rural happiness in the US was never to be the privilege of the few, but was to be the common property of every member of every family, thanks to domestic mechanization. The good life offered by early visionaries of the railroad-age such as Catherine Beecher, is of enjoyable industry for the entire family, the cultivation of the mind as well as cotton and vegetables; and it already depends, in 1869, on a notable level of mechanical sophistication. As James Marston Fitch pointed out in his key study of the redoubtable Beecher in *Architecture and the Aesthetics of Plenty*, the house she describes in 'The American Woman's Home', is firmly visualized as a true machine for living in, and already boasts such characteristic gadgetry as a pair of Franklin stoves on the main floor and a hot-air stove in the basement, while the domestic economy practised therein with such devoted industry depends, by implication (as Fitch indicates), on equipment such as the Mason jar.

If Catherine Beecher is indeed one of the Founding Dames of the suburban way of life, then the spread of that way of life from coast to coast depended not only on back-porch technologies (to which I shall return in a moment) such as fruit-preserving, but also on one other major factor which is astonishingly missing from most generalized histories of US culture – mail-order shopping. Whatever Messrs. Colt and Winchester (two more characteristic gizmo-names) may have done to subdue the West, it was Messrs. Sears and Roebuck who made it first habitable and then civilized. Yet their crucial contribution rates no more than the most passing reference, unsupported by discussion or index-reference in Max Lerner's giant coast-to-coast national-economy-sized bromide, *America as a Civilization.* The Sears catalogue is one of the great and basic documents of US civilization, and deserves the closest critical study wherever the state of the Union is discussed.

One thing the student will observe is that the catalogue rarely fails to quote, along with the price and so forth, the shipping-weight of all mechanical kit. This point has its significance in the history of American technology: where distances were great and transport difficult, costs of freightage could overwhelm the economic value of a low-grade product. Whatever was shipped had to have a high selling price, or social value, relative to its bulk and weight, otherwise it was not worth the trouble. Thus, mill-cut timber was only the base material for the balloon-frame house that sheltered the West – what made it possible to give up building log-cabins was, above all else, the incredibly cheap wire nails that began to come in around the mid-century, and were shipped everywhere in bulk by barrel and bag. Here was a product whose social utility rested upon its cheapness and reliability and vastly outweighed its shipping charges. Furthermore, it was a fixing-device that required general native cunning rather than specific craft skill to employ, and so it came readily to the hand of the householder employing back-porch technologies comparable to those his wife was employing in the kitchen. For this is another key characteristic of the gizmos that changed the face of America: they do not require high skill at the point of application, they leave craftsmanship behind at the factory. Ideally, you peel off the packaging, fix four bolts and press the Go button.

This is what makes Ole Evinrude's invention of the outboard motor so triumphantly American an event. To fit an inboard motor to an existing boat requires craft skills and mathematical aptitudes of a sort normally found only in places with a long tradition of boat-craft, as in the maritime cities of Europe or New England, where boatyards, shipwrights and the encrusted wisdom of ancient mariners was freely available. But every portage made by the pioneers took them one more river away from any such raft-infrastructure, their boats would normally be the first and only on their particular stretch of water (as are a high proportion of US boats to this day). Their back-porch technologies were unlikely to include either the tackle or the skill to bore a shaft-hole through a keel or transom, fit tube and shaft, make it watertight, calculate (let alone fabricate) the pitch and diameter of propeller, and so forth. But you can order a stock outboard from the catalogue with the right propeller for its own power and your size of boat, fix it with two clamps, add fuel and pull the starter. So ideal, and so American is this solution, that other one-shot aids to the back-porch technologist have proliferated – to cite only one, the adapters that make it possible for any hot-rod-crazy to fit any engine to almost any gearbox and transmission. Warshavsky's current catalogue has three pages of them.

Abstract and consequences of the gizmo

At this point we have seen enough of the basic proposition, to formulate some generalized rules for the American gizmo, and examine its consequences in design and other fields. Like this: a characteristic class of US products – perhaps the most characteristic – is a small self-contained unit of high performance in relation to its size and cost, whose function is to transform some undifferentiated set of circumstances to a condition nearer human desires. The minimum of skill is required in its installation and use, and it is independent of any physical or social infrastructure beyond that by which it may be ordered from catalogue and delivered to its prospective user.

As a class of servants to human needs, these clip-on devices, these portable gadgets, have coloured American thought and action far more deeply – I suspect – than is commonly understood. The US tourist hung about with expensive cameras, most of them automated to within an

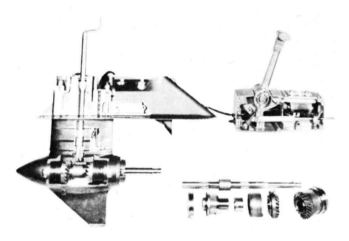

7 Evinrude's new Selectric Shift outboard.

8 An Army helicopter in Viet Nam.

inch of their lives, is a common figure of fun from Jerez to Macao, from Trondheim to Trincomalee, but he is, perhaps, a more tragic figure than a comical one, for it is difficult not to suspect that presented with scenes from cultures that he does not understand he hopes to gizmo them into comprehensible form by pointing the little black box and pressing the trigger. It may not reduce the world to a pastoral, but it will make standardized Kodachrome sense on a screen in the living-room, and it's a lot simpler than learning the language. And if you *must* learn the language, sitting down at a language-lab will give you a gizmo'd knowledge of the tongue far quicker than walking the streets of Amsterdam trying to strike up conversations in Dutch with passers-by (who always turn out to be Chinese-speaking Indonesians, anyhow).

Because practically every new, incomprehensible or hostile situation encountered by the growing American Nation was conquered, in practice, by handy gizmos of one sort or another, the grown Nation has tended to assume that all hostile situations will be solved with gadgets. If a US ally is in trouble, Uncle Sam rolls up the sleeves of his Arsenal-of-Democracy sweatshirt and starts packing arms in crates for shipment long before he thinks of sending soldiers or diplomats – and be it noted that it was a half-breed American, Winston Churchill, who responded in terms that were pure gizmo-culture; 'Give us the tools and we'll finish the job!' Current US foreign policy, Rand Corporation/Strangelove style, revolves disproportionately (it might be argued) around king-sized gadgets whose ballistic complexity and sheer tonnage should not blind us to the fact that they are still kissin'-cousins to Colt and Winchester, and that the abstract concept of weaponry is simply Sears' catalogue re-written in blood and radiation-sickness. And, now that internal subversion has joined the ranks of 'thinkable' topics in Vietnam and Santo Domingo (not to mention Harlem and Georgia) don't the departments of State and Interior wish there existed some opinion-forming gizmo (guts by IBM and RCA, box-work by Eliot Noyes, graphics by Paul Rand) that could be parachuted down, untouched by human hand, to spread sweetness and light and democracy and free-enterprise for fifty miles around ground-zero. It would beat ugly Americans any day.

It might work, at that – remember how the transistor radios that have replaced Field-Marshals' batons in every *poilu's* knapsack helped De Gaulle rally wavering troops in the last agonies of the Algerian crisis. But there are many situations that can't be resolved by gadgetry, however inspired, and the general reliance of the US on gizmo solutions (helicopters in Vietnam, recoil-less rifles in Domini-

9 General Electric's Mariner transistor radio.

ca) appears to Old World observers to have landed America in more messes than it has cleared up. This is not to say that Old World methods such as back-stage arm-twisting or political blackmail would have done any better. It is just that gadgetry is unfamiliar to Old World diplomats and is an easy target for blame.

Unfortunately, gadgetry is also unfamiliar to many of those entrusted with the formation of higher opinion and the direction of academic study in the US, and loses thereby the kind of intellectual support and scrutiny it deserves if it is to produce its promised benefits in the changed circumstances of today. I have already cited one failure of Max Lerner; let me cite another and then leave him be. In positively the worst chapter of *America as a Civilization*, that on architecture and design, he claims that the US has failed to produce a great domestic architecture, because

Great architecture is based on belief. Americans have not yet developed a way of domestic life sharply enough differentiated so that a system of belief can be built on it, and in turn give rise to a distinctive architecture. But they do believe in their system of technology. To put it differently, Americans have had greater success with the arts of consumption and comfortable living than with the problem of their life purposes. Wherever they have built structures connected with production ... there has been a sureness about them absent from the recent fumblings with domestic architecture.

10 Waste King's waste-disposer unit.

11 A 19th-century photographer and his equipment.

12 Polaroid Land camera.

There, if ever, was a man with his finger on the Go button but didn't know it. Even at the time he was writing (1956–7) the under-window air-conditioner and the under-sink waste-disposer had differentiated US domestic architecture from all preceding domestic architectures and introduced new freedoms in design that the pioneer Modern architects never enjoyed, while the consequences have more to say about the life-purposes of most Americans than all the University humanities programmes joined end-to-end. Americans believe in technology and that is where to look for the greatness of their domestic architecture – as every envious housewife of Europe, Asia and South America could tell you. In the process, the structure of the US house becomes little more than an undifferentiated shell within which the gizmos can do their work, and its external form acquires a slightly improvised quality, an indecisive shape. But this is not necessarily to be brushed off as fumbling – it may be necessary experimentation or temporizing until a definitive shape (or some convincing solution of a non-formal kind) emerges to fix the style of the gizmo-residence – experiments like Harry Weese's row-houses in Old Town, Chicago, where the air-conditioners have been built into cupboard-backs that are the least permanent, most easily altered, parts of the structure.

Instances of failures to comprehend the extent and potential of gadget culture are all to easy to multiply, but my concern here is more with the results of this lack of intellectual grip. One outstanding example is the failure to question the present dwindling independence of the gizmo, its increasing reliance upon an infrastructure it could once do without. While the walkie-talkie has cut men free of networks and wiring, the outboard motor persistently grows in sophistication and dependence – it has acquired a dash-mounted control panel and control lines, a steering harness and wheel, external fuel tank and pipe-runs and, occasionally, external electrics as well. As it becomes more integrated with the boat structure at large, it doubtless acquires something of that mystical 'unity' that Old World pundits and New World academics believe to be the essence of 'a good design', but as it passes out of the capabilities of the back-porch technologist and into the hands of the skilled shipwright, its social usefulness is severely qualified. Again, while Dr. Land's Polaroid camera is finally extricating photography from the Victorian impedimenta that has lumbered it since the time of Daguerre, Detroit is producing increasingly limp-wristed automobiles that find it harder and harder to function away from the smooth concrete of the freeway. I don't wish to sound like William Buckley calling for a return to the hairy virtues of the frontier at a time when increasing affluence and improved social techniques make more expensive and interdependent solutions possible, but there are one or two counts on which these present developments might be held up for closer examination.

Wilderness in search of gizmos

One such count is foreign aid: many of the development countries, especially in Africa, are in a condition sufficiently analogous to that of the West in the early Sears Roebuck epoch, for American experience to have directly useful relevance. Instead, such countries find themselves being bullied into sinking aid funds in massive infrastructure of a kind the US got along without for several generations, whereas small sophisticated devices that can work without much capital investment under them might produce better immediate results and leave the ground free for even more sophisticated developments in these countries later on. Many Africans are disappointed and suspicious about this

US attitude which they regard as the extension of Anglo-French colonialism by other means. In particular they suspect that the aim is to create road surfaces on which the current Detroit product will look less ridiculous than it does on the dirt roads over which Soviet and East German vehicles can bump along regardless, and the other thing they suspect is that the money is being directed into heavy investment in order to keep it out of consumer goods industries that might compete directly with the US. One African I know rolled it all up neatly into a big ball of dung by saying 'If the money was ours to spend without Washington's "advice" we would build a factory to manufacture the Japanese Toyota, which retains all the virtues which the Jeep has lost'.

The Jeep makers could doubtless rebut this statement till they were blue in the face, but the fact remains that the Jeep image has lost its ruggedness, has ceased to hold the reputation of a pioneer (and not only in Africa, to judge from the number of Toyotas one seems to see in the mountain states of the US). And there are also some hesitancies, among those who administer or influence aid, that make them unwilling to introduce the independent US gizmo in undeveloped lands; chiefly, a certain squeamishness about introducing familiar brand-names into territories where they might be regarded as dollar imperialism. There is, for instance, a distinct visual and cultural shock in suddenly coming on a Coca Cola dispenser in Latin America or the Arab States, it is apt to look like a visitor from Mars even in the more rural or desert parts of the USA. It has an almost surreal independence of its rough surroundings as it sits snug in its stylists' chrome and enamel, compact, self-contained – an alien. To many sensitive souls it is an offense that they would rather not see perpetrated; and it also implies a criticism of its surroundings.

For whatever unpleasant capitalist habits of mind it may exemplify, it always, in such surroundings, guarantees a higher level of hygiene and technique than the native culture affords. Coke is not a product that can be dispensed through system of hollow reeds and dried gourds supported in a structure made of adobe blocks, any more than there was ever a wood-burning outboard motor. It imports into surroundings that are – for worse or better – less highly-developed, a standard of technical performance that the existing culture of those surroundings could no more support unaided than could the Arkansas territory when it was first purchased. Unfortunately, much of what has just been said is equally true of Coke machines that stand in some of America's older cities, and this brings up another point about the present crisis of the gizmo that is worth discussing here.

The city as pre-gizmos archaeology

North America's cities of pre-Industrial foundation – Montreal, Boston, New York, Philadelphia through to New Orleans – could be regarded as the archaeological remains of a culture that ought to have died when the gizmos came in. They represent the kind of enormously massive infra-structural deposits that are left behind by handicraft civilizations, for (in the absence of rapid communications and compact artificial power-sources) the only way to get anything even half-way clever done was to pile men up in vast unhygienic heaps (and anyone who has seen the recently published sootfall statistics for East side Manhattan will know that they are still unhygienic today). On such man-warrens were built the only concepts of civilization that we know, but this does not mean that alternative structures of civilization are not possible, and on this basis the culture of

13 *Japanese Toyota Land Cruiser Estate Wagon*, 1975.

14 *Willys-Overland Jeep*, 1966.

15 The ubiquitous Coca Cola dispenser.

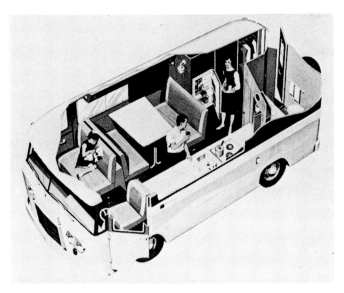

16 A cut-away view of the interior of the Clark Cortez camper.

the gizmo, with its accompanying catalogue and distribution network, will bear looking into.

And it is being looked into, at this very moment, by every egg-head who claims a 'discriminating attitude toward the mass media'. In, say, Chicago, he consults the catalogue (radio programmes in the *Daily News*) presses the Go button of his gizmo (AM/FM transistor portable) and connects himself to the distribution net (WFMT your fine art program) for the 'Well-Tempered Clavier'. The distributive civilization of gizmo culture is here already – and if that does not sound a very original observation thirty years after Frank Lloyd Wright's injunction to 'Watch the little gas station' let me re-phrase his accompanying deduction that cities are out-moded in a different key. If the nation is to continue defining its purpose as the pursuit of rural happiness, and if its population is to continue expanding at the present rate, then it may soon become necessary to re-suburbanize existing urban sites and to reduce them to quasi-rural population densities. You have only to go up to the Cloisters or Fort Tryon and look around you, to realize that Manhattan Island would be the most paradisal of American Gardens if only they would get New York off it. So I exaggerate? But not very much; there are many semi-urban areas – the centre of Denver, Colorado, for instance – that could still be re-arranged to both their immediate and future advantage provided they do not get buried any deeper than at present, in old-fashioned urban infrastructure. The future, at a modest guess, is going to require a much more flexible distribution of American citizens on the ground, and this is going to be much easier to effect if they can pick up their culture and ride than if they are pinned to the ground by vast masses of Lincoln Centre style masonry.

The traditional American wooden house has always sat lightly on its terrain – a smart hurricane or runaway Mack truck will remove it neatly, leaving just 12 posts and 2 pipes sticking out of the lawn. This potentiality seems to trouble architects to the bottoms of their monumental souls, but it has always fascinated US technologues, from Bucky Fuller's Dymaxion houses to the Clark Cortez campers that suddenly seem to be the queens of the American road. Indeed, a self-propelled residential gizmo seems to be a kind of ultimate in the present state of US culture. The Clark's running gear is a

hot-rodder compilation of proprietary catalogue compo-nents, and once tanked up and its larder stocked it is independent of all infrastructures for considerable periods of time – it need not deposit sewage or waste every time it comes to an overnight halt, so that when it moves off again the next morning, and the grass that was pressed down by its wheels has recovered its normal habit, that piece of the face of America remains as unchanged as if four persons and a package of sophisticated technology had never been there. A piece of the American wilderness had been, briefly, a piece of the American Paradise-garden, and could then return to wild.

Name it, then we'll know what it is

No doubt this vision of a gas-powered pastorale, a great nation pursuing rural happiness down the highway, is over-simplified, but observe that it has at its heart a discrete and factual object. The Cortez exists already and can be bought ex-catalogue and increasing numbers of Americans will buy them because the most fundamental American response to dreams is to purchase a piece of equipment to make them come true. And dreams aside, the facts about the Cortez are that its residential performance is considerably superior to that of the handsome Jane Jacobs-type brownstone in which I am writing these words, and its mobility is far superior to that of even the most sophisticated trailers because it is just one single compact unit running on only four wheels. For design people at the Aspen Conference this year to respond to the Clark Cortez only with complaints about its colour-scheme or 'It's an ugly brute,' seems a pitifully inadequate response to what may be one of the most portentous events in the history of the North American continent.

Maybe portentous, or maybe not – but in the absence of a general theory of the gizmo by which to evaluate it, we do not know. The number of breaks in the wall of academic ignorance mentioned earlier has been small indeed, even in the twenty years or so since Sigfried Giedion first tickled the topic in *Mechanization Takes Command*. The subject still lacks a radical theorist who will range freely over departmen-tal barriers and disciplinary interfaces and come back with a comprehensive historical account of the rise of portable gadgetry, and deduce from it some informed projections of the good or evil future it affords.

Perhaps his first task might be to think of a better name for his topic than 'Gizmology', but it may be difficult. The original impetus to write this article came from the impact of a single very precise and concrete image – a man carrying a portable welding plant across the Utah salt-flats with one hand – and the impact of this image was extremely specific. Not 'This man is carrying a portable gadget of typically US format,' but 'This man is carrying a welding plant'. The whole gizmo bit revolves around such unique and discrete objects, named after the specific functions they serve, and this indeed is the prime utility of the whole approach: whatever you want to do, the precise gadget is in the catalogue. But because the whole bit is made up of these genuinely independent parts, each as private and aloof as the Coke dispenser in the Casbah, it remains extremely difficult to generalize about them, even to find them a generic name which will, after they have been a hundred years in the field, acknowledge their nation-wide importance on the changed face of America.

2.6. (THINKS): THINK!

Still in search of the meaning of mechanized gadgetry and a way of describing it, Banham focuses, in this short article originally published in New Statesman, *October 11 1963, on the styling of IBM and Olivetti machinery emphasizing the sophisticated skills that go into designing objects which convey this contemporary machine aesthetic.*

You probably get more design skill and visual sophistication for your penny in a toffee-paper than in an IBM 1400, but when you add up all the pennies that go into the price of a computer at current rates, you get a fantastic amount of design skill and about the most visually sophisticated product on any market. Yet the public image currently lags a long way behind the hardware in production: cartoonists and TV scene-designers still show relatively palaeolithic computers covering whole walls with flashing lights and loops of wire dangling out of untidy boxes racked in serried ranks on industrial shelving. The reality has long since emerged from this Neanderthal jungle, and the kind of computers that Ministries, nationalized industries and big business are now installing tend to be very keenly styled, Mod and generally with it.

For a start, they are no longer 'giant brains': although the so-called desk-sized computers offered by firms like General Precision imply a pretty grandiose concept of 'desk', transistors and miniaturization have shrunk computers from the bulk of industrial plant to something nearer that of domestic appliances, and in the process their appearance has improved in inverse ratio to their bulk. At the Business Efficiency Exhibition last week, the impression created by the pace-setting IBM-machinery and the closest British pursuers like the ICT-Ferranti 1300 or English Electric-LEO KDF6 was a fairly consistent one of tidily detailed box-work in cool Ivy League colours with restrained bright-work and trim, and studied simplicity in any components that stuck out or had to be handled: the sort of design that can be left to retire into the background discreetly, but can stand being pushed into a position of prominence where necessary.

But there was also the impression that whatever this style of design was intended to say, it was being communicated outside the normal world of accountancy. Tech-man spoke unto tech-man, through the medium of designers who prided themselves on not being just packagers, but on having a fair idea of what went on inside the thinking boxes. Just as well, for the points where the internal workings break surface (control panels and such) are the moments of truth in computer design, and many a man who will get by on other products is not up to such moments. Thus Olivetti, on their very handsome ELEA computers, broke with their tradition of handing out the box-work to Marcello Nizzoli for a quick sculptural work-over, and called in Ettore Sottsass instead. Untypical of Milanese designers (at the material time he was driving an egg-powder-coloured Anglia as a send-up of *buon gusto milanese*), Sottsass designed in the closest collaboration with the tech-men who were doing the works, instead of just arting up the outside after they had finished, and then, apparently dissatisfied with his own version of the control panel, handed it on to the Hochschule at Ulm.

They did a typical Ulm job on it (described in the current issue of the Ulm *Zeitschrift*) which has caused some raised eyebrows in the business, but their fundamentalist approach to both keyboard-design and the symbols to go on the keys is a fair sample of the seriousness with which computer

1 *IBM 224 Portable Dictation Unit,* 1965

2 *IBM Executary 271 Dictation Machine,* 1968.

3 *IBM 72 Golfball Electric Typewriter,* designer Eliot Noyes, 1961.

4 *Olivetti ELEA Computer.*

business approaches industrial design. What remains for some design historian to elucidate one day is the precise chicken-egg relationship that lies at the heart of this situation. IBM's undisputed leadership rests very largely on their permanently retained consultant designer, Eliot Noyes. One meeting with him is enough to destroy any illusions that IBM styling is only a crafty sales pitch. It may be that too, but Noyes is a profoundly serious, not to say moral, designer, who trained under Gropius at Harvard, and IBM products look the way they do because he believes they should, and is prepared to sit tight and hold on until IBM believe it too.

It is an uncommon relationship between designer and corporation on the present US scene, and it has already become difficult to see how it started – did IBM pressure Norman Bel Geddes to let Noyes take their account with him when he left Geddes's office, because they wanted a serious designer, or did they, having acquired Noyes through the normal accidents of office politics, allow him to persuade them to take industrial design seriously? Whatever the answer, the historical fact of Noyes's intervention remains, and with it, the crucial influence of IBM on the appearance of computers.

Smart but serious is the word, and where IBM leads the industry follows, so that when Labour's glorious scientific revolution breaks, the machine that replaces your secretary and sets her free for full-time pre-marital sex, will probably look less like a battery hen-house full of war-surplus W/T equipment than a tastefully two-toned filing cabinet with cooling louvres, discreetly wired to what appears to be a typewriter with ideas above its station.

2.7 RADIO MACHISMO

Banham is fascinated by miniaturization, by the reduction of high technology into a small box which is then styled in accordance with public aspirations. The transistor radio is a good example of this combination of advanced technology with sophisticated styling, and Banham makes it the subject of this piece of symbol analysis. This article originally appeared in New Society, August 22 1974.

Remember the transistor radio? It was the main weapon in the War Between the Generations until Marshall McLuhan discovered it to be a cultural phenomenon, which then excused us from paying it any further attention. But what's happened to it since we all stopped looking?

That's the right word: looking. Although you might think that the *hearing* of a transistor radio is the most important aspect, the trannie happens to be about the most advanced piece of technology that is bought on impulse and must therefore – in a market economy – have maximum visual impact at point-of-sale. It's that visual impact of the trannie seen in the radio-shop window that lures you in to ask the man to unlock the display and put the batteries in.

So how does it look? The answer is: different. The last time we were all paying attention, back in the early sixties, the trannie was a remarkably unified product. The only market differentiation was that required to separate the trannie-trade from the rest of the radio business, which was settled, middle class and adult. So, while hi-fi and TV slipped into domestic furnishing styles and were made of furniture materials like wood, transistors became appropriately identified with portable personal gear, and got into leather and stuff. Around 1964 you could write a blanket specification for the styling of practically all the lines on the market: 'Good Design' having died on the counter (what ever happened to all those award-winning Ultras?), everything was black leather, buckles, extension aerials and large knurled chromium knobs. And there matters stuck for some time – my Toshiba 1c-70, bought in 1970, is identical in style with the first Toshibas I remember.

But that static, single image has had it now, splintered along with a splintering market. The straight transistor radio is now competing for the same mad money against cassette recorders, cartridge stereo, car radio, digital clocks; and the trannie market itself has suffered a basic split since the advent in the United States of two different kinds of pop music broadcasting: Top Forty Singles on AM, and Progressive album Tracks on FM. As soon as the split in broadcasting appeared, a new style of transistor emerged too – the first FM models began to back up, cautiously, toward the 'Good Design' type of styling, more sculptural and less boxy in shape (though to make the sound-quality good enough to justify the FM, you still had to balance them, face down, across the top of a jug).

From then on, the market has gone on fractioning – or so the styling implies, a classic example of one of those mass-markets that is really a whole lot of minorities. Even real old-time, Duke-of-Edinburgh-style elegance is back; Bang and Oluffson (the Volvo of electronics) have one so elegant you can't tell what it is, a completely anonymous plastic box that might well contain paper tissues, did it not appear to have a sliderule glued to one edge.

That's not the real trannie market, of course; that's just an executive toy for the man who already has hi-fi. The real market is more weird, more instructive, more unsettling. A visit to your local radio shop will reveal not only trannies

combined with cassette recorders, but trannies *pretending* to be combined with recorders, pretending to be walkie-talkies, or large costume jewellery, or abstract sculpture, or space-equipment.

Transistor engineers are therefore torn between sound-quality (make it big) and portability (keep it small) and ever tempted to the Gordian solution of chopping up the box, applying the sound direct to the ears via a headset and letting the residual circuitry dangle where it will. The current offering in this line is by Sony, and is the most minimal yet, little more than the top end of a stethescope and a box about the size of a Zippo lighter hung round the neck. However, there are certain dimensional constraints that are difficult to avoid, whatever you pretend your trannie to be. Speakers less than about 2½ inches in diameter tend to sound tinny, however well made, and decent reproduction of lower registers needs a certain bulk of air in the box-work (unless you're adept at balancing your radio across the top of a jug or tooth-glass to increase the reverberation-volume). But who needs the un-radio?

Worse, the un-radio lacks the physical bulk to make any positive statements visually. If you are going to hang a trannie about your person then better, it seems, Panasonic's 'fashion' models, one spherical on a chain, one a cylinder with corners on a chain, and one they apparently hope you will wear round your wrist (ankle?) – a huge lopsided bracelet that twists apart to reveal the speaker in one exposed end and the tuning dial in the other. It looks like one of those brainwaves about a supposed girlie-bopper market that only occur to male designers (like the ill-fated 'boy-watcher' sunglasses of the late sixties) and isn't, visibly, causing screaming queues to form outside radio-shops. Still, Panasonic may be right – they were the first to read the FM market correctly, and for that reason one should, perhaps, pay attention to what they are about at the other end of the market spectrum: radio machismo.

Current male-chauvinist trannie styling runs to a proliferation of knobs, switches and controls (all real, many of them necessary) and, above all, subsidiary indicator dials with genuine moving pointers and calibrated scales, over and above the actual tuning display.

The trend, indeed the idiom, is close to what's been happening to male chauvinist car instrument-panels of late; rampant diallism and the matt-black/metal-bead frame can be found in many recent Fords and in the kind of super-car interior that turns up in cigarette advertising. Much of the idiom however, comes over from 'serious' electronic gear like medical apparatus and recording studio consoles.

Now, however, the idiom seems to be borrowing from, or trying to approach, the appearance of less appealing kinds of serious electronics. Maybe it's always been at it, but there is one new trannie – too new to be in Panasonic's British catalogues though it's in the shops – that seems to make it explicit, the GX300. This comes on so aggressively macho that it seems improper to call it by the familiar endearment 'trannie'. For a start, it is gratuitiously powerful; its output of over three watts is sufficient to make the average domestic interior uninhabitable, and if you wanted to use it for house-to-house fighting, it looks the part.

If that sounds a bit far-fetched, then observe that elsewhere in the Panasonic catalogue (and probably in your local shop too) there's a portable TV that calls itself 'Commando', finished in bullshit-drab and with its screen and controls concentrated on the narrow front of a case that would drop straight into the instrument racks of a tank or counter-insurgency strike-aircraft. But in the case of the GX300, it seems more than just the everlasting army-surplus aesthetic or generalized Vietnam funky chic. GX300 is one of those rare pieces of transistor styling that looks more massive than it is; presents itself in the ads as being absolutely crammed with advanced circuitry; described itself in codes and acronyms (Ic-and-FeT/Mic-Mixing/DL) rather more than most; has an eleborate double grille for its concentric speakers like the aerial-dish of some kind of hand-held radar; and, particularly in the black finish, looks not only armour-plated but as if it would go on working under three feet of Mekong mud.

That's not just any old Vietnam then: the whole style suggests the good, clean, innocent early-Kennedy days in the Delta when it was not a question of mutinous GIs slogging it out waist-deep in irrigation-ditches, but of chopper-borne 'advisers' bearing down on the local insurgency manifestations with concentrated high technology weaponry expertise – and keeping their boots clean. Now that's pretty advanced nostalgia; most of us are barely out of the World War Two revival yet, and ... hey, hold on a moment: with a microphone and the mic-mixing control set right *and* three watts of power you could use this thing as a super loudhailer to broadcast classic messages about democracy and freedom like: 'Now hear this, ya slant-eyed gooks.' Never suppose that real-life product-styling is the genteel exercise they teach you at the Royal College of Art.

2.8 A GRID ON TWO FARTHINGS

Banham was often recognized in London in the 1960s riding around on his Moulton bicycle. In this first article in this selection about objects of transport, he describes this bike as a piece of good, simple radical design comparable to any designs produced by the Modern Movement. This article originally appeared in New Statesman, *October 29 1960.*

If we didn't live in a little England entirely surrounded by Eng. Lit. and terrorized by the humane-studies Cosa Nostra, Alex Moulton's mini-bike would surely be recognized as a minor cultural revolution, and Moulton himself would have been the subject of a *Monitor* Special long ago. Frankly, he's a natural for a smart workover by the dreaded Huw – he lives in a wild Victorianized Jacobethan manor-house just outside Bradford-on-Avon. The stables are full of peculiar pieces of machinery thumping lumps of rubber to bits; across the end of the stable-yard stands, unexpectedly, a new drawing-office block in a distinctly Frank Lloyd Wright idiom, and Moulton himself is apt to stroll into this scene with a canoe on his head, looking every inch the English bird-watcher. Appearances can be deceptive, however: some sort of nut he may be, but he is the kind of nut from whom the really creative ideas in technology come – his partnership with Issigonis on the Mini-Minor was practically inevitable. Yet he

also has some sort of affinity with more obviously artistic personalities: it is easy perhaps to make too much of the fact that on his desk there were two framed drawings, one of the Salute in Venice, the other an elaborate cut-away of a jet-plane, but even so it is very tempting to see him as the complementary of tech-biased artists like Anthony Caro or, nearer his own generation, Reg Butler.

Reputedly, he has a special interest in forms of transport that serve men directly and simply – hence the canoe. Hence, also the mini-cycle. The reasons for hailing it as a cultural, as well as technical, revolution are various, but the most important has to do with the unthinking statements made by thinking people when talking about industrial design. Running through most of such talk is a creepy idea (given definitive form by that master-creep, Paul Valéry) that the centuries have given a final shape, perfect beyond improvement, to certain basic tools such as the hammer and the oar, that generations of trial and error have produced working forms almost indistinguishable from Platonic absolutes. If one objected that this might be true of peasant cultures, but what about us with our advanced technology, one got the bicycle thrown in one's face. The bicycle, it was asserted, had already achieved its ultimate norm or form around 1900; by which time the penny-farthing had been

Moulton Standard bicycle, 1960.

rationalized down to the ha'penny-ha'penny of the safety bicycle, and its frame had settled into the classic diamond configuration. After this, there was nothing left to work out but better gear-changes, better brakes, and changing fashions in handlebar bends – systematic refinement of a basic structure that was beyond question. Even before the Moulton, this wasn't quite true, because there was a wave of dissatisfaction in the thirties which produced a number of experiments, such as reclining cycles, none of which has survived, chiefly because their radicalism was thwarted by their complication.

But Moulton's mini is simple as well as radical. Like the recliners of the thirties, it gets down from ha'penny-ha'penny to farthing-farthing, but unlike them it offers a simpler structure than the classic diamond, even while offering something the diamond never could – springing. The Moulton's two small wheels are sprung from a frame which is essentially a single oval tube (a condition which many lightweight motorcycles achieved years ago), but the rider still occupies the classic upright stance, which makes for better control and more efficient use of the leg muscles. The whole thing makes immediate and obvious sense to look at, to ride. Bicycle thinking can never be the same again, and there can be no more nonsense about permanent and definitive forms, for even the Moulton is capable of improvement. It is infuriating, for instance, that it doesn't come fully equipped off-the-peg – you still have to buy and fit your own lamps etc., because it has no built-in lighting system.

There is another and more intriguing sense in which the mini-bike brings on a minor cultural revolution, and this by way of a clever piece of equipment that does come with the machine. A simple ring of polythene on the chain-wheel effectively keeps clothes away from oil, and thus liberates the rider from that badge of social shame: trouser clips. You can ride the Moulton in a business suit and most of us mini-bike pioneers usually do. This is not necessarily to the credit of us, or the bike, but it has put a new class of men in the saddle, most of them ignorant of the cloth-cap and racing-pigeon culture of which cycling is (was?) an integral part.

Conceivably, with the disappearance of the proletarian cyclist (there are no bikes in Coronation Street that I can remember, and only two in Z Cars) the Moulton may bring on a breed of cyclists who are middle-class urban executive radicals. Except in foul weather it is the thinking man's vehicle for central London and the West End, quicker even than a car or a taxi for most journeys. Members of the outgoing big-wheel culture clearly recognize the Moulton as a threat of some sort: the first real hairy-knee'd cyclist to see me on mine promptly reacted with a tremendous virility bit, standing up in his toe-clips, thrashing the pedals up and down with his calf muscles coming out like reef-knots and the frame of the bike whipping this way and that as he smoked off along the North Carriage Drive. Happy days, mate. Remember me to David Storey!

It feels like the end of an epoch, like the end of vintage cars, and no doubt there will now be a vintage-bike cult. (You can get kids' penny-farthings in Gamage's.) The springing and the little wheels have no more taken the fun out of cycling than independent suspension took the fun out of motoring. But it is different. If you have been out of the saddle for a long time, as I had, you don't recognize at once how different the handling of a Moulton is from that of a trad grid, but serious use soon shows you. Because there is very little gyroscopic effect from the little wheels, the Moulton is short on inherent stability compared with big-wheeled machines, it feels loose and sloppy until you get used to it, and an appreciably greater degree of conscious control is required, especially at low speeds. But simply because there is less gyroscopic inertia, the response to control is more delicate and immediate. It's a natural for threading through traffic, turning in narrow spaces, and craftily picking your way in general. In this it is, very neatly, the man-powered equivalent of the Mini-Minor, but whereas Moulton only did the rubber springing for the car, the mini-bike is all his, so much so that it looks likely to carry his name into the whole field of small-wheeled bikes. They will all be called Moultons, whoever makes them, and thus guarantee him the kind of techman's immortality enjoyed by a Panhard, Bessemer or Diesel.[1]

2.9 THE END OF INSOLENCE

Banham is less impressed by the VW Beetle than he is with the Moulton bike, and in this piece of design criticism, originally published in New Statesman, *October 29 1960, he sets out his reasons. He points out that there are several design faults in the car's construction and performance and compares it unfavourably with Issigonis's Morris Mini-Minor. He contrasts it with the Detroit approach to styling which challenges the Establishment's tenets of 'good design'.*

In spite of everything, the design news from this year's Motor Show is that the Volkswagen, the all-German wonder-bug, is apparently unchanged. News? This is news like the continuance of Apartheid or the Chiang regime on Formosa; news that will be better when it stops.

It takes a little nerve to say this, because in the eyes of most people concerned with the theory and criticism of design, the Platonic permanence of the form of the Volkswagen is the one reassuring feature in the present state of consumer-goods design. Here, they believe, is a product with a really advanced specification (it isn't, not any more) that doesn't deprave and dazzle public taste with superficial changes of external gimmickry. This particular combination of Platonic aesthetics with ignorance of the nature of technology, summed up in the slogan 'a good design is for ever', is fading slowly, but very slowly, and it still holds sway in the seats of power – last year, for instance, the jury of the Compasso d'Oro award withheld the prize for Italian designers from Marcello Nizzoli in order to punish him for altering the style of Olivetti typewriters.

In the eyes of the International Design Establishment, the Volkswagen is a sacred cow; but, in fact, it is an objectionable vehicle from several points of view. I'm not, here, going to revive the scandals surrounding its early life as a Nazi swindle – it's the post-war history of Volkswagen as a textbook example of pure Burnhamesque managerial irresponsibility that is at the root of the trouble. The works at

Wolfsburg is neither nationalized nor owned by share-holders, it recognizes no responsibilities except to its own workers, and its consequently unrealistically low selling price guarantees it a permanent sellers' market in which it doesn't have to bother with the needs of the consumers very much.

But VW advertising, particularly in the US, cynically exploits the belief that because the VW offers no external styling changes, it gives more hidden technical improvements instead. However, when you average out the hidden technical improvements to the Volks over the 25 years of its existence, they are fewer than in most cars that have offered annual styling changes as well. In the meantime, nothing radical has been done about the car's outstanding design faults; a body that lags behind current standards of a body that lags behind current standards of accommodation and visibility (compare the Mini-Minor which gives more of both in a smaller car) and a combination of suspension, aerodynamics and weight distribution that causes its notorious instability (the 'Cha-cha-cha back-end', I have heard it called in Germany). The only way to cure these faults, and offer the public better service, would be to build a different car – and that is something Wolfsburg, in the grip of the worst case of industrial inertia in Europe, seems incapable of doing.

The sterility of the VW approach is rubbed in by the new US compact cars. It is clear that the 'Insolent Chariots' period is over in Detroit – not that the product is any less insolent, in spite of the disappearance of tail-fins – but the insolence is no longer the point. The US car as a socio-psychological melodrama in Cinerama and futuristic Metro-color is no longer the significant US car. The rich mine of lurid copy dug over by writers like Hayakawa ('Your Car reveals your Sex Fears') is worked out, and the sociologist and psychologist must stand down in favour of the technical critic who suddenly has a lot to write about – compacts with rear engines (Chevrolet), with independent rear-suspension

1 *Volkswagon Beetle*, 1961.

2

(Chevrolet, Pontiac), torsion bar rear-springing (Rambler), radically revised transmission (Pontiac). All this adds up to a technical revolution in Detroit, and the recovery of technical leadership, in the production-car field, for the US industry.

But the sociologists can't dismiss just yet. The insolent chariots have left behind at least two problems that need evaluation. Firstly, how real are Detroit's claims to consumer-orientation? Even if the answer is only 25 per cent, it still represents a bigger effort to ascertain consumer needs than any other industry is making. Secondly, would the current technical upheaval be possible without the preceding six years of aesthetic free-for-all? In a capitalist-type society, the worst problem about technical improvements is to make people want to buy them – it just isn't true about mousetraps, paths and doors; people like the mousetraps they know. But once it was found that the mass-market would buy aesthetic novelties, and once it was found what sort of aesthetic novelties they would buy, the industry was launched on a styling-binge that is still in full swing and has done two quite unexpected things. Firstly it has precipitated a number of hidden technical changes required to make cars workable in their ever more fantastic shapes; secondly it has completely pulped all preconceptions about what a car should look like, and thus opened the way for yet more violent changes in appearance necessitated by major technical revisions such as rear engines. The aesthetic revolution appears to have been a necessary forerunner of the technical.

But before indiscriminate hosannas are raised to the name of Detroit, it is necessary to be straight about the US industry's motives. Some voices at the Council of Industrial Design hailed the compacts (in the camp-fire jargon that seems to be a speciality at Haymarket House) as 'a sock-pulling-up operation,' and believed that Detroit has seen the evil of her ways. They should get stronger rose-tinted spectacles – the US industry has not altered its commercial pitch, or suffered any change of heart. It has simply

2 *Morris Mini-Minor,* designer Alec Issigonis, 1959.

3 *Rambler Ambassador V8,* 1960.

4 *Chevrolet Bel Air 4-Door Sedan,* 1962.

5 *Pontiac Tempest Sedan,* 1962.

observed that it is now possible to sell a non-insolent car on a large enough scale to turn a fairly fast buck.

In doing so, it undermines a fundamental proposition of Design Establishment philosophy. In pursuit of the faster buck. Detroit cheerfully admitted that it was giving the public what it wanted. This is known in Haymarket House as 'playing down to the lowest common denominator of public taste', and for proof they had only to point at the flamboyant impracticability of the Detroit product. But now Detroit, still giving the public what it wants, is also, apparently, playing up to the highest common factor (or whatever the correct cliché is) of public taste at the same time. The old, standardized and unquestioned, public-school-pink propositions that all common taste is bad, and all commercialism is evil, appear to need some revision.

This is not to say they need *reversal*; simple fast-buck commercialism can never be made to look good from the consumer-victim's end. But how simple is commercialism when it has in self-defence to get through a mass of consumer research and market study before it dare release a product on the world? And how can you condemn public taste as 'low' without adopting a position of snobbery intolerable in a Liberal, let alone a Socialist. The concept of good design as a form of aesthetic charity done on the labouring poor from a great height is incompatible with democracy as I see it. We need, instead, a concept of good design as the radical solution to the problems of satisfying consumer needs. We need an end to insolence on the part of our pundits, as well as at the Motor Show.

3

4

5

2.10 NIGHT, MRS. JAGBAG

It is the symbolic implications of the styling of the Mark X Jag that attract Banham to this car. Its suggestion of sex, high-class, maturity and affluence make it a perfect subject for Banham to apply his tools of symbolic analysis to. This article originally appeared in Architects' Journal, *November 29 1961.*

So many of the staples of British cultural life have died the death this last, deciduous autumn, that it is difficult to know what fragments are left to shore against one's ruin (to quote the old Wastelander). Among the more notable unsung casualties of progress, let me single out a really grand old girl, who has given 10 years' well-upholstered pleasure to the Island race, the Jagbag. The Mark X Jaguar is a great car, as far as one can yet judge, and yours truly might well be leading the rush to covet one were it not for a certain lack of wherewithal and wheretoparkit. All hail, Tenjag. But let us at least give a decent burial to its prececessor, that passed through marks VII, VIII and IX in some 10 years and remained unmistakably Jagbag through thick and thin – usually thick – because it/she is probably the most socially, culturally and even politically important car that has come out of a British factory since the War. Jagbag, uniquely, had

Sex. No other British car has ever achieved this, with the possible exception, now, of the Mini-Minor, which seems to attract a certain Humbertish devotion from large middle-aged men who probably haven't even read *Lolita*. But Jagbag had oodles of genuine grown-up sex: unmistakably English Sex of a special, affluent, post-war kind. Indeed, one would have been tempted to nominate her for the title of 'Miss Affluent Economy', were she not a little – er – too mature to have ever been a miss.

I don't think anyone ever doubted that they were Jagbag keys that were used for drawing lots in those wife-swopping, vodka-swilling seminars that *Reveille* wrote-up so enthusiastically in the mid-fifties under the memorable headline 'Birmingham Sex-key Orgies'. (Don't ask me for the rules now, but any *even* number can play.) Jagbag may not

1 *Jaguar Mark X Saloon*, 1962.

2 *Jaguar Mark VII*, 1951–2.

3 *Jaguar Mark VII*, 1955.

4 *Jaguar Mark VIII*, 1957.

5 *Jaguar Mark IX*, 1959–61.

have deserved the title of 'Adultery-buggy', any more than that of 'Spiv's Bentley', but there was something about her sleeked-down curves that seemed unmistakably married, and consorted well with appliance-affluence which is an essentially married state (like who needs a washing-machine to live in sin).

But also, Jagbag was English. Sex in cars is so intimately (if you will allow the expression) connected with Detroit, that it comes as a shock to find a wagon like Jagbag that owes nothing to Detroit in its styling, but it is true. She was an English original, remotely descended from those close-coupled sporting coupés with dropping waistlines of the late thirties, but where they drooped, Jagbag swelled; where they showed good taste, Jagbag burst with a self-confidence that must be unique in English design since 1851. No English bolide ever hit the market with such an exuberance of fleshy tin, and the market in big cars has never been the same since – prestige coachwork on Bentleys, for instance, has never recovered its poise after a phase of visible Jaguar influence in the early fifties.

Thinking, appreciatively, of some of Jagbag's handles and other external metalwork, it strikes me that she was, in some ways, a very Art Nouveau jalopy, with some of the exuberance you see in the Art Nouveau jewellery in the present show at Goldsmiths' Hall, an exuberance and conviction largely missing from the later gauds. The old Nouvers-type jewellery you immediately see being worn on a woman; you even see *where* she would wear it – and *why*. The later stuff you only see being worn by a woman who is herself posing as a cool decorative adjunct to some faint, tasteful Scandinavian furniture in *Design* magazine. Whatever it was we lost when ghastly good taste drove our native Nouvers underground came back, not with a bang but a wiggle, when Jagbag made the scene.

For Jagbag you immediately saw being worn by a man, you could even predict *where* he would wear her – and *why*. She was the perfect partner to the flat-cap, vodka-and-Guinness, cavalry-twilled, expense-accounted dolce vita of dual-carriage-way exurbia: the sort of car where you could usually find ear-rings between the back seat and the squab. And we shall never see her like again, for Tenjag is male, keen and rather Ivy League.

'Night, Mrs J. Old Girl. (Exit, dabbing ineffectually at incipient tear, and large chromium kiss-print on cheek.)

2.11 HORSE OF A DIFFERENT COLOUR

In this article, originally published in New Society, *November 2 1967, Banham sets out a complete stylistic analysis of the Ford Mustang, describing its genealogy, the subtleties of its form, its social imagery and meaning and its relationship to other cars of the same genre. It is highly reminiscent, in its approach, of an art historian 'going to work' on the iconography of a Renaissance painting.*

It looks as though a Detroit-built Ford may well be the ultimate reason why Vauxhall are offering the humpy body-line right across the board. On all their models, the top line of the side panel above the rear wheel now humps up into the window space above. In doing this it makes a welcome nonsense of one of ground rules of academic Pop scholarship, which assumes that bread-and-butter motor cars acquire saleable glamour, sex and zing by imitating the shapes of more spectacular models – dream cars, sporting specials, successful competition cars – in the *same* manufacturer's range.

Where General Motors' American lines are concerned (Vauxhall = General Motors Britain), the rule holds good, because the customers will see, from time to time, hot models like the brutish, muscle-bulging Corvette sports car,

the design that brought the humpy line into the GM range. But the man behind the wheel of a Viva will be lucky if he sees a Corvette on an English road in a week of Wednesdays. If there is a car that sheds reflected glory on the humpy line in England it is (whisper it not in Luton) this *Ford*.

But in a very curious, oblique and instructive way. Recent Dagenham products, like the current Ford Zodiacs and Zephyrs also affect a hump in the sill-line, albeit a far less voluptuous one than Vauxhall's. Now, that mine of motoring wisdom, the man at the end of the bar, knows where the humpy line on the Fords, at least, comes from: 'I mean, it's a sort of poor man's Mustang, right?'

Well, actually, old chap, right *and* wrong. By the strict art historian's methodology of exact formal comparison and all that jazz, the Zodiac is not a foal out of the US founder company's Mustang, but bears unmistakable marks of the paternity of a different bloodline – the Avanti, which was no kind of Ford at all, but the last dying product of the grand old Studebaker company, before its car division finally folded three years ago. The Avanti ancestry of the Zodiac is very plain around the back and fairly clear around the front. But, from whichever end you look at it, these facts are true without being the least bit relevant, because the man at the

1 *Ford Zephyr V6 de Luxe*, 1967.

2 *Ford Mustang Hardtop*, 1967.

end of the English bar is even less likely to have seen an Avanti than a Corvette. But he is increasingly likely, over the last couple of years, to have seen a Mustang, which *is* a Ford product and does, in general lines, bear some family relationship to the Zodiac's broad flat bonnet and short bobbed tail.

What gives this version of the Zodiac's parentage the conviction and strength of a sort of tribal myth is that the presumed parent is the most – wait for it – numinous motor car ever mass-produced. Of all Detroit's dozen or so postwar attempts to invent a convincing American 'sporty car', the Mustang is the only one to make good – a million and a half units is quite a herd of horse.

It had the lineaments of success from the moment it came under starter's orders. It went from dream-car prototype to production so fast that the prototype itself had to be lent out to the press for test driving. Oil-smudged slobs at the end of the US bar who laughed it off as a college girl car in 1964 – because of its tidy, compact lines, lack of brightwork and obvious attempt at European 'good taste' – were queueing up to buy the Mustang a twelvemonth later. Suddenly the Leisure People of the Age of Fun had found their transport of delight.

Inevitably it became the car driven by 'the kind of man who reads *Playboy*'. Then Carroll Shelby, the former racing-driver, found ways of tweaking it up into a competitive car for saloon-class racing, adding competition glamour (and a pair of parallel blue stripes over the bodywork) leading to a kind of ultimate accolade – Hertz bought a thousand of the race-hot Shelby horses for rent 'to approved customers' (and put a pair of parallel *gold* stripes ten inches wide over the bodywork).

As a product success story it is probably the nearest Detroit has got to the Volkswagen class, complete with a built-in product mythology that carries conviction in the teeth of common sense – like, I can see *myself* laying dollars by to rent a Shelby Mustang in Denver, Colorado, drive it up to Aspen, and down through Las Vagas to the Fun City, Los Angeles, itself. And there one can see another symbolic confirmation of the Little Horse's success. Even though Chevrolet makes models flaunting the names of Malibu and Bel Air, in both those desirable suburbs of Los Angeles they are outnumbered by Mustangs.

But what about the Mustangs the man at the end of the bar sees in England? Their story is even more remarkable in some ways. According to Lincoln Motors, who handle the

model here, only about 200 have been imported in the last three years 'through normal channels'. But there must be something like three times that number galloping about the greater London area, for a start. Obviously, they are getting in through the two standard channels of market seepage, the diplomatic corps and US forces in Britain. The trickle of 18 months ago, when I could recognize most of the few Mustangs around, has now swollen to steady stream and there is no hope of remembering t'other from which. And I very much doubt the demand is anywhere near saturated, for the Mustang appears now to be about the most compulsive car on the English market.

Without any help from the mass media either (though it has starred in no fewer than five recent French films, to the alarm of *Sight and Sound*). English columnists still see the dreary old Rolls Royce or moribund E-type (or possibly the Ferrari or Lamborghini) as the automobile of ambition. Thus, *The Observer* colour supp missed it in its pre-Motor Show survey of the market, even though it gave a plug to General Motors' Camaro, which is a desperate attempt to get the youth market back from Ford.

The Horse, in any case, is not a trendy product. It gets no promotion in Britain; its reputation has grown by word of mouth recommendation. Our local kerbside tycoon, who has had a couple through his hands recently (both with out-in-the-sticks US dealers' names still on the bootlids) develops a slight expression of religious awe and says, 'It's just a beautiful car', and the word 'beautiful' is pretty ambivalent in this context.

Visually it is, of all American cars, the one most likely to please the (slightly conservative) tastes of European motoring professionals. Not only in its external lines but inside as well. When you get behind the wheel you see an array of what John Bolster of *Autosport* describes as 'proper round dials'; and in general the cockpit puts you in mind of a motorcar and not, as one man said lately of the Aston Martin, the library of an old manor house.

But though it is a convincing stab at a Grand Touring car in looks, gait and (to some extent) handling, the Mustang can still pass as a full four/five seater. In most Fun-to-drive GT cars, like the amazing toy-sized Honda S-800, there is no room for any kind of fun except driving, but the Horse has bags of room to fall about and pursue traditional back-seat pursuits. In the drop-head versions – like the one driven by my barber – you might have to tuck your legs in a bit during such pursuits since the stowage for the hood, when folded,

3 *Ford Mustang 2 + 2 Fastback*, 1967.

reduces the seat space, but no one will complain; being convertible is part of the Mustang image from Sunset Strip to Apex Corner.

In any case, being able to fill the back with swinging bird-life is a bit of a fringe benefit, if I correctly observe the Mustang as actually driven over here. It is a one-man car, a driver's car, and expert's car. It is not a getaway-people car, full of flailing silk scarves, sulking falcons, flying sand, Eastern promise and stuff. It is the car of the ones that have got away, and know they did it by their own talents.

Looking at, say, Marty Feldman ('Rhomboid Goatcabin' of *The 1948 Show*) idling his Mustang at the lights in Tottenham Court Road, it strikes one that there is very little show-off about the Mustang bit, none of the conspicuous consumption of the old Tom Maschler Success Man approach to car usage. The Horse – as I read the signs – is the mount of the profoundly self-assured. To cite an example well-known in these pages, Peter Hall, wonder boy of English town planning, is about to buy a Mustang to commute between London and Reading. Being seen in a Mustang appears to be beside the point; driving it is the point, the whole cult is a bit private.

Yet the fact, now inescapable, that the Mustang is the focus of a private cult in England, points to a change of mind that must be of public consequence. It is the first specific model of American car to acquire this status in any European country. Cult cars in Europe have always been European

produced, expensive and rare (I once knew a man who had been judged unfit to possess a Hispano-Suiza, but he couldn't get one anyhow). Or there have been generalized admirations for 'the Detroit product' at large, whether among the hot-rod and drag-racing crowd, or the pioneer students of Pop at the ICA, in which it hasn't really mattered which particular model it was, as long as the tail fins were high, the colours ripe, and the front grille vaginal.

Ford's little horse, however, is admired in its own right, on the basis of direct experience or the judgment of one's fellow professionals; and its admirers are prepared to lay out at least two thousand nicker to get one. To have acquired this kind of esteem in the teeth of the universally bad reputation that lumbered American cars in the eyes of serious drivers only five years ago, is solid tribute to the real virtues the Ford people built into the Mustang.

But it is an even more startling tribute to a new open-mindedness among exactly that class of English intellectuals and professionals who found US cars so loathsome a mere five years since. It's quite like the changed attitude to Los Angeles – instead of damning the place out of hand without having visited it, they now admit its faults but observe that it is one way, and a workable one, of making a city, because they have been there and seen that it works. So too, no one pretends that the Mustang is faultless, but it is still known to be 'a beautiful car'. It's not just that the car is a horse of a different colour, the driver has changed too.

2.12 I'D CRAWL A MILE FOR . . . PLAYBOY

Still within the context of the ad-man's tricks which say a lot about human behaviour and aspirations, Banham looks at Playboy *magazine which 'sells' the female nude to the public. He discusses the role of the typography and the layout in this sales effort and gets beneath the surface of the appeal of this glossy mag. This article originally appeared in* Architects' Journal, *April 7 1960.*

Of course I buy it for the giant fold-out full-colour pin-ups – *Playboy's* 'Playmates' are one of America's greatest gifts to Western culture, and you know how I go for culture. And a very distinguished body of women they are too – one I particularly remember, who added new dimensions to the vernacular term 'Broad' was a Fuller from Boston, like R. Buckminster ditto – obviously a most talented family.

But if I was a working hypocrite I could find a dozen other reasons for keeping abreast of Playboy. Its interpretation of the 'male interest field' is considerably wider than say *Esquire's*: while it keeps one foot firmly planted in the bedroom door – a stance that *Esky* has now abandoned – the other covers a lot of ground. For instance, *Playboy* handles some really hard stuff – quite a lot of Pentagon ears must still be humming after a Hit-them-where-they-live piece about radio-active fall-out and another must have hurt Washington dead-heads even with its title: 'The Cult of the Aged Leader'.

Item: it makes foul swipes at up-coming public idols; and recently took to pieces the much publicized reputation of Miss Shirley McLaine for repartee, with both scholarship and refreshingly ungentlemanly mockery. In fact its performance on the wit and scholarship kick is notable. Nice pieces they have on, e.g. writing on walls, including the Pompeian founders of the art, the original Kilroy (the American 'Chad') and an interview with a slogan-writer of world championship class.

Items, visual funnies – *Playboy* is one of the basic platforms for Feiffer, but it has other strong cards, including Gahan Wilson, a real weirdie who deserves to be better known in sick circles over here, and Shel Silverstein who is, I figure, a plain nut with a fancy beard.

Item, to read: though too much of *Playboy's* fiction is the male equivalent of 'women's reading' and wears the lineaments of slightly-too-easily-gratified desire, violence, etc.; there is also a distinctive line of *Playboy* fiction, and near-fact, planted in the music-biz end of the beat generation (*Playboy* has its own jazz festival) and the Sheckley edge of science fiction.

Item, to look at: *Playboy's* typography and layout is among the most ruthless and imaginative that is commercially available, comparable British material just doesn't exist, but Bill Slack's cover for the *Motropolis AJ* lay a close second.

Item, architecture and interior design. (I will repeat that to show I am not kidding – architecture and interior design.) *Playboy* has over the years discussed and illustrated quite a lot of furniture, culminating in a Playboy Bed (where else did you expect it to culminate?) that makes most European dream beds look very thin and faint. It has also shown plans and perspectives (some perspectives!) of two projected buildings – the Playboy Penthouse and Playboy's Weekend Hideaway, neither of them by any designers you have ever heard of, but none the worse for that, and considerably better than any equivalent projects that one can remember in the *Home and Garden* magazines. Quite a lot of furnishing information is also transmitted (*a*) via features on hi-fi and (*b*) in the backgrounds to the giant full-colour fold-out pin-ups, one of whom was photographed recently in the Guggenheim spiral.

But chiefly what sends this consumer of *Playboy* is an institutional advertisement which begins 'What sort of man reads *Playboy* . . . ?' From this I have discovered quite a lot of very flattering information about myself. For instance I am one of those 'for whom a dinner date is a regular and important event', with a 'beautiful girl' – Furthermore I don't care about the size of the bill – this is because I 'enjoy an income higher than other man's magazine readers', or possibly because I 'live in 168 important metropolitan areas'. But best of all, and for this I am forever grateful to *Playboy*, my age has remained steady for some months now at 28.3 years.

2.13 COFFIN-NAILS IN HANDY PACKS

From the commercial symbolism of cars Banham moves here to another form of advertising, packaging – in this case cigarette packs. He describes the ploys of the ad-man in distinguishing between different brands of cigarettes through packaging design and the way in which the packs determine the consumers' idea about the product. This article originally appeared in New Statesman, *23 March 1962.*

Somewhere in the groin-deep slush of instant sex and spray-on status that slops around the multi-million-pound business of persuading consumers to smoke cigarettes, there lurk some hard facts. One is crucial and basic, though never aired in public – 99 smokers in a 100 can't tell one brand from another once it is alight and burning (cf. the well-substantiated observation that 'there is no bad beer'). Because of this rock-bottom addition-fact, the cigarette industry needs the advertising industry as does no other sector of the consumer-goods market. Indeed, tobacco and advertising have a very long partnership to look back on – the earliest known illustrated ad in English shows a clutch of 17th-century cancer-prospects dragging the weed and belting out hard-sell punch lines like 'This tobacco smoaks well!'

Insofar as any brand has distinctive characteristics ('personality', in Mad. Ave parlance) it is because public opinion believes them to exist, sometimes because folk-lore has built them up – e.g. Gold Flake have a half-century reputation for being extra-strong – sometimes because advertising has spread the word. A brand exists in an ideal condition of unmistakable personality in the ads, but from then onwards it's downhill all the way. The last point in this easy descent to the ash-tray and oblivion where human skill can do anything to bolster a fag's personality is in the design of the pack, and this places cigarette packets among the most instructive design-exercises there are.

The last time a cigarette is even Brand-X is in the act of being extracted from the packet – after that it is strictly Brand-Zero. As a result, pack design becomes a study in anti-ergonomics; the product must be made difficult to extract. Early in the fifties, Madison Avenue realized that a skilled US consumer could get a cigarette into his mouth without being conscious of the brand at all – he tapped the bottom of the soft pack to make a nail pop up, and raised the whole pack to his mouth, seeing only the torn top, not all those crafty visuals on the side. Hence the flip-top pack, comparatively proof against Wild West skills, and a mechanical ritual to be consciously performed every time, with the pack in view. Ads counter-presented this new manoeuvre as a superior skill, to be learned as an aid to improved peer-group status. Alas for ingenuity, the flip-top pack was anti-ergonomic in other ways too – the corners of the hard box, when stuffed into the traditional American shirt pocket, dig into the surrounding rolls of affluent flesh every time the smoker folds himself into the driving seat of his car.

On the English scene, awkward boxes have been with us ever since the old paper Woodbine sack went out, and the flip-top, which is an improvement on our traditional slide-box, will probably persist here after it has finally faded state-side – we use a different pocket. Nevertheless, with annual consumption escalating at the present rate, the market offers some glittering prizes for hard selling, even in a state of semi-monopoly, and English pack-design is under close scrutiny – chiefly because the time is thought to be about ripe for a new brand to make a sensational raid on the market and, on the evidence, pack-design will have a big part to play in its success (unless intelligent government action on the Physicians' Report halts the gold rush).

This scrutiny has brought up some illuminating facts about the movements of popular taste during this century, for there seems to be a genuine correlation between the visuals and the sales. Four brands in the last 50 years have exhibited the kind of wild, compulsive growth that is every manufacturer's ambition: Gold Flake went big-time in the early 1900s, the legendary gasper of pioneer aviators and racing mechanics; Players crashed the market in the twenties, a real runaway success; in the 'B' division, Capstan made a sizeable killing a little later, and in the years immediately following the last war, the years when Dunhill, a rank outsider, made a wild raid and then faded, Senior Service ('product of the master mind', and all that jazz) carved out a piece of the market that was big enough to worry the Imperial Tobacco establishment.

Now there is already a pattern in the very names of these brands. Gold Flake is, effectively, a description of the type of tobacco employed – a pretty naive line. Player's Navy Cut is still a tobacco-type, but the salt-water image is there and was always played up in the ads. Capstan is a pure brand-name, and generalizes the nautical image; and Senior Service adds the top dressing of ward-room snobbery to the hairy he-man stuff implicit in the Navy bit. The visual design of the packs paces this development pretty closely, though at a remove of about one human generation from the birth of the style in which it is couched. Nicolete Gray long ago pointed out that the basic Gold Flake pack was a living fossil from the golden age of cigar-box chromolithography – it was, in fact, about 30 years behind the high style of its times when it underwent its 'growth period'. In the twenties, Players grew at record speed in a pack whose style (especially the back) was pure provincial Art Nouveau – as also was Woodbine, the 'B' grower of the immediately preceding war period. Capstan, another 'B', doesn't quite fit the pattern, but Senior Service fits it with positively Marxist determinism – it is a depressingly accurate epitome of the ghastly good taste of the thirties, complete with air-brushed vignettes and half-educated architectural lettering.

Now, the question that is ulcerating the advertising agencies who handle cigarette accounts at present is this: will the next one follow suit, or is the pattern broken? Gold Leaf, the most conspicuous newcomer, certainly does not seem to fit (though it is not an 'A' brand, of course) and its brand-name takes us almost back to Gold Flake. The chances are that the break may be real, and the reason why is pretty certainly the telly. Whereas the mass-market of the first 50 years of the century was utterly undisturbed by the high-style exoticisms and jazz-modern fashions of Abdullah or Black Sobranie (the most enduring monuments to the Diaghilev epoch), Pop taste is visually a thousand per cent more sophisticated since TV has brought a constant stream of smart, with-it imagery into every home.

Even though there is no obvious correlation between the twitching screen and the newest packs, Guards has had a moderate success with a pack that looks uncommonly like the opening caption for one of the smarter discussion series. Agencies that backed a continuation of the clinical-white snobbery of the Senior Service approach appear to have got bitten, but that does not mean that a Ben Casey/Kildare pitch might not be a keen proposition if someone can think of a non-carcinogenic blend.

However, leaving the neuroses of the agencies on one side, cigaratte packets seem to add confirmation to something that is now glaringly obvious to everyone who is actively involved with popular visual taste at the WEA and evening-class level. There has been a revolution. It may not be the desirable revolution that Centre 42 is working for, but the old 30-year time-lag, so reliable, so infuriating, between accepted high-style and accepted Pop-style seems to have been broken at last. The British public, which used to be visually numb, like an atrophied limb, is now visually knowlegeable in a disorderly way, and is in some state of visual exercise. The time-lag appears to be down to 10 years, 5 years, nothing at all in some fields. It looks as if the free market in coffin-nails has lasted just long enough to provide the statistics to confirm this.

2.14 TRIUMPH OF SOFTWARE

As another route into the public imagination Banham turns his attention to mass-market films which are aimed as directly at the public imagination as the cigarette ads. Barbarella, for Banham, succeeds through the absolute contemporaneity of its imagery which consists of flexible, blow-up, 'software' environments. Banham places the film within the context of radical Pop architecture. This article originally appeared in New Society, October 31 1968.

If we *needed* the concept of a fur-lined spaceship (and we did, even if we didn't know it), we have it now. We also have a female astronaut stripping off in free fall, beginning very conventionally with the gloves like any old gipsy rose. And behind her, in the fur-lined control module, there are a rococo nude in plaster and an airlock door panelled with a section of Seurat's *Dimanche à la Grande Jatte*. And all this before the credit titles are properly out of the way, to sum up what *Barbarella* is going to be all about for its devotees; thus:

Item: an unexceptionably straight-up-and-down view of sex – Jane Fonda's clean little surf-girl face (Nancy Sinatra might have been even better in the part!) and Terry Southern's sanitized *Candy*-coloured script combine to produce a love-object about as kinky as the All England Lawn Tennis and Croquet Club.

1 *Barbarella*, 1967, Jane Fonda in the fur-lined software environment of the spaceship.

Item: a preoccupation with a kind of environment that, if not always fur-lined, is always with-it – so much so that it will become what the film is remembered to have been about in the rather specialized circles where it is remembered.

And item: a trickle of visual jokes – art-jokes, rather – that need an audience of at least DipAd complementary studies level. Since the movies are the one visual art-form whose criticism we entrust to the visually ignorant, all this art-jokery completely missed the assembled body critical at the press show, and I would like to congratulate the four people who laughed in the same places as I did, not one of them a major weekly or daily critic as far as could be seen.

Predictably, therefore, *The Guardian* doubted if it would ever become a cult movie. I have news for you, mate: old, cold news. *Barbarella* has been a cult movie for months, ever since the first stills were in *Playboy* and the colour supps, and were pinned up in architecture student pads and studios across the world. For *Barbarella*, unlike most feature movies, which are about two years behind the visual times for unavoidable mechanical reasons, is barely twelve months out of date. Style-wise, it falls about halfway between the Million Volt Light-Sound Raves at the London Roundhouse at the beginning of last year, and the great Arthur Brown/Jools/Inflatable rave organized by Architectural Association students there at the end of the year.

Compare Stanley Kubrick's *2001*, since everybody does. My spouse's verdict that this film's psychedelic (eh?) sequences 'would have been great if they had been at

Hornsey two years ago' marks the point at which Kubrick most nearly caught up with the live visual culture of now. The rest of the movie was like Pompeii re-excavated, the kind of stuff that Richard Hamilton had in his *Man, Machine and Motion* exhibition back in 1955. All that grey plastic and crackle-finish metal, and knobs and switches, all that ... yech ... *hardware*!

But *Barbarella* is the first post-hardware SF movie of any consequence. By one of those splendid coincidences that used to make German historians believe in the Zeitgeist (and which English historians always miss) the film was premiered here in the same week that a company called Responsive Environments Corporation went public on the New York stock exchange. Whatever the company is about, *Barbarella* is about responsive environments, of one sort or another, and so has been the architectural underground for the last three years or so; and from where I stand, I can't see how this could avoid becoming a cult movie. Responsive environments in the sense of not being rigid and unyielding; articulated only by hinges between disparate rigid parts: an ambience of curved, pliable, continuous, breathing, adaptable surfaces.

Fur is exactly such a surface. Of all the 'materials friendly to man' it is the friendliest, because it is kissing cousin to our own surface and grows in some of our friendliest places. But it also has, in the most objective and quantifiable terms, physical properties that would make it worth inventing if it did not exist: flexible, shock-absorbing, heat-insulating, acoustically absorbent and selectively responsive to reflecting light. (Also smelly and difficult to keep clean? So are you, *hypocrite lecteur*!)

It is extremely difficult to think of a better material to line a spaceship or any other vehicle in which human flesh is going to be tumbled about during magnetic storms, free fall or rough re-entries. Or tumbled about in that grand old Shakespearian sense of the word; Barbarella gets it once in/on furs, and again in an angel's nest lined with what has to be moss, the vegetable kingdom's nearest equivalent.

Both fur and moss, however, exist already; no point inventing them. What has been invented, and recently enough to have been almost totally overlooked by the movies, is the inflated or otherwise distended or tensioned transparent plastic membrane; and this is *Barbarella*'s other great environmental hang-up. Rightly so, because inflatables too are ... yes, friendly. I actually heard that precise word applied during an evening illuminated balloon-happening in Los Angeles. The balloons were the army-surplus sort that get advertized in SF magazines, around eight feet in diameter, blown to a merely floppy condition with an air/helium mixture that made them only marginally buoyant.

Trying to hold them steady against the light night-wind was a bit like trying to handle a plump, drunk, amiable, unstable girl at a party. Suddenly you'd find you were half-smothered in bulging, yielding, demanding plastic that wouldn't go away when you pushed it. And there was this bird came up (I think she'd been sniffing the helium) and said could she borrow a balloon because they seemed kinda, well, you know, friendly; vanished with it into the professionally designed landscaping; and reappeared about 20 minutes later, weeping and freaked out, with its exploded remnants.

Barbarella digs these (and other) aspects of inflatables in depth and at length. She sleeps (lit and photographed from below) on a transparent membrane that dimples to her form. The sails of the ice yacht become erectile when the wind blows, and the fur-trimmed tumble takes place in the yacht's translucent 'tail'. In the wicked city of Sogo, inflatable

2 *2001*, 1968.　　　　3 *Barbarella*, 1967, Wicked city of Sogo.

bolsters bumble loosely about the interiors; bodies are trapped, or rescued, through transparent flexible plastic tubes; the Black Queen manifests herself out of an exploding plastic bubble, and her dream-chamber is a bubble furnished with smaller bubbles and giant thistledown (vegetable fur again) from which she and Barbarella escape during the final Gotterdamaround in a bubble of innocence.

The whole vision is – significantly, I suspect – one in which hardware is fallible, and software (animate or otherwise) usually wins. Barbarella's spaceship is more often broken down than not. The electronic gadgetry in David Hemmings's revolutionary HQ always goes on the blink when he needs it. Milo O'Shea's positronic ray machine fails to make him master of the city. More to the point, his Excessive Machine fails to kill Jane Fonda with pleasure – instead, the insatiability of her flesh burns its wiring and blows its circuits, thus giving O'Shea the best line in the script: 'Have you no shame?'

All along, brittle hardware is beaten by pliable software. Barbarella out-yields the Excessive Machine, and the monumental structure of the city of Sogo finally falls to subterranean software: the dreaded Mathmos. Roughly speaking, the Mathmos is (cut-price French metaphysics aside) a blend of a Mark Boyle/UFO light show, detergent commercials, and a circa-1940 pulp novel trying to describe orgasm (you know: iridescent liquid fire seemed to surge up through her etcetera and like that). If you could get it in cans, it would be a great product. You could pour it on the carpet and have a psychedelic wade-in.

In the city of Sogo, however, it glints gurkily around in paramoebic blobs under the glass floors, doubling the roles of a communal libido-sewer and the London Electricity Board. 'It feeds upon our evil, and in return gives us heat, light and power.'

It has to be kept under glass, literally, because otherwise it will destroy the city. This is a conventional type of SF situation, too corny in itself to be worth commenting; but in the context of *Barbarella*, it seems to reveal something of the inner tensions between the logic of the Now and the

4 *Barbarella*, 1967, Jane Fonda in transparent membrane.

restraints of past tradition that SF shares with all other human activities, in spite of its preoccupation with futures.

At first sight, the city of Sogo is ridiculous. It doesn't look like Sodom, Sybaris or Las Vegas, which is understandable. But neither does it look like anything that could grow naturally out of the inflatable/fur-lined technology that dominates the rest of the movie, and the software culture within it. Instead, the city looks – both without and within – uncommonly like an architectural student megastructure of the post-*Archigram* age: multi-storey frames carrying nodes and capsules of living-space above ground, a labyrinth of tunnels below.

But historically this is reasonable. Both *Barbarella* in its original French cartoon-strip form, and *Archigram*'s plug-in city project are half-jokey European intellectual derivatives from basic US pulp SF. Both stand in a tradition of environmental visions that runs back visually through the comics, and verbally through texts like Isaac Asimov's *Caves of Steel* (now in Panther paperback; don't just sit there, go and buy it!), to futurist architectural visions of the nineteen-teens and ultimately to basic sources like H. G. Wells – notably *The Sleeper Awakes*, which is still a sacred text among architects.

This tradition conserves an essentially nineteenth-century vision of the urban environment – densely built, over-populated, low on privacy, violent, serviced by public transport. If that sounds just like New York, it is also a city type whose built form would make Colin Buchanan feel at home, the kind of city that most architects would prefer to Los Angeles, the city seen (like Cumbernauld town centre) as a single artifact, 'le plus grand outil de l'homme' (Le Corbusier: how did you guess?). Asimov had the vision and craft

to construct an alternative city in another book of his, *The Naked Sun*; but it is a pretty rare thing in SF. *Barbarella* holds determinedly to the grand old Wellsian tradition, and Sogo is seen, in distant views, as a singular construction on top of a hill.

Is seen as a piece of hardware, that is. And just as present technology and culture make it possible and necessary to construct alternatives to the high-density architect-preferred city, so the extrapolation of present culture and technology, along the vectors implicit in *Barbarella* (and *Archigram* too), makes the survival of the Wellsian artifact-city inconceivable. *Archigram* has acknowledged the logic of its situation by progressively abandoning its megacity visions in favour of ever more compact, adaptable and self-contained living capsules which, by last summer, had shrunk to the proportions of a rather complex suit which could be inflated (for real; the prototype worked) to provide everybody with their own habitable bubble of innocence.

The dramatic structure (for want of a better phrase) of *Barbarella* does not lend itself to such gradualism, nor its internal logic (eh?) to such commensense solutions. It is intolerable that a lump of hardware like the city of Sogo could coexist with the living, breathing vision of a friendly, sexy, adaptable personal environment. The Black Queen pulls the plug on the Mathmos and the whole hardware scene goes down in boiling flames.

Milo O'Shea presides over this final solution at the console of his positronic ray machine, screaming defiance at his fate with a grand raving Wagnerian glee. He reminded me, somewhere deep down inside, of one or two characters who might be president of the International Union of Architects in about a generation...

2.15 SUMMA GALACTICA

The sci-fi film Star Wars *provides Banham with another vehicle through which to discuss contemporary Pop culture. He feels that it appealed, through its simple and archetypal plot, to a vast cross-section of society, and captured the public imagination by sticking to and updating well-known and loved literary and dramatic conventions, thus deliberately locating itself right in the centre of Pop culture. This article originally appeared in* New Society, *October 27 1977.*

Picture, if you will, a heroine dressed all in virginal white, who never gets raped or even kissed, in an exploitation movie that has already grossed so much at the box office that *Jaws* looks like a minnow and the *Exorcist* like a Wayside Pulpit. The mind boggles. But then *Star Wars* (which doesn't hit the UK till December but whose pre-publicity is already all around us) is a boggling movie – especially if you fail to pick up the clues to its deceptive simplicities early enough.

The last possible moment at which you can hope to get on, and hang on, is probably where the bar tender points through the throng of variously fur-covered, balloon-headed, pig-nosed, cyclopean, and even more extraordinary creatures yet ... points, that is, through the normal crush at his murky, extra-galactic cantina at the fastidiously detailed (made in Britain!) gilt robot in the doorway and barks, 'We don't serve their kind in here!'

It's an old joke, as comfortingly familiar in science fiction as a mother-in-law joke would be in vaudeville. But it has a new twist now, because – obviously – Android Lib would see to it nowadays that the Equal Rights Amendment applied to automata, as well as to men, women, gays, goys, Jews, blacks, yellows, Hispanos, Amazing Hulks and things with five tentacles coming out from under each ear. The Biological Chauvinist Piggery of the whole episode pushes the frame of reference back before 1968 or so. *Star Wars* may well be the first historical costume drama of SF, and as thoroughly researched as *Roots*. Which makes it about the most complicated simple-minded movie ever made.

This simple-mindedness is the true reason for its stunning success, however. It's a straightforward interstellar Western. It is a rattling good yarn with an entirely surprise-free scenario, unencumbered by characterization or acting (apart from some Rommel impersonations by Peter Cushing), but driven at breakneck speed by real pacey-pacey cutting, and a soundtrack that rarely leaves you time to think.

Not that there is much, at that level, to think about – except that, since Kubrick's *2001*, the pundits have come to expect that any expensive SF movie has got to be a vehicle for pretentious cracker-mottoes about Man, God, Destiny and all that. So Alec Guinness's *Star Wars* valedictions, 'The Force be with you', have been scrutinized up, down and sideways for evidence of a New Deism, or even worse, when all they are, in truth, are SF conventions.

For, outside its rattling good yarn, *Star Wars* is about science-fiction conventions – all of them, a kind of *summa galatica* of downright Thomist encyclopaedism and inclusiveness, subject only to the *terminus ante quem* implied by the datedness of the bar-room sequence. This is SF before J. G. Ballard and his quality reduced it to the level of literature: SF of the period of John W. Campbell Jr's most authoritative editorial years at *Astounding* (later, *Analog*) magazine; the period, roughly, from Asimov's first robot stories to Frank Herbert's *Dune*.

George Lucas (of *American Graffiti*), who wrote and

1 *Star Wars*, 1977, Princess Laia (Carrie Fisher).

2 *Flash Gordon*, 1936.

Opposite
3 *Star Wars*, 1977, Bar-room sequence.

4 *Star Wars*, 1977, R2D2 and C3P0.

directed, knows all that stuff. Too few of those who have wasted good newsprint trying to explain 'the phenomenon of *Star Wars*', seem to know any of it at all. Most were thrown completely off-track by the statement (by whom?) that Lucas had originally intended to make a Flash Gordon movie. The more one looks at *Star Wars*, the less likely that appears. Literally 'appears', because the movie's visual sources are nowhere in that area. Its imagery comes from the non-comic-strip pulps like *Astounding* and *Galaxy* in the fifties and sixties, from their great illustrators and cover artists like Chesley Bonestell and Kelly Freas, and *above all* from the written words themselves.

This is an intensely, attentively, literary film. Which is what has made so depressing the failure of the literary critics, even in the *Times Literary* (you should pardon the expression) *Supplement*, to realize what it is all about. Regular cinema audiences don't seem to have this problem, and Lucas pays them the compliment of never supposing for a moment that they will. The narrative pauses neither to explain its references nor to underline its allusions. There's no time, and should be no need.

Most of the first quarter of the story takes place on the arid planet of Tatooine, where the two robots have been deliberately marooned with their crucial strategic information, in the hope that someone who knows what it is all about will pick them up and send the info on to the rebels. In the event, they are picked up by the Jawas, diminutive figures in quasi-Capuchin hooded habits with curious loops and lengths of plastic tubing protruding here and there from their garb.

Now, this was not just a fancy of the costume department. Practically all the audience within our earshot flashed on the fact that this was a reference to Frank Herbert's *Dune* ecology, where the desert folk, the Fremen, wear special gear that conserves and re-cycles all their body water.

To my knowledge, none of the regular critics have picked up this reference, or the fact that it apparently extends and resolves the problem left behind at the end of the *Dune* trilogy. The problem was: can the Fremen preserve their ancient and noble warrior culture without a reversal of the ecological process that is turning their desert into irrigated farm land? The implication of *Star Wars* is, so to speak, 'Neither!' The desert has returned, but the mighty Fremen have been reduced to tinker bands of midget secondhand-robot dealers, travelling in armoured vehicles whose silhouette against the sky looks deliberately reminiscent of old-fashioned gypsy caravans.

An interesting and cynical concept, but surely a bit much to be riding on the back of a rattling good simpleminded yarn? No, this is the level at which *Star Wars* is complex, and sustainedly erudite. For instance, I knew I had come across the Jedi knights somewhere before, and was only momentarily deflected by Alec Guinness's first appearance in pre-faded Zen strip. The Jedi Order's mixture of chivalric

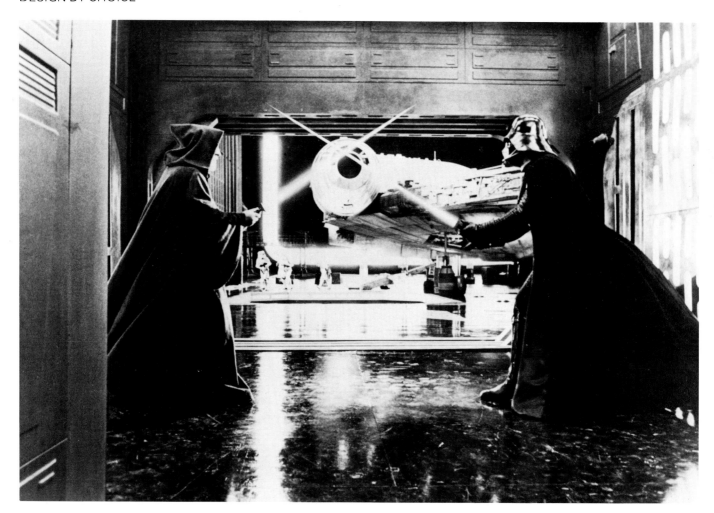

5 *Star Wars*, 1977, Ben Kenobi (Alec Guinness) fighting Darth Vader (David Prowse).

dedication and mod technology has got to come, not from Tolkien, as *TLS* correspondents aver, but from Ernst Juenger's *On the Marble Cliffs*. I don't suppose anybody much around the team that made the movie, or around us in the cinema, had ever read it, either in the original German or in translation, yet it's been soaking into SF since the early fifties.

That concept has some uncomfortable overtones. It got Juenger into trouble in some quarters because it smacked of Nazi revanchism, postulating as it did an oath-bound secret corps d'élite defending the inner secrets of western culture. That's a theme that runs through more than just SF of course. It's already there in most readings of the Arthurian legend. (Was it Clive James who pointed out what a creepy band of fascists the knights of the Round Table would appear today?) Anyhow, what seemed to reinforce the Juengarian connection was that the decor of the final sequence – and this is something every pundit *and* most of the audience picked up – unmistakably recalls Leni Riefenstahl's *Triumph of the Will*, banners and all!

Shocking or not, this sits well with the chivalric theme that informs most of the movie, and nowhere gets in the way of the cowboy aspects of the yarn. But chivalry does do something funny to the ending, generally. Thus, after the final crucial action sequence which – for all it takes place in spacefighters over the topography of an artificial Death Star – is a classic Western gulch ride, with the hired gun, who was thought to have taken his bounty and split, coming back to ride shotgun on the hero and keep the baddies off his tail

. . . after all that does boy get girl, or girl get boy? Neither and both. The princess Leia goes off with both Luke Skywalker, the hero, and Han Solo, the hired gun, arm-linked between them, just good buddies and as pure as the Coke commercial the tableau suspiciously resembles.

And that's the nearest thing to sex in the whole movie, and a great tribute to Lucas as a science-fiction scholar. The princess, played by Carrie Fisher with all the emotional depth of an underdeveloped Polaroid, remains throughout an unsullied figure in her virginal white Roman nightie, and shatter-proof hair-do which seems to be something to do with early pictures of Eleanor Roosevelt. But when the action gets rough, she mucks in with gun and boot.

A tomboy? No, the exact phrase is: 'You're a real brick, Laia!' To put it any higher would make her sound too much a Joan of Arcturus, and she's not spooky enough for that. But she is certainly as remote and unreachable as any mistress of a medieval troubadour, even when she is slopping around in peril in the waste-disposal system of the Death Star (in a glorious send-up of Wajda's *Kanal*: is *nothing* sacred?).

In a movie which has been lavishly over-praised for its special effects, and grimly over-scrutinized for philosophical mystifications (and will occasionally rejoice British viewers by its resemblances to *Dr Who*), the pure white princess is the touchstone, not only of devotion to a chivalric ideal, (i.e. dumb but noble) but more than that, of true scholarship. She is not a nostalgically idealized girl-figure like those in George Lucas's previous, and equally excellent, *American Graffiti*. She is an accurate reading of the way heroines really were in the brave science-fiction days of old. *Star Wars* is not nostalgia; it is history.[1]

NOTES

1.2 SANT'ELIA

1 CTI guide, *Lombardia*, 1936 edn., sub *Como*.

2 The Sant'Elia bibliography available to a student working in London is as follows: Pevsner, *Pioneers of the Modern Movement*, 1st edn., p. 228, note 8; Giedion, *Space, Time and Architecture*, 3rd edn., pp. 319–20, 442–3; *Dopo Sant'Elia*, essays by various hands (notably G. C. Argan), Milan, 1935, RIBA; P. M. Bardi (editor), *Belvedere*, Florence, 1933, RIBA; Alberto Sartoris, *l'Architetto Antonio Sant'Elia*, Milan, 1930, Courtauld Institute and V & A, much altered and republished, with important illus., as *Sant'Elia e l'Architettura Futurista*, Rome, 1943–4, V & A; *Casabella*, 1933, no. 82, p. 2, and 1934, no. 90, p. 2, RIBA; *Architettura*, vol. X, p. 325, RIBA; Bruno Zevi, *Storia dell'Architettura Moderna*, Florence, 1950, pp. 224–31; Manfredi Nicoletti, *L'Architettura Liberty in Italia*, Bari, 1978. This bibliography may not be all-inclusive, and the author would be glad to hear of other Sant'Elia literature in England.

3 The French text is in the V & A Library.

4 The best and most reliable text is in the first edn. of Sartoris, *op. cit.* The author hopes to publish full and accurate English translation of this and other Futurist documents in due course.

5 *Architettura, loc. cit.*

6 I am indebted to Joseph Rykwert, for the suggestion that these drawings might be found in Como.

7 *Space, Time and Architecture*, p. 319.

8 Dr. Franco Carpanelli has kindly checked the Bolognese records, and points out that Sant'Elia graduated from the *Scuola Superiore di Belli Arti*, and that there was no Faculty of Architecture at Bologna in 1912, nor ever has been. On the face of it, this turns the search for engineering influences back to Milan, unless the School of Fine Arts at Bologna was remarkably in advance of its time.

9 *Ibid.*, p. 443.

10 'Man Made America', *Architectural Review*, special issue, December 1950, p. 407.

1.4 MENDELSOHN

1 This is not to depreciate the importance of *de Stijl* outside Holland. Its influence on the International Style is undeniable, once van Doesburg had exported it from its native country, and once the pure rectangular aesthetic devised by himself and Mondriaan had been cross-fertilized with the impure, but mechanistic, rectangular aesthetics of the Dadaists (Hans Arp, Kurt Schwitters) and of the Russian abstract artists (Malevitsh, Gabo). In Germany these three movements produced a sharp and convulsive change in the aesthetics of Modern architecture, historically symbolized by the entry of Moholy-Nagy (a scholar of all three movements) into the Bauhaus staff. But in Holland there was no convulsive change; *de Stijl* won common acceptance by compromise (de Klerk being dead, and van Doesburg out of the country) with existing styles, as in the case of Dudok's romantic rectangularism. On the stylistic peculiarities of the Dutch architectural scene in the twentieth century, see J. P. Kloos, 'The Dutch Melting Pot', *Architectural Review*, April 1948.

2 We now know that the difference between Le Corbusier's vision of the grain elevators, and Mendelsohn's cuts deeper than this; Corbusier had seen only Gropius's newspaper-clippings and photographs of them, but Mendelsohn saw the elevators themselves, on his visits to Buffalo and Chicago in the autumn of 1924. In Buffalo (though not Chicago) it is still possible to stand where Mendelsohn stood to take most of his photographs and see the same elevators, virtually unaltered, and thus relive the impact they made on him at the time.

3 These strictures were written without immediate access to a copy of Zevi's *Storia*, and are inaccurate in detail, but their general validity remains, and is, indeed, reinforced by an article which Zevi has subsequently written in *Metron* 49–50. This is the first extended memorial notice of Mendelsohn's work to appear in any language, and in it he now concedes some development away from Expressionism. But this is dated from 1924, and the Expressionist canon has therefore to include the Charlottenburg villa, the Sternefeld House and the Hat Factory at Luckenweld. This seems to imply the use of the word Expressionism as a term describing the architect's supposed state of mind, rather than the manifest nature of his constructed buildings. The art-historical value of this usage is rendered very suspect by the fact that Zevi does not discuss the impact of the Dutch and American visits – or even mention them!

4 Although there is a difference between the exact acceptance of the word *Borax* in English and American Usage it means, in general, a bulbous pressed steel and/or moulded plastic manner, somewhat related to purely functional streamlining and normally enlivened by close-spaced horizontal or vertical striping, usually of chromium plate. The term is used in the English sense in this article (not in the narrower American sense) first introduced in an article in *Architectural Review* for August 1948, where the reader will find illustrations which make the Mendelsohnian affiliations very clear. For the views of Max Bill see his book *Form*, published by Karl Werner, Basel.

1.5 THE LAST FORMGIVER

1 *The Guardian*, September 11, 1965.

2 *Architects' Journal*, September 29, 1965.

3 As set out at some length in *Modulor II*.

1.6 MACHINE AESTHETIC

1 Since this article was written an English translation has appeared (*Best Wheel Forward*) of the autobiography of the distinguished French car-designer J. A. Gregoire, who was responsible for basic research on frontwheel-drive problems. In it he gives an account of the rather eccentric design methods employed by Ettore Bugatti – he had wooden models made of various assemblies, and then altered them according to purely visual criteria. This is far from the methods of precise calculation of which Le Corbusier speaks, and equally far from the methods actually employed by most design teams, but it is surprisingly and revealingly close to accounts we have of the compositional procedures of Mies van der Rohe, Victor Pasmore and Piet Mondriaan. One may also cite Gregoire for an engineer's opinion of one of the cult-objects of the Machine Aesthetes – 'I consider a number of American engines, surrounded by forests of wires, accessories, and bits and pieces, and designed without thought for line … nearer to beauty than the elegant Bugatti engines' (for which, cf. *Towards a New Architecture*, p. 262).

1.7 STOCKTAKING

1 This was the first of a series of studies ('History and Psychiatry' was a later one) commissioned by the editors of *Architectural Review* to usher in that promising-looking decade, the nineteen-sixties. The introductory paragraph was written by the *Review's* editorial power-behind-the-throne, H. De Cronin Hastings, and shows that instant grip of concepts and situations that made him in his heyday probably the greatest architectural editor who ever lived. (1979)

1.9 TOWARDS A POP ARCHITECTURE

1 'On Trial' was also a commissioned series, and this was virtually a commissioned article within it, since it derived from the insistence of Sir Hugh Casson that the emergence of Pop painting must automatically presage a Pop architecture – a wilful transference of Kenneth Clark's views of the Renaissance that must now appear as historically naive as my own views of the 'neutrality' of technology! (1979)

2.4 DESIGN BY CHOICE

1 There was one exception only to this programme, the free-standing cupboard unit, which Le Corbusier had, in fact, designed as a prototype for manufacture by Thonet.

2 The *Unité* was originally designed to house the unfurnished proletariat.

2.8 A GRID ON TWO FARTHINGS

1 Alas for prophecy, as they say; 'Moulton' never quite made it into

the pantheon of legendary technological names. Ironically, the reason why not is one of the classic stories of marketing success. After some hesitancy and harrumphing, Raleigh finally bought out the Moulton bike patents and produced the Mark III, probably the best (certainly best-made) Moulton ever. Then, in search of a bigger slice of the kids-bike market, they commissioned Ogle Associates to devise an irresistible birthday-boy machine. The result was the dreaded 'Chopper' with its springing, fancy wheels and 'ape-hanger' handle-bars, and its success was so unprecedented that the Moulton production lines had to be cleared to accommodate the demand. And that was the last of the Moulton, apart from odd hand-built examples from Alex Moulton's own experimental shops at Bradford-on-Avon. (1979)

2.15 SUMMA GALACTICA

1 My animadversions on Ernst Juenger produced loud protestations from defenders of his *anti*-Nazi reputation, but after I had apologized in print for any pain or confusion I had caused, a couple of people who (like me) hadn't read *On the Marble Cliffs* for years said, funny, but that's how they remembered it too. All too often in the Pop media (and that includes paperback editions of major authors like Ernst Juenger), a particular image or sequence will stick in the public memory, even when it is irrelevant or contrary to the author's intended message. The one virtue of *2001*, among major SF movies, was so to belabour its theme, and black slab gimmick, that there was no mistaking Kubrick's message (which was conventionally pietistic, anyhow) and even film-critics understood it. But richly referential and joke-filled products like *Star Wars* and *Barbarella*, heavily dependent on purely visual cues, references and puns, largely eluded professional movie-critics – to such an extent that my reference to who-laughed-when at *Barbarella* earned me a rebuke (from John Crosby) for 'elitism'. Yet the jokes in question, particularly the use of Kandinsky shapes for the musical notation of a fugue, would be immediately accessible to anyone who had undergone an introductory course on Twentieth Century Art – and that's quite a large body of the populace by now. We, the mass consumers, are not a bunch of ignorant twits any more. (1979)

BIBLIOGRAPHY
of Writings by Reyner Banham

1952 'Italian Eclectic', *Architectural Review*, October.
'The Voysey Inheritance', *Architectural Review*,
December.

1953 'Casa del Girasole', *Architectural Review*, February.
'Painting and Sculpture of Le Corbusier', *Architectural Review*, June.
'Howard Robertson', *Architectural Review*,
September.
'Simplified Vaulting Practices', *Architectural Review*,
September.
'Pelican World History in 48 Volumes', *Architectural Review*, November.

1954 'Object Lesson', *Architectural Review*, June.
'Mendelsohn', *Architectural Review*, August.

1955 'Facade-Elevational Treatment of the Hallfield Estate', *Architectural Review*, January.
'Vision in Motion', *Art*, January.
'The Machine Aesthetic', *Architectural Review*, April.
'Sant'Elia', *Architectural Review*, May.
'Industrial Design and Popular Art', *Civilta delle Machine*, August.
'Vehicles of Desire', *Art*, September.
'New Brutalism', *Architectural Review*, December.

1956 'Footnotes to Sant'Elia', *Architectural Review*, June.
'Not quite Architecture, not quite Painting or Sculpture either', *Architects' Journal*, August 16.
'Ateliers d'Artistes – Paris Studio Houses and the Modern Movement', *Architectural Review*, August.
'This is Tomorrow', *Architectural Review*,
September.

1957 'Futurism and Modern Architecture', *RIBA Journal*,
February.
'Ornament and Crime – the Decisive Contribution of Adolf Loos', *Architectural Review*, February.
'One and the Few – the Rise of Modern Architecture in Finland', *Architectural Review*, April.
'Mondrian and the Philosophy of Modern Design', *Architectural Review*, October.

1958 'Top Pop Boffin', *Architects' Journal*, February 20.
'White of Perspective', *Architects' Journal*,
February 20.
'Author! Author! PhD', *Architects' Journal*,
March 13.
'The Cool Young Men', *New Statesman*, March 29.
'Space, Fiction and Architecture', *Architects' Journal*,
April 17.
'Frames for Big Business', *New Statesman*, April 26.
'Tridon', *Architectural Review*, April.
'Eiffelmanship', *New Statesman*, June 7.
'Don't be a Square, Bo T', *Architects' Journal*,
June 19.
'The Jet Jetty', *New Statesman*, June 21.
'Plucky Jims', *New Statesman*, July 19.
'Hoist Yourself Petard Kit', *Architects' Journal*,
July 31.

'Machine Aesthetes', *New Statesman*, August 16.
'Questions of Proportion', *New Statesman*,
August 30.
'Home of Taste', *New Statesman*, October 11.
'Legislate for Life', *New Statesman*, November 1.
'The Partisan', *New Statesman*, November 8.
'Unesco House', *New Statesman*, December 6.
'Corb goes to Liverpool', *New Statesman*,
December 20.
'The Triumph of Style', *New Statesman*,
December 27.

1959 'Counter-attack in Aberdare', *New Statesman*,
January 10.
'New Model Parliament', *New Statesman*,
February 7.
'Back Home in Nadaville', *Architects' Journal*,
February 12.
'Architectural Wit', *New Statesman*, February 14.
'The Glass Paradise', *Architectural Review*, February.
'Well-detailed Dane', *New Statesman*, March 7.
'Dream Houses', *New Statesman*, April 4.
'Lecturing at Ulm', *Architects' Journal*, April 16.
'Master of Freedom', *New Statesman*, April 18.
'Rhein-Ruhr Rundschau', *Architects' Journal*,
April 23.
'History/Theory of Architecture', *Architects' Journal*,
April 23.
'Neo-Liberty – the Italian Retreat from Modern Architecture', *Architectural Review*, April.
'Return to Pimlico', *New Statesman*, May 16.
'About Perret', *New Statesman*, May 30.
'Hope Deferred', *Architects' Journal*, June 18.
'China Sea less Salt', *New Statesman*, July 18.
'Thought is Comprehensive', *New Statesman*,
August 15.
'The Descent of F3', *Architects' Journal*, August 27.
'Futurist Manifesto', *Architectural Review*, August.
'On Tair Carn Isaf', *New Statesman*, September 19.
'Architecture from 1800–1950', *Burlington Magazine*, September.
'The Small Revolution', *New Statesman*, October 17.
'Thus Spake Finagle', *Architects' Journal*,
October 22.
'From AA to Zucalli', *New Statesman*, November 28.
'The Double-Headed Monster', *New Statesman*,
December 5.
'The Centre of London's Common Life', *New Statesman*, December 12.
'First Time on any Stage', *Architects' Journal*,
December 17.

1960 *Theory and Design in the First Machine Age*,
Architectural Press.
'So this is FJ?', *Architects' Journal*, January 7.
'Eighteen Thousand Marbleheads', *Architects' Journal*, January 14.
'Cluster at Bethnal Green', *New Statesman*,
January 23.
'Drayneflete-on-Cam', *New Statesman*, February 20.
'Pocket Piazza', *New Statesman*, February 27.
'Stocktaking', *Architectural Review*, February.

'Balance 1960', *Arquitectura (Madrid)*, February.
'Alienation of Parts', *New Statesman*, March 5.
'I'd Crawl a Mile for . . . Playboy', *Architects' Journal*, April 7.
'Ears and Eyes', *New Statesman*, April 30.
'The Medium', *Architects' Journal*, May 5.
'The Road to Ubiquopolis', *New Statesman*, May 28.
'History and Psychiatry', *Architectural Review*, May.
'Perret Ascendency', *Architectural Review*, June.
'Persuading Image', *Design*, June.
'The Church Stimulant', *New Statesman*, July 23.
'Cose Aint What They Use T'Essere', *Architects' Journal*, August 4.
'Venezia-Incurabili', *New Statesman*, August 29.
'Fold, like the Arab', *Architects' Journal*, September 27.
'Too Brief Chronicle', *Architects' Journal*, October 27.
'The End of Insolence', *New Statesman*, October 29.
'St. Catherine's College, Oxford', *New Statesman*, November 5.
'WORLD, the; book to change, a', *Architects' Journal*, December 8.
'Monument with Frills', *New Statesman*, December 10.
'House and Land', *New Statesman*, December 24.
'The Formgivers', *New Statesman*, December 31.
'Milan Triennale', *Domus*, December.
'Futurism for Keeps', *Arts*, December.

1961 'A Gong for the Welfare State', *New Statesman*, January 6.
'H.M. Fashion House', *New Statesman*, January 27.
'Furnex 61', *New Statesman*, February 10.
'A Genuine Shambles', *Architects' Journal*, February 16.
'Ravished Groves of Academe', *New Statesman*, March 3.
'A Model Essay upon the Varieties of Anticipation as Exemplified in the Works of Fred Hoyle, Genius', *Architects' Journal*, March 23.
'Ego-Image Adjuster', *New Statesman*, March 24.
'Pirelli Building, Milan', *Architectural Review*, March.
'The Last of the Goths', *New Statesman*, April 7.
'Counter-Attack. NY', *Architects' Journal*, May 4.
'Handsome Doesn't', *New Statesman*, May 19.
'History of the Immediate Future', *RIBA Journal*, May.
'Black and White Magazine Show', *New Statesman*, June 2.
'The Vertical Community', *New Statesman*, June 30.
'Architecture – Fitting and Befitting', *Architectural Forum*, June.
'Rude Barn', *New Statesman*, July 21.
'On First Looking into Wanshavsky', *Architects' Journal*, July 26.
'Snaps', *New Statesman*, July 28.
'Design by Choice', *Architectural Review*, July.
'The Urbanistic Pitch', *Architects' Journal*, August 23.
'Transistorama', *New Statesman*, September 1.
'Apropos the Smithsons', *New Statesman*, September 8.
'Not Even One More Time', *Architects' Journal*, September 20.
'Gropius', *Arts*, September.

'The Cult', *New Statesman*, November 17.
'Night, Mrs. Jagbag', *Architects' Journal*, November 29.
'Urbanism, USA', *Architectural Review*, November.
'Homage to Sir Edward Robertson', *New Statesman*, December 8.
'Europe on the Coffee Table', *New Statesman*, December 22.
'Park Hill Housing, Sheffield', *Architectural Review*, December.

1962 Guide to Modern Architecture, *Architectural Press*.
'On Criticizing Architecture', *The Listener*, January 4.
'Seed of Daedalus', *New Statesman*, January 12.
'Joke Tap', *Architects' Journal*, January 31.
'Coronation Street, Hoggartsborough', *New Statesman*, February 9.
'Leeds Leading', *New Statesman*, February 23.
'What Architecture of Technology?', *Architectural Review*, February.
'Fear of Eero's Mania', *Arts*, February.
'Aimez-vous Marienbad', *Architects' Journal*, March 7.
'Coffin-Nails in Handy Packs', *New Society*, March 23.
'The Master of Taliesin', *New Statesman*, April 6.
'Painters of the Bauhaus', *The Listener*, April 19.
'Unspeakable KG Factor – Designing for Pleasure in Use', *Industrial Design*, April.
'On Trial', *Architectural Review*, April–May, July–August.
'Carbonorific', *New Statesman*, May 4.
'Coventry Cathedral', *New Statesman*, May 25.
'Rapid Transit Pioneers', *Architects' Journal*, June 27.
'Kidder Smith's Conspectus', *New Statesman*, June 29.
'Morse and Stiles', *New Statesman*, July 13.
'The Spec. Builders – Towards a Pop Architecture', *Architectural Review*, July.
'Big Doug, Small Piece', *Architects' Journal*, August 1.
'Old Number One', *New Statesman*, August 3.
'The First Prodigy', *New Statesman*, August 24.
'Seattle World's Fair', *Architectural Review*, August.
'Coventry Cathedral – Strictly Trad.', *Architectural Forum*, August.
'Festival Site to Let', *Architects' Journal*, September 5.
'England His England', *New Statesman*, September 28.
'A Thought for Your Pfennig', *Architects' Journal*, October 10.
'Sons of the Cardinal', *New Statesman*, October 26.
'Obsolescent Airport', *Architectural Review*, October.
'Underdone Underpass', *New Statesman*, November 2.
'The Mysterious Affair of the Baronet's Reputation', *Architects' Journal*, November 14.
'Come Over to Paddo', *The Listener*, November 15.
'The Trouble with Eero', *New Statesman*, November 23.
'Kent and Cabability', *New Statesman*, December 7.
'On the Gore', *New Statesman*, December 14.
'Report on the Design of Morse and Stiles

Dormitories for Yale University', *Architectural Forum*, December.
'The Environmentalist', *Program*, Spring.

1963 'How to Sneer at Cripples for Fun and Profit', *Architects' Journal*, January 9.
'The Stones of New York', *The Listener*, January 31.
'British Railways', *Architects' Journal*, March 6.
'The Reputation of William Morris', *New Statesman*, March 8.
'The Embalmed City', *New Statesman*, April 12.
'Department of Visual Uproar', *New Statesman*, May 3.
'Remove Corb-Coloured Spectacles', *Architects' Journal*, May 22.
'Think Kieft, Think Fast', *Architects' Journal*, May 22.
'Six-Legged Dragon', *New Statesman*, May 24.
'Europe – the Relevant Continent', *Architectural Review*, May.
'First Master of the Mass Media', *The Listener*, June 27.
'The Urban Scene – a Call for Action', *Architects' Journal*, July 3.
'Thunderbox: the Times Building', *New Statesman*, July 12.
'The Conformist Union', *New Statesman*, August 2.
'Don't Just Stand There Trembling', *Architects' Journal*, August 14.
'Shalimar in Walden', *New Statesman*, August 16.
'Home Thoughts from Abroad', *Industrial Design*, August.
'The Chairs', *Architects' Journal*, September 25.
'At Aspen – On the American Image Abroad', *Design*, September.
'(Thinks): Think!', *New Statesman*, October 11.
'Dymaxicrat', *Arts*, October.
'A Grid on Two Farthings', *New Statesman*, November 1.
'Back in the Saddle', *Architects' Journal*, November 6.
'Harvesting', *New Statesman*, November 8.
'No Dave', *New Statesman*, November 15.
'A Flourish of Symbols', *The Observer Weekend Review*, November 17.
'F.O.', *New Statesman*, December 27.
'Who is This 'Pop'?', *Motif* 10.

1964 'Multi-joke', *Architects' Journal*, January 8.
'Slum Zoo', *Architects' Journal*, January.
'Earthmovers', *New Statesman*, February 7.
'The Style for the Job', *New Statesman*, February 14.
'Norway on the Raw, 1', *Architects' Journal*, February 19.
'Norway on the Raw, 2', *Architects' Journal*, February 26.
'How I Learnt to Live with the Norwich Union', *New Statesman*, March 16.
'The Rule of Lore', *New Statesman*, April 10.
'Dr. Doomsday', *Architects' Journal*, April 29.
'On the Road and on the Scene', *New Statesman*, May 15.
'At Swiss', *New Statesman*, May 22.
'Let Them Eat Steak', *New Statesman*, June 5.
'Farewell Old Column', *Architects' Journal*, June 10.
'All the Fun of the Flop', *New Statesman*, June 26.
'Brands Hatch', *New Statesman*, July 17.
'Peoples' Palaces', *New Statesman*, August 7.

'A Designer's Pugwash', *The Listener*, August 27.
'Aspen Papers', *Industrial Design*, August.
'Speed and the Citizen: Urban Rapid Transit and the Future Cities', *Architectural Review*, August.
'Word in Britain: "Character" Labs. for the Department of Engineering at Leicester University', *Architectural Forum*, August.
'Tall Classic', *New Statesman*, September 18.
'St. Catherine's College, Oxford', *Architectural Review*, September.
'Gesampt Flanzweik', *New Statesman*, October 2.
'Condit's Chicago', *Arts*, October.
'Clean Paul', *New Statesman*, November 6.
'History, Theory and Criticism', *American Institute of Architects' Journal*, November.
'Hot Houses', *New Statesman*, December 4.
'The Atavism of the Short-Distance Mini-Cyclist', *Living Arts* 3.

1965 'Boss Span', *New Statesman*, January 8.
'Crowther's Acropolis', *New Statesman*, January 15.
'Extreme Environment', *New Statesman*, February 12.
'Zoo à la Mode', *New Statesman*, March 12.
'Liverpool Leading', *New Statesman*, April 16.
'Form Fuddles Function', *New Statesman*, April 23.
'A Home is not a House', *Art in America*, April.
'La Kermesse Mécanique', *New Statesman*, May 28.
'Missing Persons', *New Statesman*, June 25.
'Replanning Britain: New Look for Westminster', *New Statesman*, July 30.
'The Missing Motel', *The Listener*, August 5.
'Kandy Kulture Kikerone', *New Society*, August 19.
'Carry on Gatters', *New Statesman*, August 20.
'Chill Dawn in Colorado', *Industrial Design*, August.
'Fiscal Pursuivant, Proceed', *New Society*, September 9.
'Aviary: London Zoo', *Architectural Review*, September.
'The Great Gizmo', *Industrial Design*, September.
'Homo Serendipitans', *New Society*, October 7.
'Corbolatry at County Hall', *New Society*, November 4.
'Pop and the Body Critical', *New Society*, December 16.
'Servants of the Public Will', *Ulm: Zeitschrift der Hochschule*, December.
'The Missing Motel: Unrecognized American Architecture', *Landscape*, winter.
'A Marginal Redefinition of Modern', *Bartlett Society Transactions*, V4.
'Clip-on Architecture', *Design Quarterly* No. 63.

1966 *New Brutalism: Ethic or Aesthetic?*, Architectural Press.
'Architecture in Freedomland', *New Society*, January 6.
'Coronado: or Don't Smoke in Bed', *Architects' Journal*, February 2.
'Grudge Racing Tonite', *New Society*, February 3.
'Zoom Wave Hits Architecture', *New Society*, March 3.
'The Gadget People', *New Society*, March 24.
'The Science Side', *Architectural Review*, March.
'BOAC at JFK', *Architects' Journal*, April 28.
'An Added Modern Pleasantness', *New Society*, April 28.

'Lair of Soane', *New Society*, May 26.
'No more Plain Wrappers', *New Society*, June 30.
'Motherwell and Others', *Architectural Review*, July.
'Brown Angels a Go-Go', *New Society*, August 4.
'Aesthetics of the Yellow Pages', *New Society*, August 18.
'Old Futuropolis', *Architects' Journal*, August 31.
'The Last Formgiver', *Architectural Review*, August.
'Aspen, Quote, Unquote', *Print*, September.
'Frank Lloyd as Environmentalist', *Arts and Architecture*, September.
'US Automobile Painting', *Art in America*, September.
'Technology: a Boon and a Danger', *American Institute of Architects' Journal*, September.
'The Outhouses of Academe', *New Society*, October 6.
'Vinyl Deviations', *New Society*, December 1.
'Unlovable at Any Speed', *Architects' Journal*, December 21.
'Ghoultide Greetings', *New Society*, December 22.

1967 'Erno Meets the Munsters', *New Society*, January 26.
'Message is not a Monkee', *New Society*, February 23.
'Norse but not Coarse', *New Society*, March 23.
'Chairs as Art', *New Society*, April 20.
'Transport Now: Anti-Technology', *New Society*, May 4.
'The Electric Environment', *Interior Design*, May.
'Towards a Million-Volt Light and Sound Culture', *Architectural Review*, May.
'Town Planning, Experiments and Utopias', *Bauen und Wohnen*, May.
'L'Homme à Expo', *New Society*, June 1.
'Shades of Summer', *New Society*, June 29.
'Future of Art from the Other Side', *Studio*, June.
'Flatscape with Containers', *New Society*, August 17.
'Beyond Expo '67', *The Listener*, September 7.
'Le Corbusier – Guru of Our Time', *New Society*, September 14.
'On a Distant Prospect', *New Society*, September 28.
'Eheu Carnabia', *New Society*, October 12.
'This Property is Condemned', *New York Review*, October.
'Horse of a Different Colour', *New Society*, November 2.
'Vitruvius Over Manhattan', *New Society*, December 7.
'Rudolph Schindler', *Architectural Design*, December.

1968 'Reyner Banham's Grand Festival', *Design*, February.
'Not a Young-Mobile', *New Society*, March 7.
'Somewhere Totally Else', *New Society*, March 28.
'Monumental Windbags', *New Society*, April 18.
'Disservice Areas', *New Society*, May 23.
'College of Aspen '68', *New Society*, August 1.
'Cap'n Kustow's Toolshed', *New Society*, August 22.
'Los Angeles', *The Listener*, August–September.
'Bus-Pop', *New Society*, September 5.
'Cambridge – Mark 2', *New Society*, September 26.
'The Bauhaus Gospel', *The Listener*, September 26.
'Triumph of Software', *New Society*, October 31.

'Dark Satanic Century', *Architectural Review*, October.
'Environment of the Machine Aesthetic', *Design*, November.
'History Faculty, Cambridge', *Architectural Review*, November.
'Pub-shape and Landlubber Fashion', *New Society*, December 5.
'First Bus to Psychedelia', *New Society*, December 12.
'English Brutalism – Selection of Writings', *Zodiac* No. 18.

1969 *Architecture of the Well-Tempered Environment*, Architectural Press.
'Natural Gasworks', *New Society*, January 9.
'Non-Plan – an Experiment in Freedom', *New Society*, March 20.
'Californian Livery', *New Society*, April 3.
'Beyond Sir's Ken', *New Society*, April 17.
'Representations in Protest', *New Society*, May 8.
'On Victorian Lines', *New Society*, June 19.
'The Gutenburg Backlash', *New Society*, July 10.
'Softer Hardware', *Ark* 44, Summer.
'Folie de Grandeur', *New Society*, August 14.
'Dunesaga', *New Society*, August 28.
'Unavoidable Options', *New Society*, September 18.
'Joe Levy's Contemporary City', *New Society*, November 6.
'Last Professional', *New Society*, December 18.
'Bauhaus Era – Between Art and Technology', *Architecture in Canada*, December.

1970 'Household Godgets', *New Society*, January 15.
'Journals to the Trade', *New Society*, April 2.
'In the Van of Progress', *New Society*, April 30.
'Power of Trent and Aire', *New Society*, May 28.
'Sing Me to the White House', *New Society*, June 18.
'The Crisp at the Crossroads', *New Society*, July 9.
'A Hole in the Ground', *New Society*, August 13.
'Put Out More Towers', *New Society*, October 1.
'Sailflyer's Rest', *New Society*, November 5.
'On the Leger Exhibition', *New Society*, November 26.
'Wilderness Years of Frank Lloyd Wright', *RIBA Journal*, December.

1971 *Los Angeles – The Architecture of Four Ecologies*, Penguin.
'Play Power', *New Society*, January 7.
'Historian on the Pier', *New Society*, January 14.
'Shoo-Fly Landing', *Architectural Design*, January.
'Fur Out Trip', *New Society*, February 4.
'Bennet's Leviathan', *New Society*, April 8.
'LA – the Structure Behind the Scene', *Architectural Design*, April.
'A Proper Shambles', *New Society*, May 20.
'Floreat Ballspondia', *New Society*, June 24.
'A & PhoT: Big Sig in the Roman Underground', *Architectural Design*, June.
'Thomas Cubitt – Master Builder', *New Society*, August 5.
'The Master Builders', *The Sunday Times Colour Supplement*, August 8.
'Had I the Wings of an Angel', *New Society*, August 12.

'Glass of Fashion', *New Society*, September 9.
'Demon Tweak', *New Society*, September 30.
'Hermann in Eden', *New Society*, December 9.

1972 'Prevento Mori', *New Society*, January 20.
'Immoral Uplift', *New Society*, February 24.
'New Way North', *New Society*, May 4.
'Treasure House', *New Society*, May 25.
'Past Perfect', *New Society*, June 27.
'Big Brum Artwork', *New Society*, July 13.
'See it Their Way', *New Society*, August 17.
'Only an Academic Flywheel', *RIBA Journal*, August.
'Rank Values', *New Society*, September 14.
'LL/LF/LE v. Foster', *New Society*, November 9.
'Big Shed Syndrome', *New Society*, December 21.
'Monaco Underground', *Casabella* Nos. 368–9.

1973 'Proof of Baillie Scott', *Architectural Review*, January.
'Nostalgia for Style', *New Society*, February 1.
'Paleface Trash', *New Society*, February 22.
'A Quiet Bridge', *New Society*, March 15.
'Force of Example', *New Society*, May 10.
'Redbrick by Mail', *New Society*, May 31.
'The Late Twentieth-Century Hotel', *New Society*, August 23.
'Death and Life of the Prairie School', *Architectural Review*, August.
'Iron Bridge Embalmed', *New Society*, September 6.
'The Parkhill Victory', *New Society*, October 18.
'Preserve us from Paranoid Preservers', *The Observer Magazine*, October 21.
'Mythology Afoot', *New Society*, November 15.
'A Real Golden Oldie', *New Society*, December 13.
'Fitch–Viewed from Marlboro/Indian Country', *Architectural Design No. 9.*

1974 *The Aspen Papers*, Pall Mall.
'Old Wheels for New', *New Society*, February 7.
'Troglodyte Metropolis', *New Society*, March 7.
'Sundae Painters: Decorated Ice-Cream Vans', *New Society*, April 11.
'Problem × 3 = Olivetti: Criticism', *Architectural Review*, April.
'Signs Municipal', *New Society*, May 9.
'Megastructure – Civic Design at Bay', *Society of Architectural Historians' Journal*, May.
'Barnsbury-sur-Mer', *New Society*, June 13.
'Nice, Modern and British', *New Society*, July 18.
'Radio Machismo', *New Society*, August 22.
'Godzilla in Halifax', *New Society*, September 19.
'A Walled City', *New Society*, October 24.
'Gentri-Mini-Mania', *New Society*, November 28.
'Sex and the Single Lens', *New Society*, December 19.

1975 *The Age of the Masters: A Personal View of Architecture*, Architectural Press.
'The City Moses Made', *The Times Literary Supplement*, January 17.
'The Great Wall of Tyne', *New Society*, February 6.
'Les Trous of Paris', *New Society*, March 20.
'Money into Form', *New Society*, April 24.
'Ovaltine and Oake', *New Society*, May 22.
'The Great Good Windy City', *The Times Literary Supplement*, June 13.
'The Purified Aesthetic', *New Society*, June 26.
'Megastructure', *Architectural Design*, July.
'A Dead Liberty', *New Society*, August 7.
'Up in Sybil's Place', *New Society*, September 4.
'Establishing the Precedents', *The Times Literary Supplement*, September 19.
'On the Sixth Day', *New Society*, October 2.
'Arnolfini Mark 3', *New Society*, November 20.

1976 'Come in 2000', *New Society*, January 8.
'A Question of Magic', *The Times Literary Supplement*, January 23.
'Repro Time is Here', *New Society*, February 12.
'National Monument', *New Society*, March 18.
'The Mesa Messiah', *New Society*, May 6.
'Bricologues à la Lanterne', *New Society*, July 1.
'The Tear-Drop Express', *The Times Literary Supplement*, July 23.
'Where are you, Universal Man?', *RIBA Journal*, July.
'Ground Scraping', *New Society*, August 12.
'The Open City and its Enemies', *The Listener*, September 23.
'Castle on a Mall', *New Society*, October 28.
'The True False Front', *New Society*, December 2.
'News of Nowhere', *New Society*, December 9.

1977 *Megastructures: Urban Futures of the Recent Past*, Thames and Hudson.
'Goat Island Story', *New Society*, January 13.
'Euston Arch of the Air', *New Society*, March 3.
'Zapped in Buffalo', *New Society*, March 10.
'Lair of the Looker', *New Society*, May 5.
'Enigma of the Rue de Renard', *Architectural Review*, May.
'Country and Wet Bed', *New Society*, June 23.
'Valley of the Dams', *New Society*, July 21.
'A Suburb of the Sea', *The Times Literary Supplement*, August 12.
'The Four-Wheel Life', *New Society*, August 18.
'Grass Above, Glass Around', *New Society*, October 6.
'Summa Galactica', *New Society*, October 27.
'Eupepsia, Tex', *New Society*, December 22/29.

1978 'Pevsner's Progress', *The Times Literary Supplement*, February 17.
'The Geist in the Machine', *The Times Literary Supplement*, September 15.

ACKNOWLEDGEMENTS

We would like to express our gratitude to all of those who have in some way contributed to the publication of these essays. In particular our thanks go to: *Architects' Journal, Architectural Review, Art in America, Industrial Design* (1960/1965, Design Publications Inc., 717 Fifth Avenue, New York, NY 10022), *The Listener, Living Arts, Motif, New Society* and *New Statesman*, who have allowed copyrighted articles to be reproduced.

Thanks also go to the following archives, photographers, and the owners of illustrations for allowing their work to be reproduced: Akademie der Künste, Berlin 31–32 (1–9); Archigram 12, 64–65 (1–4); Architectural Press 34–39 (1–10), 47 (3), 50 (4–6), 54 (14); Alfonso Avincola (A.L.A.) 133 (1); Braun Aktiengesellschaft 99 (2); François Dallegret 56–60 (1–6); Design Council 13 (top), 53 (12), 104 (7), 106 (9), 119; John Donat 72–74 (3–5); Charles Eames 99 (1); Environmental Communications cover; Foster Associates 10, 19, 80–81 (1–2), 83 (photos John Donat), 82 (3–4); Mario Ghisalberti 24 (1–2); James Gowan 71 (1–2); Lucien Hervé 9, 40, 45 (1); Charles Jencks 43 (4–5), 52 (8 and 10), 133 (1), 135–136 (3–4); Knoll International 15, 99 (3); Denys Lasdun & Partners 75 (1), 76 (2 and 4), 77–78 (5–10) (photos Donald Mill), 76 (3), 79 (12) (photos John Donat); Raymond Loewy 46 (2); National Film Archive 95, 134 (2), 137–140 (1–5); National Motor Museum 13 (below), 91–92 (1–2), 102–103 (5–6), 113 (13–14), 121–123 (1–5), 124–126 (1–5), 127–129 (1–3); Eliot Noyes Industrial Design Inc. 115 (1–3); Olivetti 14, 105 (8), 116 (4) (photo Salo Dino); Walter Dorwin Teague Associates 62. Other photographs are reproduced from the original publications in which the essay appeared or are from the Academy Editions archives.

INDEX